Boss Ruef's

San Francisco

Boss Ruef's San Francisco

THE STORY OF THE UNION LABOR PARTY, BIG BUSINESS, AND THE GRAFT PROSECUTION

by Walton Bean

UNIVERSITY OF CALIFORNIA PRESS

Berkeley, Los Angeles, London

UNIVERSITY OF CALIFORNIA PRESS
BERKELEY AND LOS ANGELES
CALIFORNIA

UNIVERSITY OF CALIFORNIA PRESS, LTD.
LONDON, ENGLAND

ISBN 0-520-00094-3

PRINTED IN THE UNITED STATES OF AMERICA

6 7 8 9 0

For Beth and Charles

Preface

THE shortcomings of American city government have been major problems since the days of Aaron Burr, if not earlier. But these problems were especially acute in the age of industrialization and urbanization between the end of the Civil War and the rise of the progressive movement in the early twentieth century. It was an age in which large cities, large corporations, and large organizations of labor grew so rapidly that government and law could not keep up with them. One symptom of this condition was an increase in the power of the city boss, an extra-legal figure who could furnish a bridge between the lagging institutions of politics and the overwhelming demands of expanding economic organizations. It was an age in which corrupt alliances between big business and politics were a menace to democracy throughout America. And it was within this period that Lord Bryce, in *The American Commonwealth,* and Lincoln Steffens, in *The Shame of the Cities,* wrote classic accounts of boss rule.

The role of the city boss was filled by many remarkable personalities, of whom William M. Tweed of New York, "Czar" Martin Lomasney of Boston, Ed Butler of St. Louis, and "Doc" Ames of Minneapolis are well-known examples. But San Francisco, always cosmopolitan, impish, and proud of its special flavor, might have been expected to produce a political boss as colorful and out of the ordinary as the city itself. Abe Ruef had a brilliant intellect and a good university and legal education, and he left a detailed and valuable set of memoirs. He was of Jewish ancestry, which was equally unusual among prominent American city bosses. And he rose to power through

vii

a phenomenon almost unique in American history—a Union Labor party, elected, under his skillful guidance, to complete control of the city government. Ruef, whose interest in labor was primarily opportunistic, was largely responsible both for the party's temporary success and for its subsequent disgrace, which damaged the cause of labor in politics throughout the nation.

The San Francisco story has a special significance, also, in that so much can be known about the actual inner workings of boss government under Ruef. Through a remarkable combination of circumstances, one of the longest, ablest, and most determined graft prosecutions on record succeeded in laying bare the roots of the problem in pitiless detail. A crusading editor, Fremont Older of the *Bulletin,* persuaded a millionaire, Rudolph Spreckels, to guarantee the very large expenses of the investigation. Older then persuaded President Theodore Roosevelt to lend the services of an already famous team—William J. Burns, the federal government's star detective, and Francis J. Heney, one of its best special prosecutors. When an assassin's bullet temporarily disabled Heney, Hiram W. Johnson distinguished himself as Heney's substitute, and was thus launched upon his political career.

The leaders of the prosecution adopted Lincoln Steffens' theory that big business was chiefly responsible for the corruption of politics; and in the light of this theory, they gave immunity to a number of Union Labor politicians, and set out to put a number of leading captains of industry in prison. Most of the powerful forces of the business community sympathized with the indicted corporation executives, and opposed the prosecution. The trials occurred during the aftermath of the disastrous earthquake and fire of 1906, and the emotional tensions of the time heightened the bitterness of the struggle. It was a dramatic story of class and personal conflict. Before it ended, it had unfolded a panorama of urban society, and provided a case study of boss government, municipal corruption, and the difficulties of reform.

The most important sources for each chapter are given in the notes beginning on page 319. A manuscript of the book, containing a much more fully and specifically detailed set of footnotes, is in the Bancroft Library, University of California, Berkeley.

For many valuable suggestions on the whole or extensive parts of the manuscript, I am indebted to the late Frederic L. Paxson, and to John D. Hicks, Lawrence A. Harper, Carl Bridenbaugh, Arthur Knodel, and Sigurd Burckhardt. During the early stages of writing, the late Max Radin inspired me with some of his own enthusiasm for the narrative possibilities of the story.

Few books could owe as much to the constant interest, advice, and encouragement of the author's wife as this one owes to Beth Phillips Bean.

For access to documents or other important information I am especially indebted to Howard Jay Graham, Franklin Hichborn, Stanley W. Moore, Rudolph Spreckels, Helene M. Hooker, Ella Winter, George Mowry, Hiram W. Johnson, Jr., Edward I. Sugarman, and Noel Sullivan. The staffs of the Bancroft Library, the California State Library at Sacramento, the San Francisco Public Library, the Stanford and Yale university libraries, and the Haynes Foundation of Los Angeles were notably helpful. And to all the other friends, old and new, who helped in the making of this book, I wish to express my deep appreciation.

Contents

xi

ILLUSTRATIONS

Boss Ruef's
San Francisco

CHAPTER I

A reformer turns opportunist

M A N Y city bosses have been endowed with native cleverness, but few have been highly literate. Tweed, for example, had only the rudiments of an education. Ruef, on the other hand, was an unusually cultivated man.

Ruef was born in San Francisco on September 2, 1864, the only son of a fairly wealthy family. His parents, born in France, had come to California in 1862. His father, Meyer Ruef, operated a large dry goods store on Market Street in the 'sixties. Later he prospered as a dealer in real estate, and was listed in the city directory as "capitalist." Abraham was a precocious boy, and he graduated with high honors from the University of California at eighteen, the age at which most young college men of his generation were matriculating. His curriculum at Berkeley was in classical languages; he spoke several modern languages fluently, and he took an intense intellectual interest in philosophy, art, and music. Although he was never to be more than five feet eight inches tall, he was rather striking in appearance during these early years. His hair was dark and curly. As soon as possible he began to wear a mustache, perhaps in order to modify two aspects of his features—youthfulness, and a rather prominent nose. He had a ready wit, and an affable and ingratiating manner, and his slight frame was vibrant with energy. Constantly active in student affairs, he was one of the founders of the students' co-operative store and permanent secretary of the class of 1883. After graduating from the university's Hastings College of Law in San Francisco, he was admitted to the bar in 1886.

In the course of his studies, the fledgling lawyer had acquired a sincerely idealistic ambition to work for the reforming of politics, which, he knew rather vaguely, were not all they should be. With several young friends who were like-minded, including John H. Wigmore, home from Harvard for a summer, and Franklin K. Lane, Ruef formed a club for the study of civic problems, the Municipal Reform League. They corresponded with other such groups. One of these, as Ruef recalled, had a corresponding secretary named Theodore Roosevelt. They burned to put their ideas into practice, and planned an active ward and precinct organization to beat the bosses. The little group disbanded when Wigmore returned to his studies at Harvard in the fall. Wigmore was later to become Dean of the Law School of Northwestern University, and *Wigmore on Evidence* was to be a great legal classic. Lane was destined to be Secretary of the Interior. Both Lane and Wigmore became life-long crusaders for better law and better government. The youthful idealism in Ruef's ambitions was not to be so long sustained.

Ruef first took part in real politics, according to his memoirs, in the primaries of the Republican party of San Francisco in the elections of 1886. He had just opened his law office, and it was the first year in which he was old enough to vote. Attracted by a newspaper announcement of a meeting of the Republican club of his district, he made his way at eight in the evening to the advertised address on Sansome Street. This proved to be a dark and dangerous-looking three-story boarding house for sailors, under the cliffs of Telegraph Hill. It was a district where shanghaiing was still practiced, and it took all Ruef's courage to knock. The boarding house keeper led him with a lantern to an upstairs room and introduced him to the only person present, a saloonkeeper. The two men said that a meeting of more than a hundred and fifty Republicans had already adjourned, having elected these two as officers with unanimity and enthusiasm. As the disappointed Ruef turned to leave, he was asked, "Young man, can you write?" Giving an affirmative answer, he was designated secretary of the district Republican club and furnished with a vivid account of the meeting, which he wrote down and carried to the office of a newspaper. His glowing account of a large and intelligent gathering was published the next morning just as he had written it. Not until later, he asserted, did he realize that there had been no such meeting, and that so forbidding a place had been scheduled in order that no one would attend and his two hosts might elect each other.

Impressed by his abilities, the faction which controlled the district club rewarded its promising young adherent with the captaincy of two precincts in the primary campaign for the election of delegates to the San Francisco Republican convention. He was soon to discover, among other things, the significance of the fact that California, like most states, had not yet attempted to regulate party primaries by law. Legally, the party was a private enterprise. In the city and county of San Francisco, the central organization of the Republican party was the county committee. The "primary branches" were the Republican clubs, one in each district represented in the Assembly, the larger house of the state legislature. These district clubs were organized and recognized by authority of the county committee, which was, in turn, made up of one representative from each club. In practice, the party bosses maneuvered the selection of all the officers in this machinery.

Primaries for the election of convention delegates were conducted by the district clubs, under the auspices of the party, not of the state. Most citizens other than the bosses' followers regarded the primaries with apathy, or cynicism, or both, and seldom voted in them. As a result, they were perfunctory affairs, unless rival factions of would-be bosses arose. Ruef discovered eventually that such was the case in 1886, and that he was enlisted in a faction led by Jim McCord, superintendent of the Sutter Street Railroad, which was disputing the mastery of the incumbent Republican leader, Bill Higgins, and his lieutenants, Phil Crimmins and Martin Kelly. McCord's rebellion was secretly financed by the state political machine of the Southern Pacific Railroad, which had chosen to demoralize the San Francisco Republicans in that year in order to insure the election of "Blind Boss" Chris Buckley's Democrats.

In such circumstances, the absence of legal restraints on the primaries gave free reign to violence and fraud. Meetings turned into pitched battles between rival gangs of "rockrollers," little standing armies of bosses' mercenaries, known also as "the push." Fists, clubs, and rocks were used freely, although guns were usually considered unethical. Polling places could be located at inaccessible spots and kept open only at inconvenient hours. In any case, the boss who controlled a safe majority of the party's committee could handpick its subcommittee on returns and contests, which named the election officers. Years later, Martin Kelly claimed to have preserved as a curiosity a ballot box with a false bottom, capable of concealing enough pre-stuffed ballots to ensure a majority. It was an unnecessary refinement in primaries, since the ballots were "counted" behind locked doors. Ruef came to suspect that one real purpose of holding such elections at all was to discover the "safest" districts, in order to apportion them the largest representations in later conventions.

Ruef was elected a delegate among the minority permitted to the insurgent faction. He had worked hard and honestly in his own precincts, and he was eager to attend, partly from a kind of horrified fascination with politics, partly from a lingering hope for their reform. The municipal convention of 1886, however, completed his disillusionment. True, the externals of the machinery worked with finesse and even with some dignity. Few of the delegates were mere roustabouts. Many were merchants, manufacturers, and professional men, flattered at being in politics, quite willing to be "bellwether delegates," taking the program of the bosses and voting for party nominees whose names they might never have heard before. The long slate for elective city and state offices was monotonously rubber-stamped by the regular majority.

The political scene, as Ruef found it in the 'eighties, was hardly attractive to young men of principles. The machinery of boss politics in San Francisco had the general characteristics of the institution as it had evolved in most large American cities. It had been part of the transit of civilization from the East to the Pacific Coast. In California, the subservience of politics to big business was especially facilitated by the dominance of a single great corporation in the state's economy. Most of the railroad mileage in California was merged under the name of the Southern Pacific, a holding company whose charter, granted by the state of Kentucky, empowered it to do almost anything except to operate in Kentucky. The Southern Pacific, allied with lesser corporate interests, notably public utilities, maintained a confidential political organization of which the bosses of both major parties in California were satellites. The management of this not entirely invisible government was then in the hands of Charles F. Crocker, who had been entrusted with it as a compromise in a feud between Leland Stanford and Collis P. Huntington. From his offices in San Francisco, the younger Crocker dispensed the loaves and fishes which meant success to practical politicians. Not only did the railroad control the party organizations, but it played them against each other and secretly fostered new factions to keep the old ones in check. As Ruef recalled it, the railroad's money "was the power behind almost every political throne and behind almost every insurgent revolt."

According to his memoirs, Ruef first became associated with the leading Republican party bosses of the city as the result of a deathbed request from Boss Bill Higgins, one day in 1888. Ruef relates that the old man called him to his bedside and expressed great concern for the future of his Republican party organization. His lieutenants, Phil Crimmins and Martin Kelly, had been trained to inherit it, but they had grown up in the rough school of politics south of Market Street, and were lacking in finesse. Ruef made a promise to call at their headquarters in Crimmins' saloon.

There, in one of the rooms set aside for conferences, Ruef had a long talk with Martin Kelly, with whom he was destined to be associated, as a servant and later as a rival, for years to come. At the time of Ruef's first conference with him in Crimmins' saloon, Kelly was thirty-eight, a stout, genial, bearded man, easily and frequently cartooned as a boss.

Kelly offered Ruef a junior partnership in a going concern, and the reasons he gave for doing so were as flattering as he could make them. Ruef's education and abilities, he said, would add polish and eloquence to the combination of Crimmins and Kelly, who "knew men better than books." Then he made the point, which, as Ruef recalled it, was most effective. On his way through the saloon, Ruef had noticed a judge who was up for reëlection, engaged in convivial conversation with a group of the voters, reporters, and politicians who crowded the bar. The career of a young lawyer, Kelly suggested, would be substantially helped by an acquaintance with judges before whom he practiced, and whom he might have done much to elect. Ruef had a vision of power and success.

From that evening in 1888, on through the decade of the 'nineties, Ruef was a "comer" in Republican politics. His law practice grew with his political importance, and brought material prosperity which he increased by investments in real estate. He became obsessed with the dream of going to the United States Senate.

Fascination with politics made him a tireless worker. Occasionally he forgot to eat and sleep. He learned the methods of Kelly and Crimmins, and when it suited his purposes he served them by making their nominating speeches and writing their platforms. Often, however, he was found in independent "reform" factions of the party, mainly because his growing ambitions made him impatient at being a mere tool of the regulars. "But the people were apathetic," he wrote, "and so I drifted with the machine. Whatever ideals I once had were relegated to the background."

In his own right, Ruef became boss of the "Latin Quarter," where he was soon a familiar and popular figure. In the school of ward politics, he mastered the various methods of garnering votes. He was active in every possible social organization. He studied the strange psychology of patronage, the moth-like fascination of the job seeker with the glamor of even the lowliest and least secure public office. It was, he observed, "a craze . . . as enslaving as the drink or drug habit," and he marveled at the often repeated pattern of a young man ruining his life by deserting a safe and promising trade or business for the mirage of a poorly paid and temporary political job. Even minor political office holders were subject to endless demands for charity, and Ruef learned that a successful boss could never refuse aid to the needy or decline to purchase tickets to a benefit. Ruef discovered, also, that one special favor bound the recipient and his friends "more tightly than a dozen general benefits to the community." Influence with police-court judges on behalf of an arrested person could produce a release form signed in blank by the judge. Friends in the assessor's office could overlook gross undervaluations of the taxable property of corporations and wealthy individuals, and cement their support for the boss. The auditor's office could expedite payment of a bill or approval of a doubtful claim. The coroner's office could modify the circumstances entered in a report of death, relating to culpability or damages. There were as many opportunities for favors as there were functions of city government.

As a platform speaker at political meetings Ruef learned to capture the most hostile and unruly audience with a combination of humor, courage, and tact. Once, when he arrived at a rally, the platform was already dotted with "uncooked omelettes," and more were obviously being reserved for him. "Throw all the rest of those eggs at one time, so that we can get down to business," Ruef suggested. "They look like good fresh eggs. That egg man cheated you if you bought them for rotten ones." The audience laughed and cheered, and a deluge of eggs soared to the platform, spattering against posts, onto coats, and even into the band's brass horns. "Are they all in?" They were. Then, without interruption, Ruef managed a speech that ended in goodnatured applause.

Boss government in San Francisco, as elsewhere, needed revenues as well as votes. In the 'eighties and early 'nineties, some of its largest levies came from public service corporations which, in turn, depended for their prosperity and even their existence on the coöperation of politicians. The board of supervisors, the legislative body of the city and county of San Francisco, had the power to grant franchises and privileges to street railroads, for example, and also to fix annually the rates to be charged the public by gas and water companies. The Democratic boss, Chris Buckley, was believed to have accepted large payments from these corporations in the guise of attorney's fees. Payments to a boss who was not an attorney could be called campaign contributions, or given no name at all. Such payments were not bribery in the legal sense because, technically, the boss held no public office. Conspiracy to pass some of the money on to persons who were legally public officials was always extremely hard to prove.

There was basis for the general belief, however, that bribery of the supervisors was systematically practiced. The boss's ability to command the largest payments from the corporations depended on his control of a "solid seven," a majority of the twelve supervisors, able to pass an ordinance, or a "solid nine," able to override a veto by the mayor. Martin Kelly's memoirs describe several instances in which he managed the bribery of the "solid seven" supervisors whom he had succeeded in electing in 1890, in the period of his greatest success. Corporate interests were sometimes conflicting, as when cable railroads opposed the granting of trolley franchises to would-be rivals, or competing gas companies sought preferential rates. In such cases, supervisors would not always stay bought.

Political corruption in San Francisco reached one of its frequent climaxes in 1891. In the preceding election, the Southern Pacific's organization had been extraordinarily liberal with funds for the campaign expenses of prospective legislators favorable to the reëlection of Senator Stanford. The subsequent scandals both in the metropolis and in the state capitol led the Wallace grand jury in San Francisco to make a sweeping investigation. This grand jury's actions were invalidated by the state supreme court on technical grounds, but in the meantime it had accomplished several practical results. Buckley and Rainey fled the country. In the next election, in 1892, a group of reformers won control of the Democratic party of San Franciso. The most durable member of this group was a young lawyer named Gavin McNab. He established the reputation of being a "good" boss, and the period of his control of much of the city government, between the election of 1892 and that of 1901, was an era of reform.

Reform was especially apparent in the administration of James D. Phelan, a Democrat who was elected mayor with McNab's support in 1896. Phelan was the son of one of the city's most prominent capitalists, and San Franciscans loved to repeat the legend of the elder Phelan's reply to a tobacconist who asked why he smoked five-cent cigars, when his son's brands were much more expensive. The father's reply was, "I do not have a wealthy father." In fact, however, James D. Phelan's own achievements in banking and real estate had also made him a millionaire in his own right. He was capable, public-spirited, and immune to the temptations that afflicted politicians of lesser character and inferior financial independence.

In the last years of the 'nineties, Mayor Phelan sponsored the drafting and adoption of a new charter. In 1856, a state law had consolidated the city and county governments, and San Francisco had been governed under this act, with a maze of amendments, ever since. The main weakness of the system of government under the old consolidation act was the absence of centralized authority. The board of supervisors was supposed to exercise both legislative and executive power, but responsibility divided among so many was evaded by all. The mayor was a figurehead. Many mayors had been upright men, but they had been helpless. Phelan and other business leaders believed that the obvious failures of government in San Francisco could be remedied by a more business-like centralization of executive responsibility, and this was one of the sweeping changes made in the "short ballot" and "strong Mayor" charter that became effective in 1900. It vested administrative authority in the mayor and in boards of commissioners, whom the mayor appointed and whom he could remove. This was an important and necessary reform; but it made would-be bosses more anxious to secure control of the mayor's office.

The era of dominance of Democratic and reform elements in San Francisco in the middle and later 'nineties was a period of lean years for the "regular" Republican leaders, Kelly and Crimmins. But in spite of their lack of success in city elections, they kept their hold on the Republican county committee, and, hence, on the counting of ballots in Republican primaries. Ruef had a hearty contempt for both men, and believed that if he could replace them in control of the Republican machine in San Francisco, it would benefit not only himself but the city and the party as well.

At the turn of the century, Ruef thought he saw his chance. For the first time, party primaries were being brought under regulation by state law. Ruef had already had considerable success in his own North Beach district in appealing to bona fide voters, whereas he had neither the desire nor the ability to compete with Kelly and Crimmins in the stuffing of primary ballot boxes. Now, he believed, with primaries under the same legal sanction as regular elections, more real voters would take an interest in the primaries, and his own abilities could be given a fair opportunity.

Ruef based his hopes of capturing the Republican convention for the San Francisco election of 1901 on a scheme for a new organization of voters, incorporated on June 8, 1901, as the Republican Primary League. "On the surface it was to be truly representative," he wrote. Besides himself, there were to be ten directors, chosen by Ruef with an eye to support from "every religion and creed, and from labor, capital, merchant, practical politician, and professional man. Each was to be given equal prominence." Ruef's knowledge of urban society and its relations with politics was rising to the level of an applied social science.

In order to secure the support of the city's leading Republican newspapers, the *Call* and the *Chronicle,* Ruef consulted their proprietors in making up the Republican Primary League's directorate. The *Call* had become one of the many interests of the sugar magnate Claus Spreckels in 1895. Shortly afterward, it had passed into the control of his eldest son, John D. Spreckels, who took an active hand in its direction whenever his own interests in Republican politics were concerned. John D. Spreckels was usually in rebellion against the Southern Pacific in matters of state and city politics, and, on the shifting sands of factional alliances, he and Ruef had occasionally done favors for each other, both in San Francisco and at the state capitol at Sacramento. In a long interview, Spreckels and Ruef agreed on a director, a friend of both, the manager of a wholesale hardware company, who "represented the mercantile and employing elements, as well as Mr. Spreckels and the *Call.*"

The proprietor of the *Chronicle* was Michel H. de Young, who had been one of its founders in 1865. Like John D. Spreckels, de Young was not on good terms with the Southern Pacific. He blamed its political machine for the repeated failure of his hopes for a seat in the United States Senate, and he was willing to encourage Ruef's bid for control of the San Francisco Republican organization, partly for the sake of causing the railroad inconvenience. When Ruef invited him to "propose a personal representative" in the Republican Primary League, de Young named a real estate executive, acceptable to Ruef as representing "the influential brotherhood of real estate brokers and capitalists generally," as well as de Young and the *Chronicle.*

Along with the Republican Primary League, Ruef's faction of the party set up its own Republican county committee and presented to the registrar of voters a rival petition for a place on the primary ballot to elect a convention as the rightful "Republican Party of San Francisco." In this, Ruef was overruled by the San Francisco board of election commissioners and also by the state central committee of the Republican party, which the Southern Pacific controlled. The railroad's state machine preferred Kelly and Crimmins to their troublesome young rival. The Kelly-Crimmins slate for convention delegates went on the primary ballot with the endorsement of the recognized Republican party machinery, and the Ruef slate without such an endorsement.

The primaries on which Ruef had pinned such high hopes were held on August 13, 1901. Less than a third of the registered voters came to the polls, and the Republican Primary League was overwhelmed by the Kelly-Crimmins machine. Ruef's elaborate and sanguine plans for becoming Republican boss of San Francisco were thus rudely frustrated. But it was just at this time that unexpected circumstances gave him an entirely new opportunity for power. The great strike of 1901 was about to precipitate the Union Labor party into San Francisco politics.

CHAPTER II

The Union Labor party

SEVERAL factors had combined to make San Francisco a "union town" *par excellence*. One of these had been the laboring men's discovery of their power in the late 'seventies. Under the passionate Denis Kearney, labor had been "embattled rather than organized." In its brief career, his Workingmen's party had elected a mayor, forced the adoption of the new state constitution of 1879, and crystallized the demands that compelled the federal government to accept the policy of Chinese exclusion.

During the 'eighties, union organization of the skilled trades in San Francisco had gone forward rapidly, aided by the fact that the remoteness of the city from other large urban centers made it difficult for employers to bring in new non-union skilled labor.

The most extraordinary successes of unionism in the last years of the nineteenth century and the early years of the twentieth came in the building trades, and were due, in part, to the leadership of a more or less benevolent despot, Patrick Henry McCarthy. Born in Ireland in 1863 and apprenticed to the carpenter's trade, McCarthy had come to Chicago and then to St. Louis in the early 'eighties. He had taken part in the organization of the Brotherhood of Carpenters and Joiners of America, and, on coming to San Francisco in 1886, had been elected president of the District Council of Carpenters. In 1898, he organized the Building Trades Council of San Francisco and governed it under an autocratic set of rules which were to keep him in power as its president for twenty-four years.

Part of the secret of McCarthy's success lay in his genius for union politics, part in his mastery of the principles of "business unionism." "I have always believed," he said, "that labor and capital should go hand in hand." The Building Trades Council existed, in his conception, not to destroy the construction industry, but to encourage it and to increase its prosperity by coöperation with the employers. He knew that his workmen had, in their skills, a highly valuable commodity to sell, and that, like their employers, they wanted the highest possible return for their commodity. He demonstrated, both to the workers and to the employers, that the highest returns were to be won not in quarreling with each other, but in combining in a joint monopoly of labor and materials, increasing the costs of both, and passing the increases on to the public. One example was particularly convincing to employers in the building industry. In 1900, the members of the planing mill owners' association locked out their workers rather than grant the eight-hour day, arguing that they could not sell lumber in San Francisco in competition with nine- and ten-hour mills outside. McCarthy showed his own business ability by organizing a large planing mill with capital subscribed by his unions. Not only did he break the lockout, but he secured admission of the union-owned mill into the association and agreed that none of his building trades unions would work in San Francisco with lumber from any but association mills. He had achieved "a corner in labor," an ingenious combination between a closed shop and a closed market.

McCarthy's unions took full advantage of their power. Not only did they command high wages, but they carefully restricted their output and spread the work. Painters restricted the size of the brush, bricklayers the number of bricks per day. Most unions limited the number of apprentices. The plumbers admitted only their own sons, and a few unions admitted no apprentices at all for years at a time.

While McCarthy's methods were autocratic and monopolistic, they did make for industrial peace. They were in interesting contrast with the methods of his contemporary, Sam Parks, boss of the building trades of New York. Parks, violent, vicious, and ignorant, had fought and snarled his way up from the ranks of the bridge and structural iron workers, whose hazardous occupation tended to select men who were rough and reckless and to make them more so. McCarthy's "business unionism," on the other hand, had made him a pillar of his community. He was a member of the board of fifteen freeholders who prepared and proposed the new San Francisco charter, and Mayor Phelan appointed him to a four-year term on the new civil service commission.

The building trades unions tended to regard themselves as a skilled aristocracy of labor, and McCarthy's organization was little concerned with the welfare of less fortunate workers, whether unionized or not. Most of the city's other unions were allied in the San Francisco Labor Council. At first, the Building Trades Council was loosely federated with this body, but it was soon to secede from it entirely and even to hold separate Labor Day parades, marching in the opposite direction on Market Street. Around the turn of the century, the Labor Council was making substantial progress in a campaign to emulate McCarthy's successes, and to share in the prosperity which the city as a whole was enjoying at the time. Wealth was increasing from the building of new industries and the growth of old ones, from the federal expenditures on the troops and supplies flowing through San Francisco toward the scene of the Philippine insurrection, and from the coming of another transcontinental railroad, the Santa Fe. The Labor Council, aided by an organizer sent in by the American Federation of Labor, experienced a record boom in the organization of new unions and in the recruiting of older ones. There was a wave of "prosperity strikes." Some of the new unions were in highly miscellaneous occupations, and the conservative Building Trades Council viewed them with alarm and distaste. Its official newspaper, *Organized Labor,* remarked that "The Labor Council [has] gathered under its wings a most varied collection of eggs and hatched some curious ducklings and labeled them trades unions." McCarthy was equally displeased when the new unions adopted the hasty tactics of "organize, demand, strike."

In the spring of 1901, the employers concerned undertook a concerted campaign to turn back the Labor Council's advance. They formed an Employers' Association, whose activities were to be as secret as possible. At first, its only visible representative was its attorney, M. F. Michael. In an interview published on May 10, 1901, he pointed out that the crux of the Labor Council's campaign was the closed shop, and announced that on this vital issue the association would absolutely refuse to negotiate. Its basic principle, he said, would be "not to refuse employment to anyone solely because he does or does not belong to a labor organization." Discussing a proposal for a conference with the mayor, he said: "There is nothing to confer upon. . . . The employers are doing nothing. They are not making any row. They simply want to run their own places. The unions want to tell them that they shall not employ non-union men. That is all. It is as if a burglar should break into a house and the owner of the house should get up and protest, and the burglar should say: 'Well, let us go to the mayor and let him say who shall have this property.' "

The main test of strength began in July, 1901, when the employers in the Draymen's Association undertook to break the power of the new teamsters' union, organized less than a year before. Two successful strikes had forced the association to grant the union a closed-shop agreement. A nonunion draying company, not a member of the association, was awarded the contract for handling the baggage for the national convention of the Epworth League in San Francisco. An attendance of tens of thousands was predicted, and hope was expressed that the baggage could be handled more effectively than at the last similar convention, when much of it had not been delivered to the delegates until the convention was over. Again, however, the company which had the contract was swamped. It called in a firm which was a member of the Draymen's Association. The latter's teamsters refused to work on a job with non-union men, whereupon the association locked out all of its teamsters and resolved to end the closed shop in the draying business.

The draymen's lockout bore the marks of employer tactics which had already become apparent in the strikes of the cooks and waiters and the journeymen butchers: the larger employers were coöperating secretly with each other and were also coercing any of the smaller employers who might prefer to come to terms with the unions on the closed shop. In such a situation, the leaders of the Labor Council debated only between a general strike and a sympathy strike of the unions closely connected with the work of the teamsters. The latter policy was followed, and the recently organized City Front Federation of waterfront unions was called out on July 31.

The great teamsters' and waterfront strike of 1901 was not, as it was sometimes loosely called, a "general" strike, but it did have drastic effects. Including the teamsters, sailors, dock workers, warehousemen, and others in the cities on both sides of the bay, the strike involved directly at least fifteen thousand men. Moreover, the strikers were in a particularly vital position in the regional economy, and they succeeded in tying up much of its commerce for two months. Nevertheless, the strike was doomed. With each side accusing the other of conspiracy and agression, public opinion was confused and emotional. Labor itself was divided, with McCarthy's Building Trades Council offering neither aid nor comfort to the strike. The farmers of the region became more and more hostile as Port Costa became choked with wheat. Strikebreaking began to be substantially effective. Farmers and farm hands came to the ports to load and move crops. Former army teamsters, released from service in the Philippines, drove wagons. When university students began to accept summer jobs as strikebreakers, W. H. Goff, President of the San Francisco Labor Council, wrote a letter to Benjamin Ide Wheeler, president of the University of California, protesting that the university was favoring the rich against the poor. Wheeler replied that the university could not intervene to deprive students of the liberty to work their way through school, since to do so would discriminate against the sons of the poor. Goff then charged that many of the young "scab stevedores" were rich men's sons working not for money but against labor.

Mayor Phelan was persuaded to use the police force to protect strikebreakers. Pickets were clubbed and arrested. The regular police were augmented by a substantial number of "special officers," and a clash between a group of these men and a crowd of strikers led to a bloody riot on September 29. Three days later, on October 2, the strike was finally ended through the intervention of Governor Gage. The terms of settlement were never made public, but the Employers' Association claimed a complete victory and disbanded, and it soon became clear that for the time being the teamsters had lost the closed shop.

By vigorous tactics, the employers in San Francisco had apparently won a victory on the field of industrial warfare, but this victory had the startling effect of forcing the unions into politics. During the course of the strike, many laboring men and their sympathizers became convinced that the machinery of government in the city was being placed at the disposal of the Employers' Association. A Superior Court injunction restrained the pickets of the cooks' and waiters' union from using the word "unfair," and from intimidating restaurant employees or patrons. The merchant who was the foreman of the grand jury was discovered to be also the chairman of the Employer's Association, and strikers complained that this made it impossible to get indictments against special policemen for assaulting pickets. The president of the Chamber of Commerce was also president of the board of police commissioners and was largely responsible for the much criticized police policies of Mayor Phelan's administration. Among laboring men, the idea began to spread that if government could be used so effectively against them, they must go into politics and elect a mayor of their own.

William Randolph Hearst's *Examiner* contributed to this trend. The *Examiner* was the only major San Francisco newspaper which supported the strike, but it had the largest circulation in the city, and its vigorous support of the strikers further increased its circulation. Hearst himself had transferred the scene of his main activities to New York several years earlier, but he had continued to take an active interest in the *Examiner* and in San Francisco. He was developing ambitions for a political career, and during this period he was an ardent crusader for downtrodden majorities. One of his best journalists, Edward J. Livernash, was labor editor of the *Examiner,* and in August and September of 1901, the paper's news and editorial columns vividly argued the striker's cause. On August 10, an editorial called "Unions Have Come to Stay" said that "The attempt of the Employers' Association to destroy the Teamsters' Union is a piece of criminal viciousness that has no parallel in San Francisco." The *Examiner* also encouraged the striking unions by giving full publicity to the utterances of Father Peter C. Yorke, who had become a kind of spiritual leader of the strikers. In addresses to labor mass meetings and in a series of articles, Father Yorke gave Pope Leo XIII as his authority for a strong endorsement of unionism. He advised the strikers to be peaceable and temperate, but he was bitter in charging the city authorities with aiding the employers; and while his advice on the subject of possible political action by the unions was ambiguous, it was apparently interpreted as encouragement for the new Union Labor party of San Francisco, which, in the meantime, had been in the early stages of organization.

The origins of the Union Labor party were obscure. As early as June, there had been talk of a "labor convention" to nominate a list of union men as candidates for city and county offices. The movement had begun among the newer and smaller unions, and its leading spirit was apparently one Isadore Less, an official of the journeymen barbers. Early in July, Less had been announced as chairman of a temporary executive committee to arrange a nominating convention. The dozen other members of the original committee had come from such unions as the cooks and waiters, hackmen, machine hands, bakers, beer bottlers, pattern makers, and tailors.

In August, after the beginning of the teamsters' and waterfront strike, the older and larger unions had begun to take a more serious interest in the possibility of political action. They regarded the whole question with mixed feelings, and they were unable to agree on the idea of making the union organizations the base of a political party, or of giving a political movement their official support. The original "executive committee," headed by Isadore Less, had called for the election of convention delegates by the union organizations on a basis of one delegate per hundred of each union's members. A large number of unions responded, but most of them were unwilling to commit themselves officially; and thus, in most cases, the electing was done by "clubs" formed after the regular meeting had adjourned. The convention, which was to meet early in September, was only haphazardly representative of a part of organized labor. Moreover, this first convention of the Union Labor party of San Francisco was to be the last in which union membership was even unofficially used as a basis of representation.

In part, the unions' disagreements over questions of political action simply reflected the disunity, the personal and factional rivalries, so characteristic of the labor movement as a whole. There was also a well-founded fear that politics would intensify the existing differences. Political arguments in the past had been so disruptive that many union constitutions forbade discussion of politics at union meetings. Walter Macarthur, editor of the *Coast Seamen's Journal,* and one of the most thoughtful of San Francisco labor leaders, believed that the experiments of British trade unions in going directly into politics had actually weakened them in their struggle for economic gains. "There can be no intermediate form of organization between the trade union and the political club," he thought. "The trade union cannot go into politics and remain a trade union." In particular, "the . . . union official who seeks public office is the bane of the labor movement."

P. H. McCarthy and his building trades unions declared themselves "sternly opposed [to] participation in politics by the organizations as an exclusive political party." Later, in 1905, McCarthy came to the support of the Union Labor party, and in 1909, under special circumstances, he was elected mayor on a Union Labor ticket. In 1901, however, he was still an officeholder in the Phelan administration, and his statements on the earliest public proposals for a labor party actually identified his political interests and those of his unions with the interests of the employer groups. "The Building Trades Council," he said, "represents many thousands of property-owners and tax-payers, who are as jealous of their interests as any . . . affiliated body, commercial, mercantile, financial, or any other. . . . [It] has always worked side by side with such bodies . . . for the selection of safe and competent officials."

As the infant Union Labor party struggled into life, a prospective foster father, Abraham Ruef, was thoughtfully calculating its possibilities and its weaknesses. When his hopes of controlling the Republican machine were frustrated in the primaries on August 13, his interest in the Union Labor party became immediately more serious. "I saw that without strong outside influence it would never succeed," he wrote, "[but that] if properly organized and handled, it might broaden from a purely local organization to one of State and even National importance." It was clear that the original sponsors of the party were inept; that organized labor in general was unable or unwilling to give the movement legitimacy and strong support; and that, if the party appealed only to labor, there was little hope for it. On the other hand, Ruef thought, with his experienced guidance and the support of at least a part of his own following, the party might elect a mayor by plurality in a three-cornered race.

Obviously, none of the outstanding labor leaders could be elected, even if any of them had been willing to accept nomination. W. H. Goff, president of the Labor Council, scotched early rumors of his willingness. Andrew Fureseth, a well-known official of the sailor's union and City Front Federation, and "manager" of the waterfront strike, not only declined to be considered, but condemned the party movement as "a sad mistake, and likely risen from resentment rather than common sense." Michael Casey, president of the striking City Front Federation, would have solidified opposition and attracted support only from the more extreme elements of labor itself. The only men who seemed available were even more obscure. There was James De Succa, president of the iron moulders' union and a man of some experience in old-line party politics. And the *Examiner* reported that several members of the musicians' union had mentioned the name of their president, Eugene E. Schmitz.

The suggestion of Schmitz was one that attracted Ruef's attention. Ruef was Schmitz's personal attorney, as well as the attorney for his union. The two men were almost exactly the same age, thirty-seven in 1901, and they had been friends for fifteen years. They had been associated in a venture in the steamship business between San Francisco and Alaska. Schmitz was also one of the directors of Ruef's Republican Primary League. It suddenly occurred to Ruef that his friend was a remarkable combination of political assets. Born in the city, and with German and Irish strains in his ancestry, Schmitz would appeal both to his fellow native sons and to the two largest blocs of voters of foreign origin. His Catholicism was an asset in San Francisco. He was a model husband and father. His connection with union labor, through the musicians' union, was not such as to alienate many business men, and he had had some experience as a business man and an employer himself. He could also be thought of as a man of culture. He was an accomplished violinist and had some local reputation as a composer. For several years he had been director of the orchestra at the fashionable Columbia Theater, and had acquired pleasing manners of dress and an easy and gracious bearing before audiences. Moreover, he was tall and striking in appearance, "a commanding figure of a man," with heavy black hair and a neat beard. He lacked higher education, but, as Ruef put it, "he was a man of natural ability, of good intelligence and keen perceptions. He possessed a tenacious memory and an unsurpassable nerve. He could 'put up' a better 'front' than almost any man I knew. I had often seen him assume a pretense which successfully covered up all deficiencies. . . . He was imperturbable. His face could completely mask his feelings."

In their first conversation on the subject of the mayoralty, as Ruef remembered it, Schmitz laughed at the idea. "I have no ability to act as mayor," he said. "I have no experience. I don't know anything about municipal affairs. I couldn't go through a campaign. I never made a public address. Besides, I haven't the means to make the fight. The whole thing is preposterous."

"You have as much experience and information as many men who have been nominated," Ruef replied, "and more than some who have filled the office. What you lack can easily be supplied. The speeches and the funds we can take care of.

"You are not rabid," Ruef went on. "Although you were on the Labor ticket, you could appeal to the conservative element who are tired of all the industrial warfare. . . . Then, you are a man of fine appearance. You are tall, well built. The psychology of the mass of voters is like that of a crowd of small boys or primitive men. Other things being equal, of two candidates they will almost invariably follow the strong, finely built man. . . . If you are nominated, people will turn naturally as you pass by and say, 'There goes the Labor candidate for Mayor.' At the theatre you will have a thousand people talking about you every night and advertising you who scarcely give you a glance now. Think it over."

A few days later, Schmitz consented. "A fortune teller had read his future," Ruef wrote, "and had prophesied that, within a year, he would hold a high and mighty position in his native city. 'I'm not superstitious,' Schmitz laughed, 'but there's no use bucking a hunch like that, especially . . . when the case looks so good anyhow.' "

In the meantime, Ruef was quietly planning his strategy for directing the organization and course of the labor convention. Scanning the list of members of his Republican Primary League who were also union members or officials, he sent for them and suggested that they and their friends seek election as delegates. Especially promising were John Shakespeare Parry, of the piledrivers and bridgebuilders; W. J. Wynn, of the machinists; and Thomas F. Finn, of the stablemen. When the "Union Labor Convention" met on September 5, Ruef's men were in a strong position. Most of the other delegates were confused and without political experience or guidance. There were angry suspicions of a "slate," and of attempts by would-be bosses to "program" the convention, but these rumors were directed primarily against Isadore Less, originator of the convention idea, and against the recommendations of his committee on organization. In effect, such rumors contributed to the election of other officers, proposed by the confidential followers of Ruef. John S. Parry became chairman of the committee on credentials, chairman of the committee on the platform, and permanent chairman of the convention, while Wynn became the convention's secretary.

In drawing up a platform for Parry to submit as a majority report from the platform committee, Ruef was careful to include only moderate sentiments and demands and to leave as much room as possible for support from outside the ranks of labor. He knew that the sight of policemen riding on the drays as guards for scab teamsters had aroused bitter feelings of resentment among the majority of the delegates, but he knew also that their radicalism was vague and incoherent. A moderate platform, if well written, could satisfy them, and Ruef wrote one which was "true to every principle of organized labor, yet conservative, pledging fair dealing toward capital as well." It called for public ownership of public utilities. So did the city charter. Some of the other planks were for better schoolhouses, the arbitration of industrial disputes, the exclusion of all Asiatics, the segregation of all Asiatic children in the schools, the initiative, the referendum, proportional representation, and the abolition of the poll tax. When the platform committee made these recommendations on September 6, the convention adopted them without difficulty. The only alternative offered was a minority report which proved to be the platform of the Socialist party and was hastily rejected.

The nominations were postponed several times. After its first session, the convention met only in the evenings, since most of the delegates were part-time and amateur politicians whose days were occupied either with their jobs or with picket duty. There was a week's adjournment, for which some delegates suspected political motives, and then another adjournment for the period of mourning after the assassination of President McKinley. When the convention met on the evening of September 20, most of the delegates supposed that it would nominate James De Succa, of the iron moulders, for mayor. Ruef knew, however, that De Succa could arouse little enthusiasm, and according to Ruef's plan, Chairman Parry called on De Succa for a speech. The leader of the iron moulders made, as Ruef had expected, "the usual stereotyped, mumbled address." For Schmitz, on the other hand, Ruef had written "a five-minute speech, full of striking epigrams." Schmitz had carefully memorized and rehearsed it, "with gestures and elocutionary effect," but he delivered it as if it were extemporized. "His theatrical experience helped him wonderfully," Ruef remarked. "His voice rang out with great dramatic force." There were cheers and applause, and "in a moment, Schmitz had become a hero, an idol." The speech stampeded the convention and gained Schmitz the nomination for mayor.

The remainder of the Union Labor party ticket was the result of a combination of personal ambitions and union and factional representations. Isadore Less, of the journeymen barbers, the original founder of the party movement, had to be content with the nomination for city auditor. Over-optimistic about his chances for election, he misappropriated funds of the barber's union for his campaign expenses. Unable to replace them, he fled the country and was later brought back under arrest.

Neither the Republicans nor the Democrats could find a strong candidate for mayor. The Republican possibilities, said the *Examiner,* were "carefully picked over by the representatives of the Southern Pacific, the Market Street Railway, and the Spring Valley Water Company," to discover a man who would "carry out the orders of the bosses with a fearless disregard of the public weal." On the evening of September 30, the Republican convention nominated Asa R. Wells, the incumbent auditor. Ruef and the other delegates of his Republican Primary League minority protested against the steamroller tactics of the machine in securing Wells' nomination, and announced that they would not support him in the coming campaign. As for the Democrats, they were aware that 1901 was an unfavorable year. The popularity of Mayor Phelan as the sponsor of the new charter and as the strongest reform mayor in the city's history had vanished during the strike. His use of the police had offended labor, and his refusal to call for state troops had offended employers. The low Democratic vote in the August primaries was an indication that the party's chances for the mayoralty would be slim, and few men cared to go through a campaign to almost certain defeat. Phelan himself had already refused to run for a fourth term. Franklin K. Lane, city attorney, was popular and promising, but he intended to run for governor in 1902 and did not choose to damage his chances for the higher office. The best man available from Phelan's group of reformers seemed to be Joseph S. Tobin, a member of the board of supervisors, a respected young man of thirty, with an inherited fortune. The Democratic convention nominated Tobin early in October.

Within a few weeks, Schmitz flowered into a remarkably effective campaigner. The only detailed and intimate account of Schmitz's early days in politics was written by Ruef long after their friendship had cooled, and Ruef may have exaggerated his own role as Pygmalion to Schmitz's Galatea, but his recollections are valuable. "Ordinarily," he wrote, "Schmitz lacked application. He was not fond of work, and always preferred to amuse himself. But he had a power of assimilating ideas and a gift of memory, and he developed a marvelous faculty of joining thoughts and sentences from many speeches, prepared for him, into new ones of his own. . . . He dressed well, but not extravagantly. He moved rapidly and everywhere. . . . He developed a remarkable self-confidence. If he sang a song, he did so with the impression that there was an entire operatic repertoire behind it. If he delivered one speech, it was as if he could deliver any kind at any time. Social attention was as nectar to him even in his first campaign."

In October, the unsuccessful conclusion of the great waterfront strike increased Schmitz's support from organized labor and crystallized the strikers' discontent into the idea that their only hope lay in political action. The City Front Federation, lukewarm or actually hostile toward the Union Labor party in its formative stages, now strongly endorsed the party's ticket and resolved that "while we are opposed to class government as such, we see no means of resisting class government by the rich except by inaugurating, for the time being, a class government administered by those who have suffered oppression by [it]." Andrew Furuseth announced his support of Schmitz. Walter Macarthur, in the *Coast Seamen's Journal,* called on all workers

to remember "the shooting and clubbing of strikers, the wholesale arrests of hundreds of inoffensive men, the surrender of the
entire police force to the Employers' Association." Before the
election, all the main union groups were supporting Schmitz,
except the Building Trades Council, and Ruef believed that
many of its members would disregard the dictates of President
McCarthy and vote for labor's magnetic new hero at the polls.

Ruef doubted, however, that votes from the ranks of organized
labor alone would insure a plurality, and Schmitz's campaign
speeches, like the platform of the party, were written with an eye
to allaying the fears of businessmen. One of Schmitz's statements,
to the *Examiner*, was typical: "We are CONSERVATIVE AND
PRACTICAL in our ideas. I deprecate violence, am in favor of
peaceful measures at all hazards, and believe in the fair and
friendly consideration of invested capital, as correlative to similar
consideration for organized labor. I am NOT IN FAVOR OF DIVIDING
THE PUBLIC INTO CLASSES." When Tobin charged that Schmitz
was another Denis Kearney, Schmitz replied cautiously: "Nothing in my career or in my associations requires me to be a defender of Kearneyism." On the other hand, he was careful to
point out, Kearney's Workingmen's party had discovered and
produced some excellent men, including congressmen and
judges.

While Schmitz was catching the public eye, Ruef was holding
a series of quiet conferences designed to gain support wherever
he could. The fact that Ruef was a man of extensive real-estate
holdings, and that Schmitz himself was at least a part-time businessman and employer of labor, tended to reconcile some
businessmen to the idea of backing a labor candidate. Some of
them noticed, also, the possible advantages of a party ostensibly
of union labor, but actually controlled by men sympathetic with
business. Ruef was able to enlist one group of businessmen in
a body. The support of the liquor interests was of great political
importance. Among the registered voters of San Francisco, there
were a thousand saloonkeepers—more than there were grocers.
In addition, there were nearly a thousand bartenders. The liquor
industry, as a whole, took a high degree of interest in politics
because of its dependence on the favor of political officeholders
in matters of licensing and other legal regulations. Moreover,
saloons were often centers of political discussions for their pa-

trons. The liquor interests had appointed a central committee on endorsement of candidates. In a conference with the members of this committee, Ruef persuaded them to support Schmitz quietly and without a public endorsement which might alienate the votes of temperance elements.

Ruef was still keeping his own role in the Union Labor party as secret as possible, and his daily conferences with Schmitz were held quietly in Ruef's informal headquarters at The Pup restaurant, at Schmitz's home, or in Ruef's law office. Although he was managing the campaign only unofficially, Ruef was contributing heavily to it, both from his rich fund of experience of campaign tactics, and from his purse. According to his own estimate, Ruef spent $16,000 of his own money on Schmitz's first campaign, while the mayor's salary was only $6,000 a year for a two-year term. Money had to be spent for the hiring of halls, for ornamental hangings, for mountains of literature, for bonfires and bands, and for thousands of cloth signs and banners for paraders. "Elections cannot be carried without money," he wrote, "and large amounts of money at that. Politics is not a poor man's game. The amount of expenditure required even for legitimate expense is enormous. It is a lamentable, yet indisputable, fact that, for any important office, the expenses of a campaign are usually more than its entire salary. Somebody with an interest must put it up. The interest may not always be corrupt, but is always selfish."

As the returns came in on election night, November 5, it was clear that the Union Labor party had elected a mayor by a safe plurality. The final returns mounted above 21,000 votes for Schmitz, 17,000 for Wells, and 12,000 for Tobin. The victory demonstration was unprecedented in duration and volume. The musicians' union sent out a call for all disengaged men to march and play at the head of parades in honor of their leader, and whole orchestras joined them as soon as evening performances ended at the theaters. In the early hours of the morning, when the outcome was certain, Ruef went to Schmitz's home to congratulate him. "We pledged eternal fealty," Ruef wrote. "We talked of the uplift of the masses and of the elevation of labor."

The remainder of the party's ticket was less successful, indicating that Schmitz's personal magnetism had been much more compelling than the union label as such. The party elected only three of the eighteen supervisors, and none of its candidates for other offices.

In the days just after his dramatic victory, even Schmitz's opponents were warm and generous in their congratulations. Mayor Phelan said that there had been merit in labor's protests, that the Employers' Association had been tactless and indiscreet, and that it was "a splendid object lesson in popular government" to see labor's grievances expressed through the safety valve of an orderly election, without suspicion of intimidation or fraud. Franklin K. Lane, in a letter to John H. Wigmore, described Schmitz as "a decent . . . young man who will surprise the decent moneyed people and anger the laboring people with his conservatism." An *Examiner* reporter, who had voted for Tobin, interviewed Schmitz and came away scoffing at the campaign predictions of disaster and a flight of capital if Schmitz were elected. He called the outcome "the best thing that could have happened for San Francisco," and praised the mayor-elect as "what is termed a fine animal, a man of boundless energy and perfect health."

In estimating Schmitz's potentialities, no one was more enthusiastic than Abraham Ruef. He knew, however, that his pupil had much to learn in the few weeks before he was to take office. With Ruef's advice, Schmitz gave out a statement that his wife was ill and that he was taking her for a long visit with her parents in Watsonville. Actually, he departed with Ruef to an obscure little hotel in Sonoma for a period of uninterrupted instruction in municipal affairs. There was one intensive course with the city charter as a textbook, and another from Ruef's wide knowledge of practical politics and law.

"We were the only strangers in the little village," Ruef wrote. "We had left our whereabouts unknown except to our immediate families. There, in undisturbed peace, we talked and planned day and night. There in the tranquil Sonoma hills I saw visions of political power; I saw the Union Labor party a spark in California which would kindle the entire nation and make a labor President; I saw the Union Labor party a throne for Schmitz, as Mayor, as Governor—as President of the United States. Behind that throne, I saw myself its power, local, state—national. . . . I saw myself United States Senator."

CHAPTER III

The first Schmitz
administration

In PLANNING the strategy of his first two years of dominance over the politics of San Francisco, Ruef subordinated all other considerations to his ambitions for the future of Schmitz and himself. In his own words, "every act" of Schmitz's first administration was carefully weighed for its "vote-getting possibilities." Schmitz was a remarkably capable *poseur,* in his official actions as well in his poses for newspaper photographers. Ruef himself had become thoroughly opportunistic. Few men in San Francisco had less actual concern for the welfare of labor, for example, and no other idealistic considerations hampered his movements. Ideas, which he formulated adeptly, were tools or weapons in the service of his dreams for his future career.

There was no further attempt to conceal the relations between the new mayor and his legal adviser. Two days after the election, Schmitz wrote Ruef a rather long and very warm testimonial letter, concluding with the assurance that "I shall . . . feel myself privileged at all times to consider you as my friendly counsellor and to call upon you whenever I may require assistance in the solution of any of the perplexing and complicated questions which must necessarily arise in the conduct of so vast and important an office." This letter, while actually one of several testimonials written at the same time to various groups and individuals, was published alone and without comment in a weekly paper a few days afterward, and this had the effect of emphasizing its importance in the public mind. When Schmitz was inaugurated on January 8, 1902, Ruef's only official position was that of attorney for the mayor's office, without salary, but his real position of leadership in the new administration was well known.

Ruef had always been accustomed to long hours, and his fascination with his new duties led him to work even harder than before. Politics, he once said, were the only form of recreation he required. In his law offices at the corner of Kearny and California streets, he wrote most of the mayor's official papers, and he had a steady stream of conferences, not only with Schmitz but with commissioners, officials, and seekers of favors or jobs. Nor did his conferences end at ten in the evening, when he left his office. They continued past midnight, during and after his dinner at The Pup, a French restaurant on Stockton Street near Market, where a dozen callers were often awaiting him when he came in. Ambition left little room for minor vices in Ruef's character. He did not smoke; and he confined his drinking to wine for dinner, and to a single small glass of liqueur, occasionally absinthe. Nor had he time to take an interest in any particular member of the opposite sex. Once there was a rumor of an engagement, during a vacation which his doctor had ordered him to spend at Lake Tahoe. Ruef turned the reports aside with his usual good humor. "I love them all," he said, "married or single."

Even Ruef's desire for money was subordinate to his political ambition. The two elements were, however, decidedly interrelated. While his political activities left him little time for his own lucrative practice, he was able to turn over most of the detail of it to an increasing number of assistants in his office, who admired their chief intensely and served him without stint. Moreover, his political position brought him wealthy and powerful clients whose needs for his legal services were slight or nonexistent, but who hoped for his political favor.

The first offer of this kind came from the Pacific States Telephone and Telegraph Company, through its confidential political agent, Theodore V. Halsey. There would be no court cases, Halsey explained, but the company might call upon Ruef occasionally for advice in matters of municipal law. Ruef was aware that this was a polite euphemism, and that what Halsey really wanted was the assurance of his friendship if rival companies should seek franchises to break the monopoly which Pacific States enjoyed. The retainer was $250 a month, delivered by Halsey, not by check but in cash. In accepting it, Ruef knew that the highest ideals of the legal profession would have required its refusal. He rationalized his acceptance, however, by noting that Halsey had asked him for no direct favors, and that in matters of franchises there were no favors in his power to grant. As yet he controlled not even a substantial minority of the board of supervisors.

Ruef found another excuse in believing that such transactions were practically universal. "In the system of exploitation of public service which has prevailed in the municipalities of this country, under whatever administration," he wrote in his memoirs, "it may be safely assumed that whenever a special favor of any consequence has been granted the corporation has paid for it," not necessarily in direct payment of money, but often in suggestions of profitable investments, in sinecures, or in attorneys' fees, sometimes with elaborate pretense of bona fide legal duties.

In general, the first Schmitz administration, while opportunistic, was not very corrupt. Its possibilities of corruption would in any case have been limited by its lack of control not only over the board of supervisors but even over the appointive boards of commissioners. Under the charter, the system of membership in these bodies was one of gradual rotation. In the police commission, for example, there were four members with four-year terms, only one of which expired at the end of each year. In 1902, Schmitz appointed only one of its members, while three were holdover appointees of Mayor Phelan. The commissioners, not the mayor, were directly responsible for appointment and removal of the chief of police. Charges that Schmitz and Ruef were responsible for police graft during the first Schmitz administration were in this sense grossly unfair. It was true that the mayor was ultimately responsible for the actions of the commissioners, and that he had the power to remove them for cause, but in the case of the holdover appointees on the police commission it would have been politically unwise to do so. Such an action would have pleased the former strikers, but conservatives would have attributed it to the sort of class sentiment which the Union Labor administration was in fact being careful to avoid.

In the case of the board of health, on the other hand, a peculiar situation existed which made it possible for Schmitz actually to gain popularity by ordering wholesale removals. In 1900, under Mayor Phelan, there had been reports of bubonic plague in San Francisco's Chinatown. The resulting excitement had gone to extremes. The whole of Chinatown was quarantined and fumigated, and the occupants of streetcars passing through it were required to remain inside the closed parts of the car. By 1902, however, it was apparent that the evidence of bubonic plague had been doubtful from the beginning. Doctors disagreed, and San Franciscans, embarrassed by their own earlier hysteria, became less anxious about the disease than about the reports of it in eastern newspapers and their effects on potential tourists, immigrants, and investors. In March of 1902, Schmitz issued a peremptory order removing the majority of the members of the board of health for having continued to publicize their belief that the disease existed in the city. He did this, however, without formal notice or a formal hearing, and on these grounds the discharged officials gained an injunction which kept them in office for several months. The mayor's action, nevertheless, was almost universally applauded by the San Francisco newspapers.

Another opportunity for a popular gesture came when the board of supervisors submitted the annual budget for the mayor's approval. In June, 1902, and again a year later, Schmitz vetoed dozens of items, and these vetoes appealed strongly to the traditional sentiments of San Francisco taxpayers, to whom any government at all was at best a necessary evil, and all public office-holders were "taxeaters." Since the eighteen-fifties, politicians had sought popularity by retaining the "dollar limit" of not more than one dollar's property tax on each hundred dollars of assessed valuation. Even the new charter had bowed to this fetish by providing that needed revenues in excess of the dollar limit were to be raised only by separate levies for special funds. Schmitz's vetoes of items in the budget had another advantage also: they could not actually injure the services concerned. It was comfortably certain that the board of supervisors—nine Democrats, six Republicans, and only three Union Laborites—would override the mayor's vetoes by votes of fifteen to three.

Ruef's strategy in party politics during the first Schmitz administration appeared at the time to be devious and complicated, but actually it was guided by fairly simple and consistent objectives. Its aims were to make Schmitz governor and Ruef United States senator, and in the meantime to secure Schmitz's reëlection as mayor until the larger achievements should be possible. Ruef hoped to accomplish his larger ambitions through an eventual alliance of Schmitz's supporters in union labor, Ruef's own following among San Francisco Republicans, and the state Republican organization controlled by William F. Herrin, chief counsel of the Southern Pacific. There was little hope of going beyond San Francisco through the Union Labor party alone.

This was particularly apparent when Ruef temporarily lost control of the Union Labor party organization in 1902. Labor's success in electing a mayor had caused the leaders of some of the larger unions, especially those in the City Front Federation, to take a more active interest in the political movement for whose original organization they had had little responsibility. There was much criticism of the way in which Ruef and his protégé, John S. Parry, had manipulated the party's first convention, and in 1902 the Union Labor Central Club was formed, with the avowed objective of "rescuing the Union Labor party from professional politicians." One of its leaders was Michael Casey, an official of the teamsters' union and president of the City Front Federation. Casey had a large following of union members, and Schmitz had been forced to appoint him commissioner of public works. Other influential backing for the Union Labor Central Club came from William Randolph Hearst and the *Examiner*. Hearst was then preparing to run for Congress in New York, as a preliminary to running for the Democratic nomination for the presidency of the United States two years later, and he was making a wide appeal for labor support. He would have liked to attach Schmitz and the Union Labor party to his own following, and to remove them from the influence of Ruef. In San Francisco, Edward J. Livernash, labor editor of Hearst's *Examiner*, was campaigning for the Union Labor and Democratic nominations for Congress. Speaking to a mass meeting of the Union Labor Central Club, he called for a purge of "the Ruefs and Parrys of San Francisco, . . . the wretched political parasites who have fastened themselves upon trade unionism in politics . . . [the] scurvy politicians, self-serving nobodies . . . having no interest in the grand purposes of unionism."

So successful was the agitation of the Union Labor Central Club in 1902 that Ruef quietly withdrew all opposition to its ticket of delegates in the August primaries. As a result, it gained control of the Union Labor party organization for the year. Livernash received both the Union Labor and the Democratic nominations for Congress, which insured his election. Instead of holding a grudge against Hearst and Livernash, however, Ruef permitted Schmitz to make a trip to New York in behalf of Hearst's campaign. At a Hearst rally of union men in Madison Square Garden, the Union Labor mayor of San Francisco spoke vigorously: "I am in New York to say to you that . . . William Randolph Hearst has done many things for which my people are thankful. If you send him to Congress you can depend upon him as you would upon any brother in your own ranks." Schmitz thus helped to swell the vote which gave Hearst a seat in the House of Representatives, and Hearst's gratitude gave Schmitz the support of the San Francisco *Examiner* for years to come. Moreover, Schmitz's return trip from New York was a grand tour. He called at the White House, and secured President Roosevelt's promise to visit the Pacific Coast in the following year. He inspected the scenes of the recent coal strike in Pennsylvania; was entertained with honor by the mayor of Chicago; addressed the annual convention of the American Federation of Labor in New Orleans; and spoke to a meeting of such labor unions as there were in Los Angeles. All this was well publicized in the Hearst newspapers, and gave Schmitz the beginnings of a national reputation.

Ruef, in the meantime, was cultivating his hopes for advancement in the Republican party through an alliance with William F. Herrin, who was now the political boss of the state for the Southern Pacific Railroad. Herrin was a man of remarkable ability, although he had become a personal devil for California reformers. His features and his beard did indeed give him a slightly satanic appearance, which did not escape the attention of hostile cartoonists. Herrin had first come into prominence as attorney for such interests as the Spring Valley Water Company, the Miller and Lux Land and Cattle Company, and the Sharon estate. When he was still in his thirties, in 1893, his ability in quiet negotiations out of court had led Collis P. Huntington to give him the most important attorneyship in the West, the post of chief counsel of the Southern Pacific. Herrin regarded it as his duty to protect and advance the interests of his client, the railroad, not merely in the courts, but in the state legislature and in state politics, and so skillfully did he blend the functions of chief counsel and chief political manager that when Edward H. Harriman purchased control of the railroad in 1901, he continued to employ Herrin.

In 1902, Herrin's foremost concern with politics was the election of a governor satisfactory to the railroad. The incumbent, Henry T. Gage, had been satisfactory enough, and Herrin would have liked to secure his renomination. For decades, however, neither the Republicans nor the Democrats had renominated a governor. This was due in part to the fact that the nominating conventions, from one term to another, were largely made up of the same bodies of office-seekers, and no governor could have had sufficient patronage to satisfy them. Such was apparently the misfortune of Gage in the Republican state convention of 1902. Herrin finally transferred his support to George C. Pardee, a physician who had entered politics as mayor of Oakland. Ruef, finding it too early to hope for a nomination of Schmitz, sought Herrin's gratitude by supporting Pardee after the latter had been nominated.

In San Francisco, Pardee's nomination for governor was peculiarly objectionable to labor. When he had been mayor of Oakland, two incidents of the disordered times of 1894 had given rise to exaggerated legends about him. One was that he had ordered firehoses turned on the San Francisco regiment of "Coxey's army" when it had been slow in leaving Oakland on its way to the national capital. The other was that he had organized a middle-class militia, armed with pick-handles, and used it against the striking members of Eugene V. Debs' American Railway Union. Neither charge was well founded, but both were widely believed. Workingmen in San Francisco had wanted the renomination of Governor Gage, who had refused to send in the state troops in the strike of 1901. Angered by the nomination of Pardee, they turned their support to the Democratic candidate, Franklin K. Lane, city attorney of San Francisco. For Ruef and Schmitz to support Pardee for governor put the Union Labor administration in the anomalous position of having to furnish a police escort to prevent violence when "Pick-handle Pardee" bravely attempted to speak to audiences in the workingmen's districts south of Market Street. In the election, however, Lane's majority in the city was not large enough to prevent Pardee's election by a slender margin in the state as a whole. This meant that Ruef's influence had held the balance of power, and put Herrin's state Republican organization substantially in his debt.

Ruef was able to cement his alliance with Herrin still more tightly when the state legislature assembled and prepared to elect a United States senator in January of 1903. It was important to the Southern Pacific to control a small group of far-western senators. By exchanging votes with other blocs in Washington, they could protect the railroad from adverse federal legislation on interstate commerce, rates, and mail contracts, while their influence over the patronage extended even to the appointment of federal judges. In 1903, Herrin's program called for the reëlection of Senator George C. Perkins, a wealthy shipping magnate. This was opposed, however, by a group of rebellious Republican legislators, and they, together with the Democrats, could have prevented Perkins from gaining a majority of the total membership. On the other hand, if a caucus of all Republican legislators could be called, all the Republican members would be bound by its selection, and Perkins could be reëlected by a majority of the Republican majority rather than of the legislature as a whole. At the last moment, the call for a caucus lacked four signatures of the number required under the rules to force it to convene. Ruef controlled four Republican members from San Francisco. He withheld them until Herrin came to him to ask for them as a special favor. Then he instructed them to sign, thereby making Perkins' election possible. In the matter of his own senatorial aspirations, Ruef was biding his time. He was still under forty.

In May, the reception for President Roosevelt in San Francisco put the personal qualities of Schmitz to a test from which he emerged with greatly enhanced prestige. The main occasion of the President's reception in the golden state, as Ruef recalled with some amusement, was a "golden banquet," on the evening of May 12. There were six hundred guests, at twenty dollars in gold per plate, "on golden service, with golden wine and golden oratory at the golden Palace Hotel." Ruef thought it somewhat pretentious. Even the table coverings were of cloth of gold, with fringes of golden tassels. Nevertheless, the *Bulletin* insisted, the whole effect was one of "elegance rather than gaudiness." Ruef knew that it was an occasion when, of all times, Schmitz must make good. He wrote a short speech, which Schmitz committed to memory. During the dinner, Ruef, who was among the guests, heard murmurs of apprehension over the impression the mayor would make. Most of the wealthier citizens of San Francisco had always doubted that labor was fit to govern, and particularly that a Union Labor official could be fit to represent the city on such an occasion as this. Ruef was proud and delighted to notice, however, that Schmitz was nearly the most self-possessed man in the room. At the table of honor, the President had adroitly directed the conversation toward music. In the speeches which followed the dinner, no one but the President spoke more graciously than the mayor. When Schmitz's "fine resonant voice" was silent, the audience of distinguished San Franciscans applauded with relief and exultation. A few were chagrined at his success, but the majority were proud of him. The next day, Schmitz rode to the Cliff House in a carriage beside Roosevelt, and on the 14th he sat on the platform while the President dedicated the Dewey monument in Union Square. The labor mayor wore "his familiar broad-brimmed black slouch hat." It contrasted with the silk hats around him, but no one could question its taste or its dignity. "Schmitz," thought Ruef, "had arrived."

For the mayoralty campaign of 1903, Ruef succeeded in recapturing the Union Labor party organization. The party convention of the previous year, controlled by the anti-Ruef Union Labor Central Club, had chosen a county committee which the courts recognized as the legal one. As the 1903 primaries approached, this body issued such resolutions as "That Abraham Ruef is regarded by the Union Labor party as its enemy and the enemy of good government, wherefore we disclaim all responsibility for him and for his minions in the public service." Among Ruef's "minions," his opponents were so unwise as to include Schmitz. In 1903, the anti-Ruef forces in the Union Labor party were composed mainly of the union followers of Michael Casey. Casey was now president of the board of public works, and his rivalry with Schmitz had become an open and bitter feud. But

Hearst had withdrawn the *Examiner's* support from the anti-Ruef movement in gratitude for Schmitz's services in his campaign for congress in New York. Schmitz, moreover, was too obviously the only Union Labor man who could be elected mayor, and when Casey's followers attempted to read Schmitz out of the party as a tool of Ruef, they invited disaster. The county committee's ticket of delegates was badly defeated in the primaries by a Schmitz ticket, and a convention was elected which renominated Schmitz with a whoop.

In the Union Labor convention of 1903, the union organizations as such had even less influence than they had had in the party's original convention. Then, in 1901, union political clubs had elected delegates on a basis of union representation, albeit unofficially and somewhat haphazardly. As a nominating convention for political offices, such a body was not legally recognized, and its ticket had had to be placed on the general election ballot for November, 1901, by a petition with several thousand signatures. The regular primary law required the election of convention delegates by local districts, and after 1901 the Union Labor party followed this more recognized procedure. The Union Labor Central Club was composed of union representatives, and in the 1903 primaries its slate of anti-Ruef-and-Schmitz delegates from the various districts was chosen entirely from union men "in good standing." When these were overwhelmed at the polls by the ticket of Schmitz delegates chosen largely by Ruef, there was a marked decline of actual union influence in the party organization.

Continuing a somewhat forlorn opposition to Schmitz during the campaign, the Union Labor Central Club issued an announcement that "we consider that we have no ticket in the field." Ruef was described as an "evil genius," an "octopus," a "would-be Republican boss" who had twice "foisted" on the Union Labor party a candidate "technically but not at heart a Union Labor man." This document concluded with a resolution which was a masterpiece of invective and mixed metaphor: "We . . . prefer to see the Union Labor party lie dormant for the ensuing year while the cancer is being removed from our vitals than to see it in disgrace with Abraham Ruef and his pliable henchmen to work the ship."

Ruef's efforts to secure a Republican endorsement of Schmitz were unsuccessful. Instead, the Republicans nominated Henry J. Crocker, a somewhat obscure nephew of one of the founders of the railroad.

When Franklin K. Lane, having lost his chance to be governor, accepted the Democratic nomination for mayor, the Union Labor Central Club endorsed him and called on all true union men to vote for him instead of for Schmitz. To reduce the number of labor votes for Lane, Ruef made use of two campaign stratagems. One illustrated the recurring importance of anti-Chinese feeling in San Francisco politics. Hearing that Lane employed a Chinese cook for his family, Ruef devised a card printed with a picture of a leering Chinaman, whom the card christened "Ah Chew," and quoted as saying, "Me cookee for Lane while Lane talkee for white labor." The other device was equally ingenious. It associated Lane with the democratic boss Gavin McNab, whom many workingmen believed to have been responsible for Mayor Phelan's order putting policemen on the scab drays during the teamsters' strike. Lane's supporters had plastered the town with billboards reading: LANE'S THE MAN! Just above or to the left of these posters, supporters of Ruef and Schmitz then pasted up placards asking: "Who is the Man who will do all he can for Gavin McNab the friend of the scab?" And Lane's own posters answered, LANE'S THE MAN! Lane insisted in his speeches that he and McNab were actually hostile to each other. But against such a well-turned piece of propaganda, his protests had little effect.

While these devices were cutting into Lane's labor support, he was also losing votes among the conservative opponents of Schmitz, who were tending to unite behind Crocker in the belief that he had a better chance than Lane of defeating the Union Laborite. Lane expressed his view of the situation in one of his letters to John H. Wigmore: "The Republican nominee represented the employers, the Union Labor nominee, the wage earners. I stood for good government, and in the battle my voice could hardly be heard."

On the night before the election, a Lane meeting opened at the Mechanics' Pavilion with most of the seats still empty. Ruef was worried that this might lead even more of Lane's supporters to desert him for Crocker in order to defeat Schmitz. At Ruef's order, the word went out to a crowd of Schmitz paraders to change their line of march, roll up their Schmitz banners, and parade to the Mechanics' Pavilion to bolster the impression of enthusiasm for Lane.

In most respects, the three-cornered race of 1903 bore a remarkable resemblance to the campaign in which Schmitz had first been successful two years earlier. He was reëlected by an even more substantial plurality.

After the election of 1901, the *Bulletin* had wondered editorially whether the German system of choosing mayors, by canvass among the men who had made good records as mayors of smaller cities, was not more scientific than the American system. "Election time," the *Bulletin* remarked on election day in 1903, "is the occasion for an emotional debauch by which the American people vary the tedium of their routine lives."

CHAPTER IV

Fremont Older's crusade

Not even the defeated candidates could have been more chagrined by the reëlection of Schmitz than was Fremont Older, managing editor of the San Francisco *Bulletin*. Older was a striking figure over six feet two inches tall, lean and vigorous, his face characterized by a flowing and virile mustache, and by an expression of energetic seriousness of purpose well borne out by his journalistic methods. Since 1895, when R. A. Crothers had hired him for the *Bulletin*, Older had greatly increased its circulation and influence by zealous support of political reform and by frankly sensationalist news policies. He claimed credit for having been the original Phelan man in 1896. He was proud of his support of the civic reforms achieved during the Phelan administration, and felt it his duty to protect them from a relapse under Schmitz and Ruef.

According to Older's own account of the origins of his long and implacable crusade to drive Schmitz out of the mayor's office, it began as the result of an incident immediately following Schmitz's first election in November, 1901. Through a mutual acquaintance, Older sent Schmitz what was intended to be a friendly message of advice. The new mayor, said this message, now "had in his hands the greatest opportunity that any politician has had in America for many a long year." If he would be sincerely true to the laboring people who had elected him, there would be no limit to what he might achieve politically. He might be governor, or senator. But, Older advised, Schmitz should beware of associating with Abraham Ruef, who would "lead him astray."

Older was angered when Schmitz sent a reply "that he thanked me very much for my advice, but that Ruef was his friend and they were going to stand together." In the meantime Schmitz's letter to Ruef had been made public. This seemed to Older to be a "letter of marque," a license to the Mayor's attorney to extort tribute from all who sought favors, an invitation to "see Ruef." It convinced Older that there would be graft in the Schmitz administration, and he began to look for traces of it.

In the campaign of 1903, the *Bulletin* supported Franklin K. Lane on the ground that only he could save the city from its relapse into corruption. As yet, Older had found little actual evidence of corruption, and his attacks on Schmitz and Ruef were in rather general terms. The *Bulletin* charged that Schmitz's appointments of commissioners had been directed toward building a political machine with patronage, and that he had "industriously undermined" the civil service principles of the charter. There was a long list of pieces of real estate acquired by Ruef since Schmitz had been elected. There was a cartoon of "Our Mayor," showing Ruef seated in the mayor's chair, surrounded by sacks of "boodle," winking, and smoking a large cigar. These attacks were ineffective. It was pointed out that Ruef was a non-smoker. Many workingmen attributed the attacks on Schmitz to anti-labor sentiment. One observer thought that the *Bulletin's* charges gave an impression of unfairness, malice, and exaggeration which actually lost votes for Lane, and that in particular many Jews attributed the attacks on Ruef to anti-Semitism.

On election night, Older watched while a crowd of Schmitz supporters, "drunk with victory, danced a carmagnole under the windows of the *Bulletin* office." Listening to their taunts, he resolved to continue his crusade until Schmitz and Ruef had been driven from power by the *Bulletin's* exposures of the graft which he now expected to increase rapidly. As a necessary preliminary, he had already done his best to purge graft from the offices of the *Bulletin* itself. He had put a stop to the practice of selling news columns for what was actually advertising matter; and he had finally persuaded Crothers that the paper's increasing prosperity would enable it to get along without further subsidies from the railroad and public utility corporations.

After the campaign of 1903, and for years to come, the *Bulletin,* in Older's words, was "doggedly in pursuit" of the leaders of the administration. News coverage of the city government was devoted almost entirely to those activities which appeared to be discreditable. News columns became editorials, denouncing Schmitz and Ruef. In 1904 and 1905, only the most sensational events of war or crime could take precedence over headlines charging graft in municipal affairs. The shooting of the race-track magnate, Frank T. "Caesar" Young, by his sweetheart Nan Randolph, one of the original Floradora sextet; the fall of Port Arthur to the Japanese; the death of Mrs. Leland Stanford under extraordinary circumstances—only such events could crowd charges of municipal corruption off the *Bulletin's* front page.

In later years, Ruef himself admitted that graft had steadily increased during this period. In his own defense, however, he insisted that it was the *Bulletin's* "constant criticism and attacks [which] weakened the moral fibre of many connected with the Labor administration [and] inclined officials to say that they might as well have the game as the name." Ruef admitted that he himself had given orders for a lax and "liberal" policy in the enforcement of some of the city ordinances, but he insisted that the motive of this policy had been to make friends. He knew that when minor officials and policemen extorted bribes for such favors, it was *bad* politics, since every such extortion made an enemy. Whatever the causes, there could be no doubt that the "moral fibre" of the Union Labor administration deteriorated after Schmitz's reëlection in 1903.

The major types of graft in American cities of the time were in the fields of franchises and rates, police powers, and public works. Franchise and rate graft resulted from the broad authority of the elected municipal legislative bodies in the regulation of privately owned public utility corporations. In previous decades, in the case of San Francisco, this had often involved bribery or other improper influence in the board of supervisors. But any opportunity for either the first or the second Schmitz adminis-tration to have received graft of this type would have been limited by the fact that only three Union Labor supervisors were elected in 1901, and only two in 1903, one of the latter having had Republican endorsement.

Though public utility franchise and rate graft involved the largest lump sums, there were other important types of munici-pal corruption, made possible through non-enforcement of city ordinances by executive agencies of city government. The most notorious of these resulted from the power of the police commission to grant licenses for the sale of liquor, the powers of the police department over gambling and prostitution, and the powers of the board of public works over public building and paving contracts and private building construction permits. It was in such matters as these that corruption became possible for the Schmitz administration in 1904 and 1905, since by his third year in office Schmitz had appointed majorities of the rotating memberships of most of the boards of commissioners. And it was this type of graft to which the *Bulletin* began to devote its constant attention.

The board of public works was composed of only three members, one of their terms expiring each year, so that by 1904 Mayor Schmitz had appointed the entire membership. This, and the fact that the mayor's brother Herbert was one of the three commissioners, led Older to instruct the *Bulletin* reporters to watch its activities with particular care. By degrees, their reports became steadily more sensational. An early example was the *Bulletin's* charge that the rock-quarrying firm of Gray Brothers was gaining special privileges by employing Ruef as its attorney. One of the quarries was located in the Telegraph Hill cliffs. Many of the poverty-stricken families who lived on the hill had complained that the Gray Brothers' blasting was undermining their houses, as well as their peace of mind, and the board of supervisors passed an ordinance to stop it. The mayor vetoed this ordinance. Later, the board of public works passed an order that only the "blue" type of rock should be used in paving the city streets. The *Bulletin* pointed out that all of the "blue" rock in the neighborhood of San Francisco was in the Gray Brothers' quarries.

The next two items to receive the *Bulletin's* attention were the condition of the streets and the awarding of paving contracts. The board of public works awarded one such contract to the new firm of F. M. Yorke, a brother of Father Peter C. Yorke, one of the original and leading advocates of the Union Labor party. When the bill was presented, it seemed excessive for the amount of work done. In an investigation by the finance committee of the board of supervisors, it was charged that F. M. Yorke & Co. had submitted the lowest bid, and gained the contract, after a verbal promise by Commissioner Herbert Schmitz that it could complete only part of the work and submit a bill for the whole of it. The company avoided investigation of the charge by accepting several thousand dollars less than it had asked, in full payment for the work actually completed. When the *Bulletin* publicized this account of the matter, Father Peter C. Yorke asked his followers in the Church and in the unions to boycott the newspaper.

In its beginnings, Older's crusade against the Schmitz administration had received only lukewarm support from his employer, who was uncertain as to the effects on the *Bulletin's* circulation and profit. An incident in September, 1904, removed the last of Crothers' hesitations. Late on a Saturday evening, as he was leaving the *Bulletin* office, he received a blow from a piece of metal pipe, which might have crushed his skull had its force not been broken by his derby hat. Falling, he was struck again, but he made a loud outcry, and his assailant hurried away. There was no attempt at robbery, and this, the *Bulletin* argued editorially, proved that hired revenge and intimidation could have been the only motives. The Schmitz administration, this editorial continued, should take warning from the retribution which the Vigilance Committee of 1855 had meted out to Casey, the gambler and politician who had shot and killed James King of William, then editor of the *Bulletin,* because the *Bulletin* "persisted in attacking the scoundrels who were then in control of the municipal government." Crothers had an understandable reluctance to take the mantle of James King of William on his shoulders, but he finally did so with fury and courage, particularly after an insult was added to his injury. The detective who made the official report of the affair told a reporter for the *Examiner* that it was "a case of too many Scotch highballs." At Crothers' outraged demand, the detective was demoted to the rank of patrolman. Later, the *Bulletin* claimed, Ruef commanded his promotion to detective sergeant. Crothers and Older hired bodyguards and returned to the attack with renewed vigor.

San Francisco, prosperous and growing, was experiencing a boom in building construction of all kinds. The *Bulletin* informed the grand jury, without effect, that the mayor had secretly been made a partner in the building company of his friend, "Jerry" Dineen; that the board of public works, under the mayor's brother Herbert, was refusing building permits to clients of other contractors under pretense of rigorous enforcement of the building code following the disastrous Iroquois Theatre fire in Chicago; and that the mayor himself was suggesting to disappointed applicants that the Dineen Building Company was more familiar with the legal requirements for safe buildings. Its prices were considerably higher. A related charge, which the grand jury did investigate, was that the board of public works had granted a permit for construction of a ten-cent theater, the Baldwin, with too many seats and too few exits and obviously unsafe from fire and panic, after Ruef had become owner of more than a third of the shares of its stock.

The most sensational of the *Bulletin's* charges of corruption in the board of public works involved the construction of a building which Fremont Older claimed the distinction of having christened "the Municipal Crib," at 620 Jackson Street in China-town. According to these charges, three partners, including George Maxwell, a former secretary of the fire department, bought an old Chinese opium den, which was then condemned by the board of health as unsanitary. The board of public works ordered it torn down at the city's expense, and granted a permit for the construction of a three-story building to be called the Standard Lodging House, and to be constructed by the Dineen Building Company. When the establishment was nearly finished, a building inspector reported that it was obviously not intended for use as a lodging house, but rather as a house of prostitution, containing about a hundred small apartments or cubicles. Herbert Schmitz, president of the board, reprimanded the inspector for being suspicious and overzealous and pigeonholed his report.

The establishment opened in May, 1904, and in November the *Bulletin* began to publish charges against it. An editorial called "Gold Mine for Graft in Dive" alleged that the cubicles were rented to women at three dollars per day in two shifts, and deduced that the annual income to the owners would be an extraordinary one for a "lodging house" in such a district. In January, 1905, under the headline "Gang Given a Brothel Corner," the *Bulletin* alleged that the police were raiding other such places in order to destroy competition for the "municipal" enterprise. At the *Bulletin's* urging, representatives of the grand jury and the district attorney's office raided 620 Jackson Street and arrested 72 women. The owners, whose identity was not yet known, sought relief in the courts through the medium of an otherwise obscure man who had leased space in which he operated a cigar stand and a perfume counter on the first floor of the premises. This person's attorneys persuaded Superior Judge Hebbard to issue a restraining order against further raids in the building, on the ground that they damaged his legitimate business. When Hebbard was criticized for this action, he returned the case to Presiding Judge Seawell for reassignment. Seawell took it himself. In July, 1905, when it finally came up on his crowded calendar, the testimony was so confusing that he could see only one way to resolve the contradictions, as to whether the place was a bona fide lodging house or otherwise. He stationed himself in front of it on a Saturday evening. "While I cannot use that as evidence," he remarked in court the following Monday, "I can and do . . . state the fact as I saw it on these premises. The condition was like that of a theatre, where you see a continuous stream of people going in and coming out." He withdrew the order restraining further raids, but the police did not seriously interfere with the operation of the place until 1907.

At first, Older's justification for calling 620 Jackson Street a "municipal" establishment had rested largely on inference. It was "unreasonable to suppose," the *Bulletin* argued, that the owners would have spent so much money on the building unless they were assured of the administration's protection; and it was "idle to think" that the Schmitz administration would have overlooked the opportunity to share in such an income. In 1904 and 1905, however, these were only suspicions and rumors. Not until 1907 was it to be disclosed that Ruef had made an agreement with the owners whereby he received one-fourth of the profits, half of which he said he paid to Mayor Schmitz.

The element of police protection in the affair of the Municipal Crib involved charges of corruption engineered through the police commission and the police department, which the *Bulletin* had not been neglecting during its campaign against the board of public works. For decades, most police officials in the larger American cities had taken what they regarded as a realistic view of the human vices of gambling and prostitution. They considered real suppression impossible, and yet they were compelled by law to make a pretense of it. As a result of this situation, some degree of "police protection" and "police graft" had become the usual compromise. More or less open prostitution, for example, had prevailed in San Francisco since the beginnings of the gold rush. Most of it was conducted in the notorious Barbary Coast, a loosely localized area north of the main business and financial district, extending in length about ten blocks in from the water-front, and in width about five blocks, mainly between Commercial Street and Broadway. The origins of the name Barbary Coast were obscure. According to one guess, it was first applied by a sailor who thought it as piratical as the coast of North Africa had ever been. By the turn of the century, the more expensive establishments, known as "parlor houses," were mainly located in another area, the Uptown Tenderloin, west of the main business district, and centering in Stockton, Powell, O'Farrell, and Ellis streets, running northward and westward from Market. "Tenderloin" was not an expression coined in San Francisco. Originally it had meant the 29th police precinct in New York City, which offered unusual opportunities for police graft, one captain having said when he was transferred there "that whereas he had been eating chuck steak he would now eat tenderloin."

Neither Schmitz nor Ruef believed in the possibility of driving prostitution out of existence, and both said so publicly. Commenting on the matter of 620 Jackson Street, the mayor was quoted as saying: "It seems to me that we must recognize the fact that the evil which this enterprise is said to represent must continue to exist here, as elsewhere, and if it must, certainly it is better that it should be located in Chinatown than anywhere else. The actual use to which the building is put should be left entirely to the discretion of the police." In a public speech, Ruef "advocated as desirable and wise the plan of concentration and seclusion in regard to such establishments."

Schmitz's appointments to the board of police commissioners were among his most difficult administrative problems during his whole career as mayor. His first appointment, in January, 1902, had been that of Harry W. Hutton, attorney for the City Front Federation. Since the main reason for union support of Schmitz in his first election had been discontent with police policies under Mayor Phelan during the waterfront strike of 1901, the City Front Federation had insisted on the appointment of its own attorney as a police commissioner. In January, 1903, the Federation had demanded the reappointment of David I. Mahoney, who had been the only commissioner under Phelan to vote against police escorts for strikebreaking teamsters. By this time, however, Schmitz had openly broken with Michael Casey and other Federation leaders. He defied their wishes and acceded to Ruef's by appointing John A. Drinkhouse, a former public administrator and one of Ruef's closest political associates. The next appointment was that of Thomas Reagan, a street paver and a political follower of Ruef. Reagan had been a delegate of the pavers' union to the Union Labor convention of 1901, in which he had worked for Schmitz's nomination. The term of the last Phelan appointee, Commissioner J. R. Howell, did not expire until January, 1905, when Schmitz appointed Dr. Joseph Poheim, a former member of the board of health, who had Ruef's friendship and confidence.

Shortly after taking office, Commissioner Reagan had become an insurance agent. The *Bulletin* remarked on the large number of saloons among his new insurance clients, and charged that the insurance they were really buying was that of the commissioner's friendship against the time when their licenses were to be renewed. About the same time, the cigarmakers' union protested to the Labor Council and to the mayor that Commissioner Drinkhouse, the sole agent in the city for a certain brand of Cuban cigar, was increasing the number of his saloon customers by intimidation. Schmitz investigated and announced that the increase in Drinkhouse's clientele was a "natural, unforced result" of his position. The mayor advised the union cigarmakers and the Labor Council not to be made the tools of "avowed enemies of the administration."

In the meantime, the *Bulletin* was making similar charges against Schmitz and Ruef themselves, in the matter of what it called "municipal whiskey," and "the local whiskey ring." The *Bulletin* began this attack by pointing out that printed on the business cards handed to saloonkeepers by salesmen of the Hilbert Mercantile Company, wholesale liquor dealers, the name of "A. Ruef, Attorney" appeared in larger type than the name of the company's president. The inner history of this affair was revealed two years later in an investigation brought on by creditors of the enterprise. It appeared that the Hilbert Mercantile Company had temporarily avoided bankruptcy by an agreement with the administration. Saloon men in the red light district were to be compelled to buy large quantities of low grade whiskey at high prices, in return for police protection. The company overextended its credit accounts however, and failed after the earthquake and fire in 1906.

All the ancient forms of Chinese gambling had flourished in San Francisco since the coming of the Chinese in the eighteen-fifties, and the infrequent attempts of the police to enforce the later ordinances against it had been generally unsuccessful. Older had a "vague intuition," and some basis in logic, for believing that there must be police graft in Chinatown, and on the basis of this belief he published charges against the administration which he was never able to substantiate. On July 30, 1904, the *Bulletin* stated the amount of Chinatown protection money as $8,000 per month, but the details of contributions from lottery companies and their agents, fan-tan tables, houses of prostitution, and opium dens, were given in such round figures as to be obviously guesses. On November 30, on the basis of a surprise raid on several fan-tan clubs by Police Commissioner Hutton, the *Bulletin* amended its figures, and under large pictures of Schmitz, Ruef, Chief Wittman, and police commissioners Reagan and Drinkhouse, it printed the headline: "These Five Men, and Only These, Have the Power to Protect the Chinese Gamblers, Who Pay $9,035 a Month for Protection." At the demand of Ruef, Older appeared before the police commission, and admitted that he had no evidence for the charge except his own feeling of certainty. More angry than ever, Older tried desperately to find evidence. The sergeant of the police squad in Chinatown was Tom Ellis, and by the device of putting Ellis secretly on the *Bulletin's* payroll, Older induced him to turn over to the grand jury $1,400 which he said he had received in weekly installments from an agent of the Chinese gamblers, Chan Cheung. Ellis testified that he did not share this money with anyone. Only Chan Cheung could have had evidence of payments to anyone higher than Ellis, and under the strongest pressures he refused to say a word.

The current grand jury was free from administration control. The chairman of its police committee was a personal friend of Older's, and he coöperated in Older's somewhat extra-legal attempts to obtain evidence. Nevertheless, the police committee's report to Foreman T. P. Andrews of the grand jury was cautious. "We are inclined to think," it said, "that the final resting place of the money is not at this time susceptible of legal proof, but is sealed in the minds of those who handle it, and that they will commit perjury out of personal interest and fear of death at the hands of their associates." The report concluded that the police department had never made a proper attempt to suppress Chinese gambling, but that the committee was satisfied that Schmitz and Ruef had no connection with it.

The police commission, after holding its own hearings on the protection charges, exonerated its own suspected members, Drinkhouse and Reagan, and placed the responsibility and blame upon Chief of Police George Wittman, who had been appointed under Phelan. The *Bulletin* had since accused Chief Wittman of complicity with Schmitz and Ruef, and when the commission dismissed him in March of 1905, the *Bulletin* did not defend him except to insist that he was only the scapegoat, and to predict a worse appointment. His successor was Jeremiah Dinan, who was promoted to chief of police from the rank of detective sergeant, over the heads of seven captains. The *Bulletin* did not deny that Dinan had made a good record as a sergeant, and that he had secured the convictions of many desperate criminals. But it charged that his methods were those of the "stool pigeon school" of police officers, based on wide and intimate personal acquaintance in the underworld, and that he had shown no signs of executive ability.

Of all the transactions of Ruef and Schmitz during the latter's second administration, the one with the most enduring consequences was the affair of the "French restaurants." Since the days of the gold rush, San Francisco's restaurants had been a distinguishing feature of the city's life. In the early period, there had been few family homes. The city's visitors as well as its citizens possessed both wealth and the taste for spending it, on fine food as well as other luxuries. Even after the turn of the century, San Francisco, with one-fifth the population of Chicago, still had a larger number of restaurants. Among these, the term French restaurant had a special meaning which did not include all of the establishments kept by Frenchmen. The *Bulletin* once remarked that the French restaurant was San Francisco's "peculiar institution." On the first floor there was a public dining room to which respectable family groups could and did come, and in which good food was served at moderate prices. On the second floor were private dining rooms, luxuriously furnished, often with couches as well as tables and chairs. On the third and higher floors were private supper bedrooms, rented as in hotels, but with less restraint. It was generally understood that respectable women did not go above the first floor.

The French restaurants of San Francisco had existed for decades, with relatively little public censure. They were a well known tourist attraction, and the city was rather proud of them, as it was of its reputation for gaiety in general. There were about a dozen of them, representing a capital investment of perhaps a million dollars, not including the value of the choice sites on which some of them stood. One of these was leased from one of the city's soundest trust companies.

For their very considerable prosperity the French restaurants were dependent on the city government for their liquor licenses. Wine, as Ruef remarked, was the "fundamental Gallic element" in French dinners. The city charter required the quarterly renewal of every liquor license by majority vote of the police commission. In March, 1904, Commissioner Harry W. Hutton began to vote against these renewals, arguing that the French restaurants were luxurious houses of assignation, and a menace to the character of the young. Only two votes in the commission were necessary to prevent a renewal, but for several months none of Hutton's three colleagues, Reagan, Drinkhouse, and Howell, would join him in an adverse vote.

Mayor Schmitz as an advisory member of the police commission, ex officio, held several conversations with Commissioner Thomas Reagan on the subject of license renewals. Reagan made a tour of inspection of the French restaurants, but he found nothing to persuade him to vote against them until November, 1904. At this time, the liquor license of Tortoni's restaurant was about to be reviewed for renewal. The cooks' and waiters' unions had been making an unsuccessful drive to unionize the establishment, and their business agents, M. P. Scott and Charles A. H. Smith, resorted to a trap to bring pressure on the proprietor. They engaged two men to have dinner at Tortoni's and to ask the waiter to introduce them to female companions who would accompany them to one of the upper floors. Scott and Smith

submitted their evidence to Commissioner Reagan, who, as a
union man himself, was sympathetic with their objectives.
Reagan in turn presented the evidence to Mayor Schmitz.
Reagan later insisted that the mayor asked him at this time to
vote not only against Tortoni's but against all other French
restaurants as their liquor licenses became subject to renewal.
In any case, Reagan voted for the resolution which revoked the
license at Tortoni's; and at the meeting of the police commission
on Tuesday, January 3, 1905, his vote added to Hutton's prevented the renewal of the license of one of the largest French
restaurants in the city, Delmonico's, on O'Farrell Street opposite
the Orpheum Theatre.

The other French restaurant keepers were now deeply worried.
Late in the evening of the adverse vote on Delmonico's, Ruef,
at his home, received a telephone call from Jean Loupy, proprietor of The Pup, which Ruef had long made his informal political headquarters during his dinner hour. Ruef informed Loupy
that he was willing to become attorney for the French restaurant
keepers, and Loupy called several of them to a meeting the next
day to suggest that they jointly employ Ruef as counsel at $7,000
per year for two years. One of the proprietors of Marchand's,
Pierre Priet, did not trust Loupy, whom he believed to be seeking a commission for himself in acting as Ruef's broker in the
matter. Priet went to Ruef in person, and on Friday, January 6,
in Ruef's office, signed a contract to employ Ruef as attorney at
$5,000 per year for two years. At Ruef's suggestion Priet signed
as "President" of a "French Restaurant Keepers' Association of
San Francisco"—an organization which had not existed before
and which held no formal meetings afterward. In one informal
conference, the members of the association apportioned their
contributions toward the first annual payment to Ruef. Pierre
Priet of Marchand's, Joe Malfanti of Delmonico's, Antonio
Blanco of the New Poodle Dog, and Max Adler of the Bay State,
paid $1,175 each; Jean Loupy of The Pup paid $300. Priet took
the total, $5,000, to Ruef. In a separate transaction, three smaller
restaurants paid Ruef an additional sum of $500.

Fremont Older was accustomed to dine at Marchand's, and
there Pierre Priet had told him of his fear that his restaurant
would be put out of business by the loss of its license. On Saturday, January 7, 1905, the day after the signing of the contract,

Older heard a rumor of it. Hurrying to Marchand's, he found Pierre in a state of happiness as deep as his earlier gloom. He had sent for the doctor, he told Older, and he was sure that "Dr. Ruef" could cure all of his troubles. On the same afternoon, Older hurried into the last edition of the *Bulletin* a front page story charging that Ruef had extorted a fee from the French restaurants for "protection."

Ruef testified later that he explained his contract with the French restaurant keepers to Mayor Schmitz shortly after the contract was made; that he told the mayor of receiving the first $5,000 payment; that he explained the source of the money and told Schmitz that if the latter would accept half of it, he would be glad to give it to him; and that thereupon he did give it to him. These statements Schmitz later denied.

To accomplish the renewal of the licenses would require the withdrawing of one of the two adverse votes, either Hutton's or Reagan's. According to Reagan, the mayor asked him privately to change his vote, but he refused to do so. He had voted against the licenses at the mayor's own request, he argued, and to reverse himself would make him appear ridiculously inconsistent before the public. On Sunday afternoon, January 15, Schmitz called a conference at his home, at which the guests were Ruef and police commissioners Reagan, Drinkhouse, and Poheim. When Reagan again refused to change his vote, Schmitz expressed some sympathy for his position, and resolved to accomplish the same result by removing Commissioner Harry W. Hutton for cause.

Schmitz had never been particularly friendly with Hutton since the City Front Federation had dictated his appointment. During 1904, Hutton's individual campaign against the French restaurants had been only one phase of a series of investigations and charges against gambling and vice, which he undertook on his own initiative, and for which his motives have remained obscure. Enemies whom he made in the course of these activities retaliated by secret investigations of Commissioner Hutton himself, and furnished the information to the mayor. Under the charter, the mayor had power to remove any appointed official simply by sending to the board of supervisors a statement of cause. The mayor's communication to the supervisors on January 25, 1905, removing Hutton as police commissioner, was one of the most extraordinary documents in the city's administrative history. While it began with general charges against Hutton's public and private character, the bulk of it consisted of a pitilessly detailed daily report of a phase of his personal life. The report demonstrated that he was living with a young woman to whom he was not married, and stated the woman's name. The document included other similar accusations.

Hutton's successor had not yet been appointed when the police commission met on the evening of February 1, 1905. Ruef appeared as attorney for four French restaurants whose liquor licenses had previously been denied renewal, and proposed a series of regulations which he himself had drawn up. These provided that restaurant and hotel facilities must be separate aspects of such establishments; that dining rooms and bedrooms must not be on the same floor; and that all hotel guests, both permanent and transient, must sign a register. As several of the French restaurant keepers remarked later, these regulations made no very substantial changes in the manner in which they had always conducted their business. By votes of two to one, the police commission adopted Ruef's proposals and renewed the licenses of his clients on their promise to comply with them.

In its accounts of what it knew and what it suspected of these proceedings, the *Bulletin* rose to new heights of sarcasm and denunciation. It asserted that Hutton's private life had "no bearing on his standing as a Police Commissioner," and was not the real reason for his dismissal. It criticized the mayor for having had "the needless indelicacy to mention the name of the woman —an act for which he would be thrown out of any club and lose his social standing, if he were a member of any club or had any social standing." Repeating its charge that Ruef had forced the French restaurants to "raise a sack" in order to "continue their reproduction of a shadowy phase of French life," the *Bulletin* insisted that Ruef's open appearance as their attorney was conclusive proof of the charge. It remarked: "As a cheerful pirate, who does his deeds regardless of what the world thinks, Abe Ruef, landsman, rivals that eminent seaman Captain Kidd."

More and more frequently, during 1905, the *Bulletin* asserted in headlines, cartoons, and editorials that Ruef and Schmitz belonged in the penitentiary.

CHAPTER V

The election of 1905

SEVERAL factors accounted for the failure of Fremont Older's attempts to turn majority opinion against Ruef, Schmitz, and the Union Labor party during the second Schmitz administration. The very bluntness of the *Bulletin's* graft charges apparently alienated the credence of many good citizens of fastidious temperament, who found them too "shocking." Persistence in the repetition of the same or similar charges tended to satiate other readers who might at first have been deeply stirred. The *Bulletin* itself described the frustration of an editor who, tired by hours spent in composing "in his mightiest fulminatory manner a broadside against the grafters," repaired to his club, where he watched a fellow member read the paper in which his efforts appeared. "The eminently respectable member reads the war news and a divorce report on the first page; turns over the other pages, glancing at the headlines; then opens the editorial page, and, seeing the expanse of type, looks at it languidly, passes it by, and plunges into the sporting column, which, being read carefully, the eminently respectable member lays down his paper and goes in to dinner."

Lack of support from the other newspapers also weakened the effect of the *Bulletin's* attacks. Though the *Chronicle* occasionally criticized the administration, its criticisms had nothing of the persistence and virulence of the *Bulletin's*. The *Call* once referred to some of the *Bulletin's* charges as "newspaper hysteria," and the *Examiner* was strongly sympathetic with Schmitz and Ruef. Moreover, the *Bulletin* did not improve this situation when it denounced the motives of its competitors. It remarked, for example, that the *Call* was "kept as a toy by a rich man [John

D. Spreckels] who prefers it as a plaything to a steam yacht or a racing stable," and that Ruef and Schmitz had purchased its complaisance with the reappointment of its owner's brother, Adolph Spreckels, to the honorific position of park commissioner. The *Examiner,* said the *Bulletin,* was "the official organ of the grafting administration," and had "the privilege of resting its head on the very bosom of Abraham" as a result of Hearst's political bargains with Ruef.

The fact that none of the other major newspapers joined with any strong enthusiasm in the *Bulletin's* crusade during this period lent color to the impression that the policies of Crothers and Older were based on mere personal spite, and Ruef seized on this as an argument. Personal invective was a field in which Ruef was well able to compete, and he replied to the *Bulletin's* attacks in kind. In the spring of 1905 Ruef accepted a challenge to a public debate with J. E. White, a little-known attorney, under the auspices of the "Progressive Reform Club," composed of some of the members of the Fourth Congregational Church. The debate, on the subject of whether the administration deserved public confidence and reëlection, was held in the Alhambra Theatre, and only men were admitted. This, according to the *Examiner's* account, was because seats were at a premium and women were not voters. At any rate, Ruef was able to speak of Fremont Older in language of "more directness and vigor than would have been appropriate before a mixed audience." Ruef's opponent discussed the previously published charges against the administration, but his manner was so dignified that Ruef himself thanked him for the "delicacy" of his remarks. After an extended defense of his own motives and actions, in a tone which the *Examiner* called "satirical and humorous rather than vindictive," Ruef concluded that "all this excitement is based upon the statement of a single man in a newspaper," and that only the medium of the press gave Older's statements more importance than those of "an imbecilic inebriate" addicted to "gross immoralities." Next day the *Bulletin* fumed that the *Examiner* had collaborated with Ruef in prearranging this form of attack, in order to take advantage of the California law under which a newspaper account of a speech at a public meeting was a privileged communication, immune from suits for libel against the publisher.

A few weeks later Ruef devised another ingenious weapon—a newsboys' strike, or rather boycott, against the *Bulletin*. Schmitz had once been a newsboy, and his rise to the mayoralty had made him the idol of the newsboys of San Francisco. Ruef had strengthened this sentiment by arranging a newsboys' banquet in Schmitz's honor, at which Ruef was the toastmaster and many prominent officials were present. On that occasion, Schmitz had brought tears to the eyes of his audience by describing how he had fought for a corner at Pine and Montgomery streets thirty years earlier, and how he had wondered whether he would ever be as famous as were some of the men who bought his papers there. On June 27, 1905, when the mayor called a mass meeting of newsboys, he had little difficulty in persuading them to declare a boycott of the newspaper which was their hero's avowed enemy. Their enthusiasm increased still further when the mayor informed them that the *Post,* the *Bulletin's* evening competitor, which Ruef had recently subsidized, would now sell them their copies at four for a nickel instead of the usual two. Immediately the *Bulletin's* circulation was virtually halted by violence against its delivery wagons and carriers, with little interference from the police. After ten days, however, Older broke the main force of the "strike" by the simple device of paying a thousand dollars to a group of its leaders.

Since the election of 1903, Ruef's political influence had continued to grow. In spite of his support of the Union Labor administration, he had succeeded in increasing his importance in the Republican party, and he continued to hope for an eventual Republican endorsement of Schmitz, first for mayor and then for governor. In June, 1904, Ruef went as a delegate to the Republican national convention at Chicago. At his departure he was escorted from the City Hall down Market Street to the Ferry Building by a triumphal parade including most of municipal officialdom—the *Bulletin* called it a "procession of tax-eaters." In one automobile was a large floral horseshoe; in another, red, white, and blue flowers formed a huge "R" which meant, the paraders explained, not "Roosevelt" but "Ruef."

In the August primaries of 1904, although three of his political supporters were later convicted and sentenced for fraudulent voting, Ruef's delegates won in both the Republican and the Union Labor columns. This enabled him to merge the two parties' nominations, and gave him control of nearly all of San Francisco's twenty-four seats in the state legislature which met in January, 1905. While a senatorship was to be filled, the time was still not ripe for Ruef's own aspirations, and in any case political practice in the state had already assigned one of its United States senators to Southern California. This practice had prevailed through the terms of Stephen M. White and his successor, Thomas R. Bard, and in January, 1905, Frank P. Flint of Los Angeles was elected to the Senate, with Ruef's support.

As the San Francisco mayoralty election of 1905 approached, William F. Herrin and other California Republican leaders were seriously alarmed by Ruef's increasing influence in the Republican party. They might have been willing to give him control of the San Francisco Republican organization if he had been willing to drop Schmitz and Union Labor, but this Ruef refused to do. In the spring of 1905, various elements formed the Republican League to prevent Ruef from capturing the Republican nomination for Schmitz; and lest Schmitz win on the Union Labor ticket in another three-cornered election, the Republican League began to plan what amounted to a fusion movement with Gavin McNab, the "good boss" of the Democratic organization.

One basic weakness of the Republican-Democratic fusion against the Union Labor party in 1905 was that it coincided with the rise of a rabidly anti-labor movement, the Citizens' Alliance, in San Francisco. This movement first came into prominence in Colorado, where its membership had included some of the most repressive of the mine owners. The ostensible organizer and leader of the Citizens' Alliance was one Herbert George, who brought it to San Francisco in 1904. While employers' associations usually paid lip service to the right of labor to organize, the Citizens' Alliance was extraordinarily frank in refusing to do so. Its demands for the open shop were so extreme as to amount to a demand that labor unions be abolished, and its initial proclamation in San Francisco contained a vigorous statement of this point of view. This document charged: "Excessive industrial organization has been diverted from its professed legitimate purpose. . . . The labor union has usurped and exceeded the sovereignty of the State, and assumes to be superior to the civil and moral obligations of citizenship. . . . The limitation of apprenticeship to handicrafts has practically outlawed our native youth. Forbidden the right to learn a trade, they must either overcrowd the professions or fester in the vices of idleness until they require the restraint of reform schools and prisons." The proclamation spoke further of the "denial of the right of non-union labor to work at will" as an "extraordinary infringement of natural right . . . enforced by boycott and by maiming and murder." It denounced the unions for attempting "an absolute control of every man's private business, by those who have no legal interest in it, and no legal right to intrude upon it."

In one of the most unionized cities in the nation this frontal assault upon unionism was at best ill-advised. It solidified labor sentiment, and gave the Schmitz administration a brush with which to tar almost all of its opponents—the charge that they were agents of the hated Citizens' Alliance. While the organization claimed to represent not the employers but "the community," it was joined by several well-known extremists among San Francisco employers. Some of these men also became active supporters of the Republican-Democratic fusion in 1905, and Schmitz's followers industriously spread the idea that the Citizens' Alliance and the fusion movement were one and the same organization.

Another serious weakness of the fusion strategy was that fusion politics made strange bedfellows. There was the wealthy merchant, Fairfax Wheelan, a reform-minded Republican who had been the chief complaining witness in the prosecution of fraudulent voters in 1904. There was the Southern Pacific Railroad's Republican organization, with which Wheelan's reformers were willing to ally themselves in order to defeat Schmitz. Finally, there was the Democratic organization under Gavin McNab, who had entered politics as a reformer in the 'nineties, and was the railroad's long-standing enemy. Fremont Older was virtually the only member of the fusion group who was, at the outset, still on reasonably friendly terms with most of the others, and as a result it fell to him to try to suggest a mayoralty candidate acceptable to all. The advance agreement was that in preparing a ticket for endorsement by both Republican and Democratic conventions, the Republicans were to name the candidate for mayor and the Democrats the candidates for all the other offices. According to Older's account, the railroad's representatives did not object to any of his several suggestions of Republicans for the mayoralty, but Wheelan and McNab objected to all of them, and Older heard reports that they had agreed to jam through a candidate of their own whom the railroad could not accept. Fearing that this would disrupt the whole fusion movement and ruin its chances of defeating Schmitz, Older felt justified in resorting to drastic measures to compel Wheelan and McNab to accept a compromise candidate. In the course of his political alliance with them, Older had acquired knowledge of their use of various tactics which it would have been politically disastrous to them to reveal. By the blunt political blackmail of threatening to publish these matters in the *Bulletin,* Older forced Wheelan and McNab to endorse his final proposal.

No fusion candidate so selected could have received very enthusiastic support from Wheelan and McNab, and no candidate chosen primarily for his inoffensiveness would have been likely to attract real enthusiasm anywhere. The selection fell upon John S. Partridge, a respectable but colorless and obscure young lawyer who held a subordinate position in the city attorney's office. While Ruef had elected a substantial minority in the Republican convention, he made no attempt to obstruct Partridge's nomination, and was in fact delighted with it. Noticing that Partridge was "pale and spare" and "devoid of external magnetism," Ruef thought him the candidate least likely to succeed against a man of Schmitz's personality.

The fusion movement failed to establish real unity among Schmitz's opponents, and its supposed connection with the Citizens' Alliance led the various factions of organized labor and its sympathizers to support Schmitz with a much higher degree of unity than before. The only noticeable labor opposition to Schmitz in 1905 came from a small organization calling itself the "United Labor League," and purporting to be a successor of the Union Labor Central Club of 1902 and 1903 in its attempts to purge the influence of Ruef from the Union Labor party. Apparently this movement was organized by one Timothy Sullivan, an electrician for the San Francisco Gas and Electric Company, who was secretly acting as a political agent for the company and for William F. Herrin. In July, Schmitz suddenly appeared at a United Labor League meeting and captured it with a speech charging that those who would use the organization against him were in the pay of the Citizens' Alliance.

The *Examiner* supported Schmitz with vigor. Former Congressman Livernash, even though Ruef's failure to support him had led to his defeat for reëlection to Congress in 1904, tried to persuade the Democrats not to join in the fusion against Schmitz. "While I detest Eugene Schmitz and Abe Ruef," he said, "whenever the shadow of policemen killing union men arises, then Schmitz looms large. The unions believe that while he is in power the police will not be at the beck and call of Sansome Street."

P. H. McCarthy and his Building Trades Council supported the Union Labor party for the first time in 1905. The agitation of the Citizens' Alliance for the open shop in the San Francisco building trades had accomplished nothing except to arouse McCarthy's rage. He issued an open letter attributing all opposition to Schmitz to "institutions under the control of Herbert George," and made his position even more emphatic by appearing in the gallery at the organizational meeting of the Republican convention, where his booming voice repeatedly interrupted the proceedings with cries of "Herbert George" and "Citizens' Alliance." The *Bulletin* insisted that Schmitz had promised McCarthy, as an added inducement, to appoint him a commissioner of public works.

Ruef did not underestimate the danger to Schmitz's prospects from any fusion candidate for mayor, even a weak one. As for the other offices, the fusion ticket seemed to have made a certainty of the defeat of anyone who would accept a Union Labor nomination. The *Bulletin* exaggerated only slightly when it sneered that "Ruef is hawking nominations about, begging people to take them." Ruef himself did not believe that any Union Labor candidate except the mayor would have the slightest chance of being elected, and as a result he tried to choose as candidates for the administrative offices men outside of the ranks of labor who might bring particular groups to vote for the mayor as well as for themselves. The most important of these choices was that of William H. Langdon for district attorney. Langdon was a schoolteacher and lawyer who was elected superintendent of the San Francisco public schools in 1902, on the Democratic ticket with Union Labor endorsement. When Ruef offered him the Union Labor nomination for district attorney in 1905, Langdon suspected that several other lawyers had already refused it; that

Ruef merely wanted the votes of Langdon's acquaintances in the school system for the Schmitz ticket; and that his chance of actual election as district attorney would be small. Nevertheless, he accepted the nomination, as he wrote some years afterward, in the hope that its incidental advertising of his status as an attorney would bring him a more successful private law practice than he had previously enjoyed.

Some of Ruef's other selections for administrative offices bordered on flippancy. Joseph A. Stulz was tendered the Union Labor nomination for public administrator, for example, "largely because of the popularity his appearance would create as 'Foxy Grandpa,'" a comic strip character who was then universally known and whom he closely resembled.

Ruef did his best to find men of established reputation who might be willing to run for the board of supervisors, but it was there that the prospects for success seemed least promising of all. He encountered so many refusals that he was forced to make up most of the slate of eighteen candidates, very haphazardly, during the last two days before they were scheduled to be nominated by the Union Labor convention late in September. Not one of the incumbent members of the board of supervisors was a labor union man, but four incumbents, all previously Republicans, accepted Union Labor nomination in 1905. These were James L. Gallagher, Charles Boxton, Louis A. Rea, and W. W. Sanderson.

James L. Gallagher, a lawyer and former city attorney, had long been associated with Ruef in Republican politics. Active and well-liked in fraternal circles, Gallagher was about to become Grand President of the Native Sons of the Golden West. In 1904, Ruef had procured Gallagher's nomination for superior judge on the Republican and Union Labor tickets, and although defeated, he received over 25,000 votes. In February, 1905, Schmitz appointed Gallagher to a vacancy in the board of supervisors. The heavy Democratic majority of eleven members of the board included several who were adept and vigorous in harrying the Schmitz administration with attacks which the *Bulletin* eagerly publicized, and Ruef and Schmitz felt keenly the lack of a strong spokesman to defend them in the board's meetings. By offering the only labor union member, Thomas F. Finn, a position as fire commissioner, Schmitz persuaded him to resign from the board of supervisors and thus made a place for Gallagher, who liked to make a speech and could make a fairly effective one. Thus Gallagher became Ruef's leading candidate for the board of supervisors in the election of 1905.

Dr. Charles Boxton was a dentist who was one of San Francisco's leading war heroes of the Philippine campaign, in which he had served as a major in the First California Volunteers. In 1901 when he first ran for supervisor on the Republican ticket, the handsome and popular Boxton was elected by the largest vote given to any candidate, and he was easily reëlected in 1903. During his second term, he supported Mayor Schmitz's policies, and was rewarded by appointments of a relative and a friend to minor city offices.

Louis A. Rea was the best known figure of the Italian Swiss element in North Beach. A painting and decorating contractor, active in improvement clubs, he was also proprietor of a small paper, the *North End Review,* which was strongly sympathetic with union labor. He was elected supervisor as a Republican with Union Labor endorsement in 1903.

W. W. Sanderson was a wholesale grocery salesman whose family name was well known in San Francisco politics. His father had been mayor in the early 'nineties, and his brother had served as supervisor for several terms. He himself was elected supervisor on the Republican ticket in 1903, but in 1905 the fusionist agreement giving nearly the whole supervisorial slate to Democrats deprived him of a fusion nomination, and he accepted a Union Labor nomination instead.

Along with these four incumbents, there were ten union members and four business men, but of the whole list of eighteen Union Labor party candidates for supervisors, not more than six or seven were known outside their own immediate circles of acquaintance.

During the month before the election, Schmitz's campaign speeches employed a vigorous strategy of warning labor not to be misled by its enemies. Slander, he said, was exactly the weapon which capital might have been expected to use against labor-in-politics. In a series of addresses to union labor rallies, he used the slogan "Vote as you march!" He also painted a vivid picture of a conspiracy in which, he claimed, the fusion movement had originated. After his reëlection in 1903, he said, representatives of the Employers' Association and the Citizens' Alliance had held a council of war in the office of Gavin McNab. McNab had told them: " 'Gentlemen, the way to beat this man Schmitz is to start out now to impress on the people that he is a grafter." All the charges of graft since that time, Schmitz asserted, were a part of the conspiracy.

It was apparent that Schmitz's appeals for labor solidarity were remarkably effective. Moreover, he had another strong argument in the prosperity which the city had enjoyed during his years as mayor. Washington Dodge, the Democratic assessor running for reëlection on the fusion ticket, tried to counter this argument in a speech in which he reported that while San Francisco's population had grown by 31 per cent since 1901, the populations of Seattle and Los Angeles had doubled, and that while annual expenditures on buildings in San Francisco had increased by 166 per cent, the increases in Seattle and Los Angeles were 250 and 550 per cent respectively. New capital, Dodge charged, was avoiding San Francisco because of its labor government. The effect of these pessimistic statements, however, must have been lessened by the fact that the growth of open-shop Los Angeles was beginning to be a distasteful subject in San Francisco, and that it was irritating to mention it.

In mid-October Ruef adopted the bold and extraordinary device of engaging the Alhambra Theatre for an evening in which he himself made the only speech, and in which he defended himself, attacked his enemies, and held his audience from eight until after midnight. Ruef paid for the printing of more than a hundred thousand copies of the full text of his speech, a document of twelve full newspaper pages, and distributed it to every household in the city. As the *Evening Post* remarked with admiration, there were few men anywhere who had the wit to hold an audience for four hours, as Ruef had done with remarkable success.

The election of November 7, 1905, gave the Union Labor party of San Francisco a stunning victory which upset every calculation, including that of Ruef himself. In 1903, when the opposition had been divided, only the mayor and one supervisor had been elected on the Union ticket without other endorsement. In 1905, with the party opposition for every office consolidated, Ruef supposed that the mayor's own chances would be less rather than greater, and that the other Union Labor nominees would have virtually no chance at all. What actually happened was that Schmitz received more than 40,000 votes and Partridge less than 27,000; Langdon received almost the same majority of more than 13,000 for district attorney; and every other Union Labor candidate including the entire board of supervisors was elected by at least 6,000 votes.

One element in the outcome was that for the first time in the city's history the entire election was conducted with voting machines. The United States Standard Voting Machine Company advertised its products as foolproof and fraudproof. In San Francisco, however, they were unfamiliar and they seemed complicated. At the left end of each machine was the straight ticket lever, simple and inviting. On the other hand, anyone who wanted to vote a split ticket was confronted with a disconcerting battery of individual levers. The rules allowed each voter only two minutes in which he must pull the final switch that recorded his vote, cleared the machine, and opened the curtain. Quite possibly, most of the Union Labor officials, especially the supervisors, were elected by the votes of citizens who would have preferred Schmitz for mayor and fusionists for other offices, but who feared to invalidate their votes among the mechanical complexities of a split ticket.

Before the election, the *Call* and the *Bulletin* had warned fusionist voters and election workers to be on the lookout for the alleged possibility of a rubber band attached from the Schmitz lever to the Partridge lever, so as to pull the latter back to neutral before it was recorded. When the returns were in, however, there were no serious accusations that this or any other fraud had actually occurred. Even the most disconsolate fusionists admitted that the outcome was the verdict of the people.

One advantage of the voting machine was that the final results were available in less than an hour after the closing of the polls. At 7:30 in the evening, a cheering crowd swirled into Ruef's office at Kearny and California streets. Two admirers lifted the little boss to their shoulders and carried him down Kearny to Market, at the head of an impromptu parade, orderly but jubilant in the unexpected completeness of victory. Among the crowd who watched with mixed feelings from the sidewalks was a rising attorney named Hiram W. Johnson.

That a Union Labor party had been elected to control of the entire government of San Francisco brought a thrill of pride and elation to labor leaders, including those who had at first been most dubious of San Francisco's political experiment. Even the very conscientious and scholarly Walter Macarthur was now so enthusiastic that he began to prepare a history of the rise of the Union Labor party and of the causes of its victory in 1905. Events overtook his manuscript, and it was never published. Its title was "San Francisco—A Climax in Civics ."

CHAPTER VI

The origins of the prosecution

THE news of the crushing Union Labor victory came to Fremont Older in the *Bulletin* office shortly after seven o'clock on election night. "I could not believe," he lamented, "that Labor would stand by men so discredited as Schmitz and Ruef. It was far out of the range of my thoughts to imagine that any great number of the business men would vote for them." Yet the vote for Schmitz in the wealthier residential districts of the Western Addition was nearly as heavy as the majority obtained among the workingmen who lived south of Market Street. With Older as he read the returns in stunned silence were his wife and his editorial writer, Arthur McEwen. For two decades, McEwen had been a well known satiric writer on California politics. He had gone to New York, but an invitation to join Older's campaign against Schmitz and Ruef had lured him back to San Francisco, and he had written many of the *Bulletin's* strongest attacks on the administration. Now, in bitter disgust, McEwen resolved to return to New York. "I wouldn't waste my time in this mud hole of San Francisco," he told Mrs. Older. "Fremont looks as if he received a mortal wound."

Later in the evening a crowd broke the *Bulletin's* windows, and jeered the Olders as they walked along Market Street to their rooms at the Palace Hotel. Toward midnight the *Chronicle* tower, across the street from the Palace, caught fire, either from a celebration rocket or from the red flare used earlier as a signal announcing the news of Schmitz's victory. To the Olders, routed from bed lest the fire extend to the Palace, it seemed that the night's air of eerie unreality had reached a fitting climax.

There followed what Cora Older called "a fortnight of sick

despair." The *Bulletin* was almost completely silent on matters of politics. Gradually, however, Fremont Older began to recover his equanimity, and as he did so he recalled one episode of the crowded campaign with new interest. It was an incident which had had little effect on the outcome, but which now seemed to Older to offer a spark of hope. On the Saturday evening before the election, Francis J. Heney had made a sensational speech for the fusion ticket in the Mechanics' Pavilion. Heney was achieving remarkable success as special assistant to the the United States Attorney General's office in the prosecution of the Oregon land fraud cases. His national reputation as a special prosecutor gave emphasis to certain passages in his Mechanics' Pavilion address.

"I personally know," Heney had said, "that Abraham Ruef is corrupt. Whenever he wants me to prove it in court I will do so." If Schmitz were to be elected mayor for another two years, graft would become so intolerable "that the people of San Francisco will send for me in whatever part of the United States I am and beg me to come back here and put Ruef in the penitentiary where he belongs."

Two days later, on Monday, November 6, Ruef wrote an open letter to Heney which was published on the morning of election day, the 7th. Denouncing Heney's charge as false, unprovoked, and politically motivated, Ruef challenged Heney to try to prove it in court, at once. "In making the statement that you personally know that I am corrupt you lied," Ruef wrote. "You cannot personally know that which does not exist. In making the statement at a time and place which allowed no opportunity for a legal showing before the date of the election which you seek to influence, you showed the same courage which put a bullet into the body of Dr. J. C. Handy of Tucson, Ariz., in 1891, for whose killing you were indicted for murder, and upon trial were acquitted because you were the only witness to the deed."

Upon reading this letter, Heney issued a public statement reiterating his claim to "personal knowledge" that Ruef was corrupt. Ruef's reply, he said, reminded him of the tearful denials of United States Senator John H. Mitchell of Oregon, whose conviction for land fraud conspiracy he had since secured. Heney also gave an explanation of his killing of Dr. J. C. Handy in Tucson in 1891. The fact was, he said, that there had been fifty witnesses to the shooting. Handy was known throughout the town as a man of powerful physique and violent temper. He had sued his wife for divorce and the custody of five children, and had publicly threatened to kill any attorney who would take his wife's case. Heney took it, whereupon Handy threatened to kill Heney with the attorney's own gun. When Handy attempted to wrest Heney's gun from him, in front of the courthouse during the noon hour, he was shot by Heney in the ensuing scuffle. The *Bulletin* published telegrams from the governor and a supreme court justice of Arizona Territory saying that Heney had been exonerated of any blame.

On Wednesday, November 8, the day after the great victory of Schmitz and Ruef at the polls, Heney appeared before the San Francisco grand jury in answer to a subpoena, and district attorney Lewis F. Byington challenged him to produce the evidence for his claim that a competent district attorney would immediately secure indictments against Ruef. Heney was forced to admit that he had no real evidence of anything actionable. There was the French restaurant transaction, but Heney knew no more of it than the details which the *Bulletin* had published, and which the previous grand jury had found to be within the law. Actually, Heney could speak only of a rumor that Ruef had proposed to Stratton, collector of the port, a scheme for the illegal importation of Chinese women. Stratton indignantly denied this rumor. Heney then charged that District Attorney Byington was not acting in good faith; that many of the grand jurors were under Ruef's influence; and that the entire proceeding had been planned in order to "leak" a story of it to the newspapers, and to bring apparent discredit on himself. In any case, an account of the supposedly secret proceedings of the grand jury appeared the next day in the *Examiner*, in which Heney's failure to produce evidence was emphasized. The same article quoted Ruef as saying that this conclusion of the episode would mean "the exit of Heney from the stage of political life," and the end of the legal reputation "which he has so recently acquired."

Heney's whole career had been studded with similar conflicts. He had been a fighter from boyhood. He was born in Lima, New York, in 1859, of an Irish father and a German mother, who brought him at the age of six to San Francisco. There he grew up in a rough-and-tumble neighborhood south of Market, in which boys frequently fought in juvenile gangs, and in which his slight physique and belligerent temper often made him the object of the attentions of bullies. As soon as he had finished grammar school, his father wished to put him to work in his furniture store, and Heney was forced to secure unaided the remainder of his education in spite of his father's opposition and refusal of support. In night school, he prepared himself for entrance to the University of California, and then spent several years in earning the money for the expenses of a university education. During these years he often tempered his frustrations and difficulties by drinking and gambling. Having gained admission to the university, Heney was expelled before the end of his freshman year—for fighting. A "non-org" student wrote an article in a campus paper, citing Heney as a perfect example of the dissoluteness of fraternity men. Heney challenged the writer to a duel with pistols, and actually engaged in a fight with him in which a gun was drawn, though not fired.

After an equally hectic interlude as a school-teacher in the mining town of Silver City, Idaho, Heney returned to San Francisco to study law. Attending the Hastings law school, he was admitted to the bar in 1883. His health broke down, however, and intense suffering from sciatica drove him in 1885 to the drier climate of his brother's cattle ranch in Arizona. There he fought Apaches, and acquired a rancher's hostility to the Southern Pacific Railroad. In 1889 he began to practice law in Tucson, where the Handy affair grew out of one of his lesser cases. He took a prominent part in land-grant litigation, and argued three cases before the United States Supreme Court. He became active in politics, and served as a territorial delegate to the Democratic national convention in 1892. In the following year he was appointed the attorney general of Arizona Territory. Soon afterward he brought charges of corruption against the governor, and when President Cleveland delayed in removing that official, Heney resigned the attorney generalship of the territory and returned to San Francisco, where he built up a lucrative practice.

In 1903, the United States Department of Justice employed Heney as a special prosecutor in California public land fraud cases, and, during the following two years, in similar cases in Oregon. In these cases Heney was intimately associated with William J. Burns, one of the ablest of American detectives. Burns was born in Baltimore of Irish parents. He grew up in Columbus, Ohio, where his father became a police commissioner and kindled his son's interest in the problems of the detection of crime. Entering the secret service division of the United States Treasury Department, Burns made a brilliant record over a period of fifteen years, especially in breaking up gangs of counterfeiters. From these experiences, as Theodore Roosevelt once remarked, Burns acquired a tendency to believe any man guilty until proven innocent. In 1903 Secretary of the Interior E. A. Hitchcock persuaded the Treasury's secret service to release Burns to investigate the fraudulent system of acquiring titles to timber-bearing public lands in the far west; and in California and Oregon the Heney-Burns team functioned with remarkable success. Their methods were direct and vigorous. Burns became an expert in reporting to Heney on the opinions of prospective jurors. By the device of granting immunity to a lesser conspirator, S. A. D. Puter, and thus persuading him to testify, Heney and Burns secured their most notable conviction, that of United States Senator John H. Mitchell, who had been political boss of Oregon for decades.

A dream of what Heney might accomplish in San Francisco flooded upon Fremont Older as he began to recover from the shock of the election of November, 1905. The idea became an obsession, and Older planned a trip to the national capital to persuade President Roosevelt to lend him the able special prosecutor. Crothers and Mrs. Older considered the project to be highly improbable, but they were worried over Older's nervous state of mind, and after agreeing secretly that he needed a vacation and a change of scene, they encouraged him to go.

Heney himself had gone to Washington in the meantime, and Older met him by appointment at the New Willard Hotel on December 2, 1905. Older's first proposal was that Heney come to San Francisco as counsel for the *Bulletin* in a libel suit which Ruef was threatening to bring against it. Heney doubted that Ruef would actually be unwise enough to present his enemies with such an opportunity to prove the truth of their assertions. He suggested, however, that it might be possible for an investigation to proceed through the office of the district attorney, under certain conditions: first, that official must be willing; second, there must be a special fund of at least $100,000 for the expenses of a large force of secret investigators, a sum far beyond the inadequate ordinary budget of the district attorney's office; third, William J. Burns must also be willing to undertake the assignment.

Heney introduced Older to Burns that afternoon, but the first reaction of the "star of the Secret Service" was negative. How could the necessary funds be raised, he inquired, when Ruef himself would have control of the city government? Older replied that he hoped to have the private support of a San Francisco millionaire, Rudolph Spreckels. Burns felt that the investigation would not be worth while unless it could reach "the big fellows," the rich men themselves, and he was skeptical that Spreckels would continue to support it if it reached men of his own class. If he could be satisfied on this point, Burns concluded, he might be interested.

The next day, Older had an interview with President Roosevelt. The President was immediately sympathetic. He himself had tilted many a lance at corruption in high places, both in New York and in Washington. Ruef asserted privately in later years that Roosevelt feared the effects of a possible expansion of the Union Labor party into national politics, and was delighted with an opportunity to discredit the new organization before it could spread. This assertion could not have been more than a speculative one, obviously motivated by Ruef's political position. In any case, Roosevelt was attracted to Older's project. He agreed that Heney and Burns would be the best men in the United States for such an assignment, but he emphasized their value to the federal government, and would make no definite promise to release them. Nevertheless, when Older left Washington he felt strongly hopeful. On his return to San Francisco he sought a conference with Rudolph Spreckels, upon whom the fate of the project for a San Francisco graft prosecution would turn.

The fabulous history of the house of Spreckels was interwoven with a remarkably large and varied part of the economy of San Francisco, and the first two generations of the house were stamped with characteristics of strong-mindedness and vigor. Claus Spreckels, as a penniless young immigrant from Hanover, Germany, came to New York in the 1840's to work as a grocery boy. In 1856 he opened a grocery store in San Francisco. Impressed by the wastefulness of the current methods of refining sugar, he experimented with better ones in a small plant of his own, and soon acquired control of all of the sugar refining which was done in the city. He broadened his interests to include the sources of the product, and by the 1870's he was in possession of the best cane sugar plantations in Hawaii, and much of the ocean-going trade of the eastern Pacific. He returned to Germany to study the methods of obtaining sugar from beets, and established vast beet ranches in the western United States.

In the 'eighties and 'nineties Claus Spreckels' stern and pugnacious temperament led him into a series of feuds with other powerful interests, in all of which he was victorious. When the American Sugar Refining Company, or "sugar trust," sought to invade his Pacific Coast territory, he launched a counter-invasion of its eastern markets by constructing a rival refinery at Philadelphia. He was so successful that the trust was compelled to buy his eastern refinery at his own price, and to agree to stay out of the western part of the country. When the Southern Pacific Railroad refused to meet his terms in the matter of freight rates, Claus Speckels subscribed the bulk of the capital for a rival railroad down the San Joaquin Valley. Much publicity was given to the many smaller subscriptions, and to the idea that the enterprise was a revolt of farmers and local business men against corporate tyranny. Soon after the road was constructed, however, Claus Speckels sold his controlling interest in it, at a large profit, to the Santa Fe.

Claus Spreckels had four sons, John Diedrich, Adolph, Claus Augustus ("Gus"), and Rudolph. Rudolph, the youngest, was born in San Francisco in 1872. When he was seventeen his father offered him a university education, or a trip around the world with a private tutor. Instead the young man chose to study the sugar industry and to aid in his father's fight against the sugar trust by taking a job in the new Philadelphia refinery. When Rudolph was twenty-two a long and bitter family feud began over the disposal of one of its large Hawaiian plantations, which had been losing money. Claus Spreckels and his two older sons, John D. and Adolph, were resolved to sell it. The younger brothers, Gus and Rudolph, insisted that if the management were turned over to them they could make it pay. Their father, infuriated, ordered the plantation sold, cut off all business and personal connections with his younger sons, and warned every banker in San Francisco against lending them money. Gus and Rudolph, however, succeeded in getting a loan from a private capitalist, bought the plantation, put it on a paying basis, and sold it at a large profit four years later in 1898.

By the turn of the century, Rudolph Spreckels, still under thirty, had become a millionaire in his own right, and his fortune continued to increase rapidly through investments in real estate and corporation securities. One of these operations involved a continuation of the feud with his father, this time in the gas, light, and power industry. The San Francisco Gas and Electric Company had enjoyed a near-monopoly for several years during the late 'nineties. In 1899, a smokestack at one of its plants began to blacken the walls of the new Claus Spreckels Building nearby. The elder Spreckels was extremely proud of this structure. It was one of the first skyscrapers in the city, and was faced with finished stone on all four sides. One day at the Pacific Union Club, Claus Spreckels approached the president of the San Francisco Gas and Electric Company, Joseph B. Crockett, and protested against the smokestack as a nuisance. Crockett replied that the club was no place to discuss business matters, and turned away. Immediately Claus Spreckels returned to his office to begin the organization of the Independent Light and Power Company, which soon built a competitive system and declared a rate war in which it captured thousands of its rival's customers.

Claus Spreckels' revenge coupled with Crockett's poor management reduced the San Francisco Gas and Electric Company to near bankruptcy. In 1900 Rudolph Spreckels decided to buy large amounts of its securities, at a low price. In the following year he took a seat on the board of directors, and by voting his own stock and his proxies won control of the company. He then forced the resignation of Crockett and a drastic reorganization. Increased efficiency under the regime of Rudolph Spreckels enabled the company to make a profit in spite of its continued rate war with his father's rival concern. Peace was concluded in the summer of 1903, when Claus Spreckels sold out the Independent to the San Francisco Gas and Electric Company. Not long afterward, having thus restored the company to a dominant position and greatly increased the value of its stock, Rudolph Spreckels disposed of most of his interests in it at a very large profit.

Rudolph Spreckels had assumed control of the San Francisco

Gas and Electric Company in January, 1902, at approximately the same time that Ruef was coming into power in the city government, and it was shortly afterward that the two had their first meeting. Apparently at Ruef's request, Charles Sutro, a stock and bond broker, brought Ruef to the office of Spreckels, introduced them to each other, and withdrew, permitting them to speak privately. Ruef then suggested that he had legal ability, and that he could be useful to the San Francisco Gas and Electric Company as one of its counsel.

His offer received no encouragement from Rudolph Spreckels, and served only to arouse his suspicion of the way in which Ruef would make use of his power in the Schmitz administration. This suspicion was much more seriously aroused two years later when, according to Spreckels, Ruef made a more startling proposal: that Spreckels should form a syndicate to buy up the whole of a pending city bond issue, and that Ruef should arrange that Spreckels' bid would be successful.

In a special election in the fall of 1903, the voters of San Francisco gave their approval to a bond issue of more than seventeen million dollars, for a city-and-county hospital, a sewer system, schools, better streets, a new jail, a public library, and additional parks and playgrounds. At the time, San Francisco had no bonded debt, which ordinarily would have made its credit excellent, and permitted its bonds to sell well above par. Nevertheless, before the bonds were to be issued in October, 1904, it became obvious to Ruef that they would be boycotted by investors all over the country. Ruef thought that this disapproval was due partly to distrust of the credit of a Union Labor government, and partly to fear that the power to spend so large a sum of money would strengthen the Union Labor party, thus increasing its chance to spread to other parts of the nation. Apparently, Ruef went to Rudolph Spreckels because of the latter's reputation for disagreeing with other capitalists, and in the hope that the entire issue might be sold with his aid.

As Spreckels later described the interview, he inquired how Ruef could guarantee that his bid would be successful, when the sale of the bonds was open to competitive bidding. Ruef replied that he would arrange a paralyzing street car strike before the bonds were to be placed on the market, and thus ensure a low degree of confidence in San Francisco at that particular time.

Spreckels registered shock, and asked whether this proposal could be seriously meant, whereupon Ruef flushed, replied that he was only joking, and went away. Outraged, Spreckels felt a strong urge to become a political reformer. He spoke with T. P. Andrews, the foreman of the grand jury, who told him that only a large special fund could make possible a really searching investigation of the inner workings of the Ruef-Schmitz regime.

Ruef's fears for the bonds were well-founded. The charter forbade the city to sell them below par, and when they were offered for sale, there were bids at par for only a trifling amount of them. A few weeks later the civic-minded ex-Mayor Phelan, who had recently become president of an Association for the Improvement and Adornment of San Francisco, organized a syndicate of bankers which bought about two million dollars' worth of those bonds intended for the purchase of ground sites, since the spending of this money would be managed by the Democratic majority of the board of supervisors, rather than by the Schmitz-controlled board of public works. Ruef planned a campaign to sell other bonds in small lots to unions and to individual working men, but this proved impractical. During Schmitz's entire term of office, only about a fifth of the bonds were actually sold.

Rudolph Spreckels and James D. Phelan were friends and business associates. Occasionally during 1904 and 1905 both Spreckels and Phelan complimented Older on the *Bulletin's* campaign against the administration. Older had his two wealthy friends in mind when he told Heney in Washington that he thought he could get financial support for a special investigation in San Francisco. Immediately on his return in December, 1905, Older conferred with them and received further encouragement. Spreckels was highly enthusiastic, and while he testified later that his original interest in a special prosecution had been directed against "the corrupt administration" and corruption in general, and not against any particular individual, Older's recollection was that Spreckels had said that if such a prosecution were to be worth undertaking, it must reach for William F. Herrin. Undoubtedly Rudolph Spreckels shared his family's opinion that the Southern Pacific Railroad was the fountainhead of political corruption in the state.

Spreckels' first plan for a special prosecution fund was that it should be subscribed to by about fifteen leading citizens of San Francisco, organized, secretly at first, into a sort of unarmed vigilance committee. He discovered, however, that apart from Phelan not one of the men he approached was willing to serve.

Heney came to San Francisco early in January, 1906, and Older arranged a conference with Spreckels and Phelan in which the two capitalists gave informal assurances of their personal financial support. On the question of the attitude of the new district attorney, it was noted that Langdon, while not informed of any plans for a special prosecution, had made strong statements to Phelan and to Older that he intended to enforce the law. Thus by January of 1906 the seeds of the graft prosecution had been sown.

CHAPTER VII

Labor and capital

TOTAL victory was the one emergency for which Ruef was unprepared. And when he found the entire slate of Union Labor supervisors swept into office, he was forced to recall with some anxiety the circumstances of their hasty selection. Only four incumbent supervisors, previously Republicans, had been willing to accept nomination by the Union Labor party. These were James L. Gallagher, a former city attorney, whom Schmitz had appointed to a vacancy in the old board of supervisors, and who would be the administration's chief in the new one; Dr. Charles Boxton, dentist and war hero; Louis A. Rea, painting contractor; and W. W. Sanderson, wholesale grocery salesman. These four were obvious choices, but the other fourteen candidates were chosen not because there was any reason to suppose that they could be elected, but rather in order to clinch groups of votes for Schmitz, as head of the ticket.

Ten seats, a majority of the eighteen, were allotted to labor union members. Although Ruef had the advice of a former president of the San Francisco Labor Council, George B. Benham, in preparing the list of candidates, few of the men selected were well known as labor leaders. Along with membership in various unions, the candidates had also to be distributed among several sections of the city, according to residence. This was a requirement of practical politics, although, under the charter, supervisors were elected at large. All in all, this part of the ticket was decidedly a patchwork, which Ruef pieced together two days before the Union Labor convention in a conference at his office with Benham, Gallagher, and Schmitz.

Two Union Labor men had come within a few hundred votes

of election as supervisors in 1903 and were selected to run again in 1905. Michael W. Coffey was a hackdriver and president of the hackmen's union, and like most of the other members of that organization he had a wide acquaintance and took an active interest in the discussion of matters of politics. Edward I. Walsh was a machine operator in a shoe factory, and an official of the shoe workers' union. Two candidates were chosen from the building trades: Ferdinand P. Nicholas, president of the district Council of Carpenters; and Max Mamlock, an electrician who was vice-president of the electrical workers.

The other union representations were somewhat miscellaneous. John J. Furey, a blacksmith, was president of the Iron Trades Council, and the owner of a fur store on Powell Street. Thomas F. Lonergan was president of the bakery wagon drivers' union. Sam Davis, whom Schmitz selected as a representative of the musicians' union, was a drummer in the orchestra of the Tivoli Opera House, and owned a small music publishing business. Jennings S. Phillips was an official of the printing pressmen's union, and chief pressman of the *Evening Post* which had been both supporting the administration and being supported by it. Daniel G. Coleman was a member of the retail clerks' union, and had been noticed by Ruef to be a lively and persuasive speaker. James F. Kelly was president of the piano polishers' union, an old time Republican, and a resident of the new Potrero district, which was not otherwise represented on the ticket.

The remaining four places were allotted to businessmen. But the attempt to find four businessmen of prominence who had never had disagreements with labor and who were willing to accept Union Labor nomination was a task which had exhausted even Ruef's ingenuity. George F. Duffey was a proprietor of one of the city's largest plumbing companies. Patrick McGushin was a saloonkeeper and a director of the liquor dealers' association. Cornelius Harrigan was a grocer in the workingmen's district south of Market, whom Ruef had never met but whose name he accepted on Gallagher's suggestion that Harrigan had made many friends in the ranks of labor by liberal extensions of credit during the long teamsters' strike of 1901. For the eighteenth place a series of offers had brought a series of refusals. The name of Andrew M. Wilson was suggested only a few hours before the slate was presented to the convention itself, and it was not until after Wilson had actually been nominated that a telephone call brought his permission to use his name on the ticket, on the promise that he should not be required to take any part in the campaign. As a furniture dealer and proprietor of a moving and storage concern, Wilson was a successful businessman. The suggestion of his name originated with Ruef's trusted legal assistant, George Keane, whom Ruef had made a state senator and the mayor's private secretary. Keane had met Wilson in a restaurant where both men came for lunch, Keane because it was near the city hall, Wilson because it was near his place of business. Except for this chance acquaintance, Ruef wrote later, "not one of us even knew what manner of man this newly nominated Supervisor might be."

Shortly after the election, Schmitz and Ruef left San Francisco to spend two weeks in Southern California, in order to hasten the mayor's recovery from a chronic sore throat induced by his rigorous schedule of campaign speaking. In the absence of the mayor and his attorney, the supervisors-elect held several conferences on the subject of their prospective committee assignments, in the course of which strong disagreements arose. When Ruef returned to the city with Schmitz late in November, he was startled by the vigor with which some of the inexperienced and previously obscure new supervisors were asserting their demands for particular chairmanships and memberships of committees. There was a remarkable demand for posts on those committees concerned with matters on which private business concerns had relations with the city government, notably public utilities, artificial lights, streets, and water rates. In particular, nearly every member of the newly elected board wanted to be on the public utilities committee. Ruef suspected immediately that many of the prospective supervisors were hoping to receive bribes, and that representatives of corporations and contractors were encouraging them in the expectation.

Ruef soon began to receive reports which confirmed his fears. Many of the members-elect knew little of the nature of their office except the gossip that supervisors in San Francisco had always received bribes. For decades such gossip had been repeated so often and so matter-of-factly that it had become a kind of folk legend, although there had been no actual evidence of it since the early 'nineties. In the fall of 1905 some of the newly

elected supervisors were so naïve in their suppositions that bribery would be their normal prerogative, that they invited some
of their colleagues to share in particular opportunities for bribery when they discovered them. In this way such reports came to
Gallagher, who took them to Ruef. Obviously some of the men
at least had gone so far as to apply for positions on payrolls, and
for commissions from merchants who wished to sell goods to the
city.

Ruef became alarmed. He could see that the open and promis-
cuous manner in which some of his hastily nominated officials
were soliciting favors would lead to inevitable discovery and
publicity. In the clumsy dishonesty of a group of men, many of
whom he scarcely knew, and most of whom filled him with contempt, Ruef could see the specter of ruin for all of his own ambitions. Calling a meeting of the suspected members in his office,
he told them angrily that what he believed them to be doing
was not only improper but criminal, and that it would lead
them and the Union Labor administration to disaster. Seeing
in their faces an unspoken reproach, that he himself had accepted
much larger amounts of money for his political influence, he
did his best to make clear to them the importance of the distinction involved. It was not illegal and it was not even improper, he
insisted, for a corporation or a person to employ an attorney who
was not a public official. On the other hand, for a supervisor to
take money privately for actions in his public capacity was accepting a bribe, and was punishable by a long term in the penitentiary. Ruef threatened that he himself would prosecute any
member of the board who should be guilty of such conduct in
the future. All the members present gave their solemn promises.
Within a few days, however, it was evident that the promises
were not being kept. Some of the members remained uncon-
vinced of the validity of the distinction between Ruef's position
and their own. Others knew that he was bluffing when he spoke
of prosecuting them himself.

Toward the middle of December, Ruef sought a solution to
this dangerous problem in a conversation with Gallagher. It was
apparent, the two men agreed, that nothing but money would
suffice. The question became that of how to devise a system of
payments to the supervisors which would involve the least possible risk of exposure. Ruef's first proposal was that he would pay

as much as $4,000 apiece to the supervisors during their two year term of office, out of his own pocket, in return for their promise not to accept money from any other source. He asked Gallagher to sound them on their willingness to accept such a proposition. A few days afterward, Gallagher returned to say that it had been rejected. Actually, Gallagher had spoken only to Andrew M. Wilson, whom he recognized as the most vigorous personality among the supervisors.

It was soon clear to Ruef as well as to Gallagher that it had been an unlucky chance which had placed the name of Wilson on the ticket. Neither had known him until after his nomination. He proved to be entirely too enterprising a businessman, holding the cynical view that valuable privileges within the power of the city government to grant were themselves matters of "business," and that those who were fortunate enough to control them should sell them like any other commodity, for what the traffic would bear.

Ruef saw that if individual supervisors were to solicit and accept bribes directly from business interests, the situation would have two disadvantages, apart from its illegality. It would involve a high degree of risk of exposure, and it would soon remove the board from his own control. Finally, in the latter part of December, Ruef and Gallagher agreed upon a plan. When, as Ruef expected, certain interests paid him large attorney's fees, he would turn over half of the money to Gallagher. Gallagher would divide this into eighteen equal shares, and pay it to the supervisors individually, without mention of its source. There was to be no discussion of specific payments for votes on specific questions, but only a general understanding that money would be forthcoming after the votes had been cast as Ruef suggested. Gallagher found this proposition to be acceptable to Wilson, and to Boxton and Furey. He did not discuss it in advance with the other members, although Ruef assumed that he had.

In his later accounts of the origins of this system of payments to the supervisors, Ruef strove to lay the blame upon the machinations of circumstance, rather than upon his own intentions. Certainly Ruef would have preferred to control the board without bribery, had that been possible.

In order that the board might present a good appearance in its public meetings, Ruef decided to bring the members together in weekly caucuses which he would attend as their volunteer legal adviser, and from which the public would be excluded. Mayor Schmitz was to be present as ex officio president of the board. After the new supervisors took office, on January 8, 1906, their regular public meetings would be on Mondays. A caucus each Sunday evening in the mayor's office would prepare the members for their parts in the public meeting the next day. In the private caucus meetings, nothing was to be said about "money matters." Rather, as Ruef put it, the caucuses were to permit "the framing of plausible public argument for every proposition submitted, and of reasons in defense of the votes of the members . . . ostensibly and sometimes actually in the public interest." The caucuses would also make possible the resolution of differences privately, and an appearance of unity and expeditiousness in public. George Keane, the mayor's former secretary, was now to be clerk of the board of supervisors, and was to keep full minutes of the caucuses as well as of the public proceedings.

The first important public matter on which the Union Labor supervisors were to pass judgment was a proposed franchise to the Ocean Shore Railway Company. This company proposed to build and operate an interurban electric line running about eighty miles along the coast, connecting Santa Cruz and San Francisco. Not only real estate promoters but also the city's newspapers were supporting the project, on the ground of its potential value in building up residential suburbs in the western part of the peninsula. A franchise permitting the Ocean Shore Railway to extend to the downtown district of San Francisco had received preliminary approval from the outgoing supervisors late in 1905, but they left the question of final passage to their successors. Two weeks before the new board took office and before its first caucus had met, Mayor Schmitz called Ruef and the members-elect to a conference at the city hall. He urged approval of the project, arguing that it would increase business, give employment to labor, and also carry out his policy of giving encouragement to home industry and local capital. Finally, he revealed that he had already given the Ocean Shore directors his personal promise that their franchise would pass.

As the conferees were leaving the mayor's office, Andrew M. Wilson spoke to Ruef privately. What, he asked, were the mayor's motives? Had not several of the Ocean Shore directors openly opposed the Union Labor ticket in the late campaign? In his reply to these questions, Ruef avoided any reference to Wilson's implied inquiry as to whether money would come to the mayor, and whether it would be shared with the supervisors. Instead, Ruef merely urged Wilson to respect and follow the mayor's decision. Actually, the question of Schmitz's motives was troubling Ruef, too. He was annoyed that the Ocean Shore promoters had not engaged his own legal services, or even consulted him, and he suspected that they had made Schmitz a present of Ocean Shore stock. On the other hand, he thought it possible that Schmitz was merely seeking to gain the gratitude of William J. Dingee, J. Downey Harvey, and other wealthy men who were interested in the Ocean Shore Railway.

The circumstances which had thrown Schmitz into frequent association with men of great wealth had exerted a deep influence upon his character. Repeatedly, wealthy men told him that they were surprised to find such gentility and polish in a Union Labor mayor. Fascinated by this experience, Schmitz thought himself well fitted to enjoy the way of life which wealth made possible. He thought it unfair that men in politics should be limited by a trivial salaried income, when they had a degree of power comparable to that of captains of industry. Such feelings were apparent in the intimate friendship which developed between Schmitz and William J. Dingee, one of the most colorful, but also one of the most unscrupulous, of California millionaires.

Dingee had begun his career as a clerk in a real estate office in Oakland. Rapidly acquiring holdings of watershed lands, he gained control of an East Bay water monopoly, the Contra Costa Water Company, and by controlling the Oakland city government in matters of water rates and tax assessments he made the company extremely profitable. One of the secrets of Dingee's phenomenal success lay in his manner of gaining influence over men in public life by tempting them to escape the financial limitations of their status. One such man was Frederick W. Henshaw, a justice of the state supreme court. In 1901, although the fact did not become publicly known until seventeen years afterward, Dingee secretly arranged the bribery of Justice Henshaw with $400,000, to reverse his vote in the case of the will of James G. Fair.

In October, 1902, Dingee met Schmitz and his wife on the

train which was carrying them to New York, where Schmitz was to speak in behalf of William Randolph Hearst's campaign for Congress. In New York, Dingee and his wife entertained the Schmitzes at their mansion on Fifth Avenue. Later they continued to entertain them in the equally palatial Dingee residence in San Francisco. For this personal introduction to the highest circles of society, Schmitz felt deeply grateful. Moreover, Dingee began to give him expensive presents, which were rumored to include a team of noble carriage horses, costly rugs, china, and silver, and various objects of art. In 1904, Schmitz appointed Dingee a park commissioner. There were other ways, also, in which the mayor sought to express his gratitude. Dingee's varied interests included nearly all of the slate quarries in California, and a large cement plant at Santa Cruz. The mayor sponsored an ordinance encouraging the use of slate as a roofing material. It was in the same spirit that he advocated the passage of the Ocean Shore Railway franchise, which would enhance the value of Dingee's properties in Santa Cruz, along the peninsula, and in San Francisco.

The decisive action on the Ocean Shore franchise was taken at the first caucus of the Union Labor board of supervisors, which was held shortly before January 8, 1906, the date of their taking office. Ruef had solved the problem of committee appointments by drawing up the list himself, and Gallagher presented it to the members for ratification. They approved it, in spite of several complaints. The enterprising Wilson, in particular, was disappointed that he was not to be a member of the public utilities committee. When the Ocean Shore franchise was introduced for discussion, Wilson expressed strong opposition to it. Privately, Schmitz had made it clear by this time that there would be no money involved. Ruef had explained to Schmitz his plan for the sharing of his attorney's fees with the supervisors, and had offered a further share to Schmitz. The mayor had made no objection to the plan in general, but he had insisted that the Ocean Shore franchise must be a separate case, and that it must be granted without any such payment, simply in fulfilment of his own promise. To avoid disrupting the administration, Ruef had agreed. The board approved the franchise, though with some resentment.

Ruef's first payment of money to the supervisors resulted from the establishment of what later became known as the "fight trust." A San Francisco ordinance required that "professional boxing exhibitions" be staged only on permits from the board of supervisors, not oftener than once a month, and under the sponsorship of "genuine incorporated athletic clubs." Actually, the contests, or exhibitions, were sponsored by individual promoters who controlled the clubs. While the number of the promoters was small, they were in such lively competition for the permits that, as Ruef remarked, the fights among the promoters over these concessions "sometimes exceeded in vigor the contests between the pugilists." Political influence was necessary for securing permits, and those who wished to succeed as fight promoters needed to have been active election workers in their respective districts. Four of the promoters, Eddie Graney, James Coffroth, Morris Levy, and Willis Britt, had supported the Union Labor ticket in several elections. Partly, at least, for this reason, they had been denied permits by the Democratic majority which had controlled the board of supervisors until after the election of 1905. In the meantime, Ruef and Schmitz had rewarded the would-be promoters as best they could. Graney's blacksmith business got the contract for shoeing the fire horses; Coffroth became secretary of the superior court; Levy was appointed secretary of the board of public works, and then a deputy tax collector. The victory of 1905 opened the way for more lucrative rewards in the field of prize fight promotion.

One evening about the first of January, 1906, Eddie Graney sought an interview with Ruef in a private dining room at The Pup. Graney proposed a scheme by which fight permits might be awarded in a more orderly manner, by eliminating the competitive conditions which had prevailed in the past. The two men agreed on the establishment of what Ruef called "a sort of holding company of the various athletic clubs," to be controlled by Graney, Coffroth, Levy and Britt. Before the end of January, all the monthly permits for the coming year were to be awarded to this group, in advance. From Ruef's point of view, the plan had advantages in addition to the rewarding of political supporters. The board of supervisors would not be troubled every month by a scramble of promoters offering improper inducements, and a dangerous scramble of supervisors to receive them. And the

"Consolidated Association of Athletic Clubs" would pay Ruef an attorney's fee of $20,000.

Graney was to have collected $5,000 from each of his three associates. Levy was reluctant to pay, until he found it otherwise impossible to gain the approval of the supervisors for a Gans-Sullivan fight which he had scheduled for the latter part of January. Finally, Graney paid Ruef a total of $18,000, which Ruef agreed to accept as payment in full.

Late in January the supervisors passed a resolution fixing the monthly dates for professional boxing exhibitions during the coming year, and awarding the permits to the favored promoters. The system was regularized still further by fixing the number of complimentary tickets which supervisors and other city officials might expect to receive. As in the case of railroad passes, prize-fight tickets stamped "complimentary" had a prestige value much higher than the price of the seat. They marked the bearer as a member of a select inner circle, and politicians found them useful for the payment of political debts, particularly to men who would have been insulted by an offer of money.

So far as the supervisors knew at the time, small blocks of these tickets were to be their only material reward for passing the prize fight resolution. Shortly afterward, however, Ruef paid Gallagher $9,000, or half of what he himself had received from Graney. This sum would have provided $500 for each of the eighteen supervisors, but Gallagher retained a 5 per cent commission, and gave $475 to each of his colleagues. Ruef said nothing to Gallagher of the specific origin of the money, or of the specific purpose of its payment, although Gallagher undoubtedly understood both. Gallagher said as little as possible to the other supervisors. Wilson, however, somehow learned the facts, and revealed them to several other members. To each of those who then complained against the withholding of commissions, Gallagher hastily paid the additional $25. He abandoned the commission idea henceforth.

Ruef, according to his own account, gave $4,500 of the "fight trust" money to Schmitz, leaving an equal amount for himself. Some time afterward, Willis Britt repented his part of the bargain, and threatened to publicize the whole matter unless Ruef returned the $5,000 which Britt claimed to have paid to Graney.

Ruef did so, with the result that the "fight trust" eventually brought him a net financial loss of $500. He regarded the loss lightly, for his primary purpose in the whole affair had been to give the supervisors an early assurance that his plan of payments through Gallagher would be carried out, and thus to forestall their much more dangerous individual projects for the receiving of money.

The actual effects of the fight trust payments upon the different supervisors were varied. One, Louis A. Rea, was a conscientious and honest man. Gallagher had never broached the subject of money to Rea until he handed him an envelope containing $475 in currency, merely with the explanation that a friend had sent it to him to help him defray his campaign expenses. Rea was puzzled, but as a fairly prosperous businessman he did not regard the amount as a large one, and he accepted it without further question for the time being, with no expectation that he would receive more. Some of the other members, however, had never before held more than $100 in their hands. Some were pleased with the secrecy and the apparent safety of the arrangement, as Gallagher cautiously explained it to them. Others, led by Andrew M. Wilson, were more covetous and more reluctant to limit themselves to this one regular channel. Moreover, in the face of Wilson's bold curiosity, Ruef's plan for the complete avoidance of discussion of specific payments for specific votes began to break down. Wilson began to discuss with Gallagher and with other members the amount of money which might be expected from the next important matter which would come before the board. This was the fixing of the gas rate.

The San Francisco charter empowered the board of supervisors to set a maximum gas rate each year, by an ordinance to be passed during the month of February and to take effect on the first of July. In 1905, as in most of the other recent years, the rate had been set at one dollar per thousand cubic feet. It was good politics for the Union Labor party to advocate reduction, and Ruef had included a plank calling for seventy-five cent gas in the Union Labor campaign platform on which, technically speaking, the supervisors were elected in November.

Within a few weeks after the election the new Pacific Gas and Electric Company completed its merger of the ownership and control of virtually all of the gas, light, and power companies of

San Francisco and the rest of central California. One of the largest stockholders in the Pacific Gas and Electric Company was Frank G. Drum. According to Ruef, it was Drum who employed him as a confidential attorney for the new company. One day when Ruef was in the office of William S. Tevis in the Mills Building, Drum entered from his adjoining office. He explained to Ruef that he represented various large interests, not only his own but those of the wealthy Tevis family, and that he could offer Ruef a position as "one of our attorneys," with particular reference to the new gas company of which Drum was a director. Ruef was impressed by this "pleasant-spoken, clean-cut, prosperous looking" capitalist, particularly when he offered a retainer of $1,000 per month, which Ruef accepted.

The question of the gas rate came before the board of supervisors at its caucus on Sunday evening, February 4, 1906, in Mayor Schmitz's office. Ruef himself claimed to have arrived at the seventy-five cent figure, after careful study, as a rate which would allow the company a fair though narrow margin of profit. He knew that a month's study by experts could hardly determine with exactness an equitable rate, and in later years he recalled with sarcasm the spectacle of earnest debate among new officials "whose only knowledge of gas probably was that it flamed when ignited." Several members argued that even seventy-five cents was too high. Mayor Schmitz advised caution and further investigation, and said that some of the principal owners of the company had called on him to assure him that seventy-five cents was too low. At this point, Ruef heard Wilson remark "in an audible whisper to his neighbor that it looked like more 'Ocean Shore.' " Other members called for an immediate vote in favor of the seventy-five cent rate which their campaign platform had demanded. Ruef persuaded the board to defer its vote, on the ground that if it proceeded too hastily and arbitrarily, before the reports submitted by the gas interests had even been read, the courts might invalidate its action.

Shortly after the board's first caucus on the gas rate, a fire in the company's central station in San Francisco caused a loss of nearly half a million dollars. Ruef believed that this might justify an eighty-five cent figure, but he felt that the supervisors would be unwilling to go above seventy-five cents except for "good reason," that is, money. He informed Drum that in order to protect the interests of the company he would need an additional attorney's fee of $20,000, which Drum paid to him shortly afterward in currency. Ruef later said he paid $3,000 of this to Schmitz, and about $14,000 to Gallagher for distribution among the supervisors. According to Gallagher, Ruef paid him $13,350, of which he retained $1,350 and paid $750 each to sixteen of his fellow members. He paid nothing to McGushin, who believed strongly in municipal ownership of public utilities, and had often spoken against any favors for public utility corporations.

Louis A. Rea had accepted Gallagher's explanation that the fight trust payment was money from "a friend" to help defray his campaign expenses. Rea had become deeply disturbed, however, when his fellow supervisors began to gossip to the effect that money would be coming to them for eighty-five cent gas. He took these rumors to Schmitz, who said that he could not believe them. When Gallagher handed Rea another envelope, containing $750, and refused any explanation. Rea took the money to Schmitz as proof. He told the mayor that he was a man of family and of good character, and asked to be permitted to resign. Schmitz persuaded Rea to leave the matter in his hands, and to refrain from resigning. Gallagher made no further payments to Rea thereafter.

At the next caucus, on Sunday evening, February 11, the members of the board showed an almost unanimous change of mind in favor of eighty-five cent gas, which they justified on the ground that the fire in its plant would cause the company serious difficulties. The board voted to fix the rate at eighty-five cents, but to delay any public announcement during a formal period of investigation. The official ordinance was not passed to print until the board's last meeting in February, on Monday the 26th.

A matter of greater magnitude than the gas rate, the Ocean Shore, or the fight trust was the affair of the Parkside franchise. Parkside was a large real estate subdivision comprising nearly a fifth of the entire Sunset district, in what were then the bare sand dunes of the far-western part of San Francisco. The Parkside promoters believed that the sale of lots in their tract could bring returns of four or five million dollars on an invested capital of about two millions, provided only that a franchise for a trolley line connecting the area with the more settled parts of the city could be obtained from the board of supervisors.

The Parkside Realty Company was organized in July, 1905, by a group of investors, of whom the principal stockholder was William H. Crocker, son of Charles Crocker of the "Big Four" and president of the Crocker National Bank. As quietly as possible, and acting through third parties, the Parkside associates had purchased a large number of lots from the several previous owners, one of whom, as it happened, was Ruef. In all, these purchases made up a tract of four hundred acres, some five blocks wide and twenty blocks long. It was about a mile south of Golden Gate Park, and extended from a point one and a half miles west of Twin Peaks to within three blocks of the ocean. The nearest car line of the United Railroads, the main street car system, ran along the southern boundary of Golden Gate Park, and the Parkside company hoped to connect its properties with this line by a new trolley on 20th Avenue. This would be merely a transfer line connecting the subdivision with the existing system, and would bring no revenue in itself. The United Railroads was not inclined to apply for a franchise, consequently, and the Parkside promoters realized they would probably have to obtain a franchise and construct a road. A street car line was vital to the Parkside scheme because the automobile was still a luxury of the rich, and the promoters planned to sell their 5,000 twenty-five foot lots to lower-income families.

After the land was finally purchased, in the summer of 1905, William H. Crocker asked William J. Dingee to arrange an interview with Mayor Schmitz. Dingee was not an investor in the Parkside Realty Company, but he was under obligation to Crocker's bank for much of the financing of his varied enterprises. In an interview in Dingee's office, Crocker explained to the mayor the potential value of the Parkside project in the development of the city, and the necessity of the trolley franchise if this value were to be realized. Schmitz inspected the properties, and in a second interview in Dingee's office he assured Crocker that he would offer no opposition, and that he believed the franchise would be secured. On the basis of this assurance, the Parkside company proceeded to spend money for the grading and paving of streets and the installation of sewer and utility systems.

On the day of the first meeting of the new board of supervisors, January 8, 1906, the Parkside Realty Company filed an application requesting the city to offer for sale to the highest bidder a franchise for a trolley line on 20th Avenue. At the next Sunday evening caucus, Schmitz told the supervisors that he strongly favored granting this petition. It would mean the difference, the mayor pointed out, between an idle waste of drifting sands and a beautiful residential suburb. The lots were designed for the homes of workingmen, and would give them an opportunity to build their residences in San Francisco rather than in Oakland or Alameda. The whole project would give employment to labor and put money into circulation. The mayor mentioned also that it was expected to produce a profit of at least three million dollars for the capitalists who had had the foresight to invest in it. At this point, according to Ruef, some of the supervisors "glanced at one another significantly, and with curious interest at the Mayor and myself." Schmitz remarked in conclusion that he had already promised the granting of the necessary franchise.

This was several days after the mayor had broached the Ocean Shore Railway matter, and the similarity of the two situations was apparent. Suspicion of the mayor's motives was now even more pronounced, and there was resentment that he had presumed to speak for the board before consulting it. The supervisors declined to take any immediate action. Ruef had not been informed of Schmitz's commitment on the Parkside franchise, and after the caucus the mayor and his attorney walked home together in earnest conversation. Schmitz explained that, apart from his friendship for Dingee, he had been thinking of the valuable political support to be gained from the gratitude of William H. Crocker. Ruef expressed agreement with this viewpoint, and promised to urge the granting of the franchise upon the supervisors.

A brother-in-law of Crocker, Prince Poniatowski, had become an intimate friend of Ruef: "both," as Crocker put it, "being French, and both being pretty clever men." Frequent meetings in the company of Prince Poniatowski had also led to a certain degree of friendship between Ruef and Crocker. After Schmitz had informed him of the Parkside situation, Ruef gave assurances to Crocker, as well as to Schmitz, that the franchise would be granted, and "without cost" to Crocker or to the Parkside company. In spite of his assurances, however, Ruef did not actually believe that a majority of the supervisors would be willing to pass the Parkside franchise without some assurance of being paid for it. Ruef and Gallagher decided not to press the matter with the board until the situation was clarified. Ruef hoped that the Parkside Realty Company would voluntarily offer to employ him as an attorney, but he did not care to solicit such employment from William H. Crocker.

During January, 1906, President J. E. Green of the Parkside company along with some of the company's engineers presented their case at several meetings of the board of supervisors and of its committees on streets and public utilities. They received no encouragement. On February 8, Green arranged a tour of inspection of the Parkside properties for all of the members of the board who might be able to go, and at ten in the morning, in spite of a downpour of rain, Mayor Schmitz and about twelve supervisors assembled with Green and other officials of the company at the city hall, and rode to the Parkside tract in automobiles which Green provided.

After two hours spent in viewing the tract and discussing its possibilities, the members of the party were driven across Golden Gate Park to a restaurant known as the Casino, where they found refreshment and refuge from the inclement weather. Wine was served, and after luncheon there was a round of speeches. Green painted a glowing picture of the future of Parkside, and Schmitz spoke of the value of the project to the development of the city. None of the supervisors present expressed any opposition, but the remarks of at least one of them, Dr. Charles Boxton, contained a startlingly palpable statement of the terms under which the board might be expected to coöperate. Since Boxton was chairman of the public utilities committee, his remarks carried particular weight. He explained afterward that he had drunk a considerable quantity of wine and that he could not remember what he had said. As Supervisor Daniel Coleman recalled it some years later, it was in part as follows:

But Mr. Green should bear in mind that we are the city fathers; that from the city fathers all blessings flow; that we, the city fathers, are moved in all our public acts by a desire to benefit the city, and that our motives are pure and unselfish. . . . But it must be borne in mind that without the city fathers there can be no public service corporations. The street cars cannot run, lights cannot be furnished, telephones cannot exist. And all the public service corporations want to understand that we, the city fathers, enjoy the best health and that we are not in business for our health. The question at this banquet board is: 'How much money is in it for us?'

It was this quotation which the newspapers described as "the black flag speech" when it was first published in 1910.

Ruef was not a member of the party which visited Parkside and the Casino. Gallagher soon informed him, however, that some of the supervisors had regarded the tour as one of "exploration" of other terrain than that of the lots, and that at the luncheon "other ice had been broken than that which surrounded the cooling wine."

Shortly after the Casino luncheon, Green decided that his company could gain its objectives only through Ruef. For the mission of sounding out Ruef, Green selected Gus H. Umbsen, head of one of the largest real estate firms in San Francisco. Umbsen was the agent for several of Ruef's properties, and Ruef was Umbsen's attorney. Umbsen was not an official of the Parkside Realty Company, but he was deeply interested in its success, since his own company was the exclusive agency for the sale of Parkside lots at a 10 per cent commission; and Crocker was "carrying" a block of Parkside stock for him. According to Ruef, Umbsen bluntly inquired of him how much money would be needed to secure a franchise from the board of supervisors, to which he replied that no money would be asked or accepted for this purpose. Umbsen's version of this interview was that he had asked whether Ruef was delaying the franchise, to which Ruef replied that he was "not the attorney." In another conversation a few days later, Umbsen asked Ruef if he would accept employment as an attorney for the Parkside enterprise, and Ruef answered that he would.

The regular attorneys for the Parkside Realty Company were the distinguished partners A. F. Morrison and Walter B. Cope, both of whom were also members of the Parkside board of directors. Cope and Ruef had known each other since 1879, when they entered the University of California in the same class. Later, Cope had been a superior judge in Santa Barbara County, and at this time he was president of the San Francisco Bar Association. Green, as president of the Parkside Realty Company, now authorized Cope to inquire of Ruef the fee he would ask for his legal services. Ruef mentioned a figure which he later recalled as $30,000, but which Cope remembered and reported to Green as either forty- or fifty-thousand dollars. Apparently, Cope had nothing further to do with the matter. It was Umbsen who then informed Ruef that the Parkside company had decided to employ him at a fee of $30,000, for two years, to which Ruef agreed.

Within the Parkside Realty Company, the executive responsibility for this decision rested with President J. E. Green, in his capacity as general manager. The company's board of directors had filed a blanket resolution authorizing the president to expend money. In employing Ruef, Green did not inform Crocker, Morrison, or Cope that he was doing so, and each of them could and later did deny that he had known of it. On the company's books, Green charged the transaction not to legal expense but to the purchase of property. A block of lots presumably worth $30,000 was owned jointly by the company's secretary, Douglass S. Watson, and by Harry P. Umbsen, a brother and business partner of Gus. Ostensibly, the Parkside Realty Company purchased this property with two $15,000 checks, one to each of the owners, and the deed was duly recorded. Secretly, however, the property was then deeded back to Watson and Umbsen, and the second deed was not recorded for several weeks. The cashing of the checks provided $30,000 in currency, which President Green instructed Secretary Watson to transfer to the custody of agent Gus H. Umbsen. Watson carried the money to Umbsen's office in an envelope and laid it on his desk. The only comment which Watson could recall that he had made on this occasion was either "Hello, Gus" or "Here is the money."

Green was asked later whether he did not feel that Ruef was extorting the money from him. He replied: ". . . It was a large fee to pay for legal purposes but we had invested a million dollars there. We expected to spend a million more and figuring it on that basis of what we could sell our property for, our returns would be four or five million and an expenditure of $30,000 to me under those circumstances, wasn't an enormous thing, the profits could afford it."

Ruef mentioned the fact of his Parkside employment to Gallagher. On March 26, 1906, the board of supervisors passed a resolution providing that a street railway franchise for 20th Avenue should be sold on May 7. The owners of the Parkside Realty Company organized the Parkside Transit Company, and prepared to submit a bid for the franchise. Later Gus H. Umbsen paid Ruef $15,000 of the agreed attorney's fee in currency, retaining the balance of $15,000 until the matter should be farther advanced. Ruef had intimated to Gallagher that each of the members of the board of supervisors, except Rea, would be allotted $750, and Gallagher himself somewhat more than that. But Ruef never actually paid any of the Parkside money to any of the supervisors. The beginning of the graft prosecution was destined to prevent the Parkside matter from being consummated during their tenure of office.

CHAPTER VIII

Telephone competition

Historians of the telephone have usually interpreted the period of competition as a wasteful and futile episode in the history of a natural monopoly. In this ill-starred era of competition in the telephone industry the granting of a franchise to the Home Telephone Company for a competing telephone network in San Francisco was one of the most colorful incidents.

The older network was that of the Pacific States Telephone and Telegraph Company, a part of the Bell system. The "Bell companies" had developed the telephone system in the United States as a monopoly, but the expiration of the original Bell patents in 1893 fathered numerous litters of independent companies which attained their most flourishing condition about 1906. In later years these independents were gradually absorbed into the Bell system, that is, the American Telephone and Telegraph Company and its subsidiaries.

Most of the six thousand independent telephone companies of the early years of the twentieth century were not actually competitive, but were merely mutual associations of small groups of subscribers in rural areas which the Bell system did not reach. About one thousand companies, however, were organized for competition and partial duplication, especially in middle-sized cities in the Middle West. The promoters of these companies based their hopes in part on the unpopularity of the existing system, whose customers had experienced frustrations through both mechanical and human elements in its expensive and often imperfect service. The new promoters argued that competition, as in other fields, would improve service and reduce rates. In practice, competition developed into a choice between half-

97

service and double expense. About a fifth of the subscribers in competitive-telephone cities had two separate instruments installed. As one historian put it, the independent promoters argued that two telephones were as natural as two ears, when in fact the telephone was not an ear but an entire nerve system, something which nature had never duplicated in one and the same body.

One of the most substantial of the independents was the family of Home Telephone companies, in which the leading capitalist was Abram K. Detwiler of Toledo. This chain of companies owned the patent rights to the dial telephone, which operated an automatic exchange and dispensed with the central office operator. The American Telephone and Telegraph Company lacked this highly important asset. Because of the superiority of the dial system over the operator, Detwiler cherished dreams of not merely competing locally with the Bell companies, but of driving them out of existence, and of supplanting the whole American Telephone and Telegraph Company with a new national telephone federation.

Detwiler succeeded in establishing Home Telephone companies in a number of cities ranging in size from Henderson, North Carolina, to Detroit, and in the early years of the twentieth century he was invading the west, the territory of the Pacific States Telephone and Telegraph Company. His plan of campaign was to enlist both the capital and the influence of leading families in each city. Only through their political, economic, and social connections, he felt, could he hope to combat the entrenched power of the Bell system. This method was almost immediately successful in establishing a competing network in Los Angeles, and the Bell company executives had good cause for alarm at the vigor of its efforts to establish itself in Oakland and in San Francisco.

In the Bell system, the parent American Telephone and Telegraph Company owned the instruments and rented them to its operating subsidiaries. In the end, during the following decade, it solved the problem of dial competition by buying up the Home companies and their properties, including their patent rights. But in these earlier years, Detwiler and his associates were unwilling to sell at any practicable price. Moreover, the Bell system had only recently undertaken the junking of its older instruments, of the type with a battery in connection with each telephone, in favor of the more modern central battery. The scrapping of a virtually new system because of still another development in technology would have presented insuperable financial and engineering difficulties. For the time being the Bell companies were forced to fight dial system competition as best they could. In each city, the most critical point in this fight was always the question of whether the city government would grant a competitive franchise.

The Pacific States Telephone and Telegraph Company employed Theodore V. Halsey as "general agent," although his actual duties were of a very special rather than a general nature. They were essentially the duties of a lobbyist, especially in the matter of combating the attempts of would-be competitors to obtain franchises, and in this capacity Halsey maintained the closest possible relations with the members of municipal lawmaking bodies from San Diego to Seattle. His qualifications included a naturally pleasant and affable manner, which his stenographer described as "always exceedingly courteous and urbane." Moreover, he was not required by the Pacific States company to submit detailed vouchers explaining his expenditures of money in the course of his special duties. He simply drew on the company's treasury by means of tags stating amounts withdrawn and signed by one of the executive officers. These tags were entered in the books, and audited, merely as special expenses "as per detail on file." The details were actually "filed" only in the memories of Halsey and the executive officers. The latter were Louis Glass, vice-president and general manager, and John I. Sabin, president of the company until his death in October, 1905. In the selection of Halsey for the performance of so highly confidential a function, it had undoubtedly been significant that Halsey, Glass, and Sabin were all brothers-in-law, having married three sisters.

In 1902, Halsey countered the efforts of the bona fide Home Telephone Company of Alameda County to gain a franchise in Oakland by organizing a fictitious "Oakland Home Telephone Company." This was incorporated, technically, by W. A. Beasly, a San Jose lawyer and close friend of Halsey's, and their dummy corporation actually succeeded in getting a franchise to establish a competing system in Oakland in 1902. Privately, Beasly sent

Halsey a document assigning ownership of this franchise to an official of the Pacific States Telephone and Telegraph Company. Beasly was furnished with several thousand dollars which he expended in the pretense of actual construction, but the project was finally abandoned and the franchise allowed to lapse. In October of 1905 the Oakland City Council granted a franchise to the bona fide Home Telephone Company of Alameda, which began actual construction of a rival system a few months afterward.

In the meantime, Detwiler as the guiding spirit of the Home companies had been gradually preparing for an assault on San Francisco, the most important position in the Pacific States system. Halsey was well aware of his danger. Since 1902 he had been employing Ruef as an attorney to the extent of paying him a monthly retainer in cash, although he had never called on the debonair little boss for any actual services, either legal or political. During the first two Schmitz administrations Ruef controlled so few votes in the board of supervisors that his intervention would have done more harm than good for Halsey's purposes. Ruef supposed that Halsey was paying him merely as a form of insurance in case the Democratic majority in the board should pass a resolution to sell a franchise for a competing system; in that case Halsey would have come to Ruef in haste, and with larger retainers, in the hope of obtaining Mayor Schmitz's veto.

In June, 1905, the Home Telephone Company of San Francisco filed a formal petition asking the city to sell a franchise. The Democratic board of supervisors kept the application bottled up in the public utilities committee, and Detwiler and his associates then pinned their main hopes on the fusion movement in the coming election. They contributed heavily to the fusion ticket's campaign fund, as did many other public utility corporations and individual capitalists. This mistake in backing the losing side, however, did not deter Detwiler, as it might have deterred a less intrepid capitalist, from making prompt overtures to the winner, who for practical purposes was Ruef.

One day in January, 1906, Ruef received a telephone call from James L. Gallagher, saying that there was a man in Gallagher's law office who wished to see Ruef there, in order to avoid the crush in Ruef's own rooms. Gallagher, while a member of the previous board, had taken a stand in favor of the proposed new telephone franchise, and he was also a close friend of one of the Home company's attorneys. When the man whom Ruef found waiting in Gallagher's office proved to be Abram K. Detwiler, Ruef thought he understood why Gallagher had not mentioned the name of the Home company's leader over a wire of the Pacific States company, a wire which might have been tapped for evidence of just such a call. Gallagher introduced his two callers and left them alone together, closing the door gently. Ruef liked Detwiler on sight. Even smaller in frame than Ruef himself, Detwiler still gave "an impression of large affairs." He was about fifty-five, "the typical business man, ready for action in his smartly cut gray tweeds, with his close-cropped iron-gray hair and mustache. He was quick of movement and precise in diction, with snapping eyes and a determined jaw."

According to Ruef, Detwiler began the conversation by congratulating him on his brilliant victory in the 1905 campaign, and by expressing satisfaction that the members of the old board of supervisors, who had opposed a new telephone franchise, were now out of office. But how, Ruef inquired, could Detwiler say this when his company had given all its support to the fusion movement? Ruef continued with some half-smiling remarks on the callousness of corporations in matters of politics, to which Detwiler replied: "I see you are a philosopher. I am only a plain businessman." He then made Ruef a very attractive offer of employment as an attorney and presented his stock of arguments in favor of the dial telephone. He said that the eyes of the whole world were upon the San Francisco experiment in labor government. So large an investment of new capital in the city would show confidence in the Schmitz administration, and increase prosperity, which was always the best politics. He hinted also at a strong political alliance of his company with the Union Labor party in the future, and offered to let the administration name the majority of the hundreds of men to be employed in the construction, installation, and administration of the new system.

In two more interviews with Detwiler in Gallagher's office, Ruef agreed to accept an attorney's fee of $125,000. Detwiler proposed at first that this entire sum be payable when the franchise was finally granted. Ruef objected that under the law this would take more than two months. He suggested, instead, a retainer of $25,000, with the balance of $100,000 to be paid as soon as the supervisors had passed an ordinance providing that a franchise be offered for bidding and sale. This they could do within two weeks, while the actual sale of the franchise could be completed only after the expiration of an additional legal period of several weeks more. Detwiler agreed. The next day, again in the privacy of Gallagher's office, Detwiler paid Ruef $25,000 in currency. "Detwiler was certainly a business man," Ruef wrote later. "It was a pleasure to deal with him in his rapid decisions and his instant recognition of conditions."

In order to come to an understanding with Detwiler, it was necessary for Ruef not merely to ignore the Home company's previous support of his own opponents, but also to ignore the fact that he himself was already employed as an attorney by that company's opponent, the Pacific States. Moreover, shortly after the election, Halsey had increased his retainer to $1,200 a month. Ruef's rationalization was that Halsey had never called on him for any specific legal services.

Ruef's acceptances of confidential retainers from both sides made him even more than usually secretive in his relations with the supervisors. The result was that while Ruef was preparing to pay the supervisors, through Gallagher, to vote for the Home franchise, eleven of them received money from Halsey to vote against it. Andrew M. Wilson appears to have taken the lead among these eleven members of the board in arranging their acceptance of money directly from Halsey, thus circumventing the established Ruef-Gallagher system of payments, without consulting Ruef or Gallagher in advance. Wilson claimed to have believed that Ruef himself was in favor of the Pacific States company and opposed to the new franchise. This remarkable series of events, however, must be explained in more detail.

Although the Pacific States company, like its would-be competitor, had given its main support to the fusion ticket in the election of 1905, Halsey had also done what he could both before and after the election to obtain the individual friendship of the Union Labor nominees. He had made payments to at least two, Boxton and Nicholas, for their campaign expenses. After the election, either Halsey, or his assistant John Kraus, or both had taken several of the new supervisors individually on conducted tours of the company's plant and to luncheon with wine. There were explanations of the nuisance that would result from telephone duplication; hints to some that friendship for the Pacific States company would be worth substantial sums of money; and hints also that Ruef favored that company's cause.

At the caucus of the board of supervisors on Sunday evening, February 18, 1906, Gallagher presented a new application of the Home Telephone Company for the sale of a franchise. Ruef had drawn up this document, and Detwiler had sent it to Gallagher. Ruef had informed Gallagher of his employment in behalf of the Home company, but apparently he had not yet mentioned any specific matters of money. In the caucus there was a lively debate, as well as considerable doubt and confusion. Several members inquired where Ruef stood on the question. He gave only the guarded reply that it was usually safe to follow Gallagher.

At this time, Halsey was paying monthly salaries to supervisors Boxton and Coleman to report to him on matters transpiring in the board. Informed of what had taken place at the caucus, Halsey felt that the critical moment was approaching, and that the time had come when he must take strong action or fail. The same Frank G. Drum who had employed Ruef as an attorney on behalf of the Pacific Gas and Electric Company was also a director of the Pacific States. Halsey told Drum that he needed a place in which to meet the supervisors for conferences, in order to present to them his arguments against telephone competition. Drum's own office was on the ninth floor of the Mills Building at Bush and Montgomery, near the heart of the financial district. For Halsey, Drum rented for a few days an empty office on the seventh floor, consisting of two rooms, one at the corner looking out on both streets, and the other room facing on Bush.

On February 23 and 24, the Friday and Saturday following the first caucus on the Home franchise, a number of the supervisors visited this office at Halsey's invitation. They came singly at various hours and entered the room facing Bush Street, which was unfurnished except for a table and two chairs. Halsey, or in some cases his assistant Kraus, handed each supervisor an envelope containing currency, usually with no more directly relevant explanation than that the Pacific States company would like to have the supervisors' friendship. Some did not examine the contents of their envelopes until after they had left the office, and one, Michael Coffey, claimed not to have opened his for several days. Altogether, eleven supervisors received a total of $51,000 in this matter, either from Halsey or from Kraus. Most of them received the money in the Mills Building.

Supervisor Wilson had received his share of this money on the morning of Saturday the 24th. Late in the afternoon of the same day, Wilson became somewhat worried and decided to tell Ruef what he had done. Ruef now told him emphatically that the administration favored the competitive franchise, and that he should not have accepted Pacific States money. Wilson agreed to vote as the administration directed, and to advise his colleagues to do the same. At Ruef's request, Wilson and Gallagher hastily called on various members at their homes, advising them to confer individually with Ruef later in the evening at The Pup. There Ruef demanded their support for the Home franchise.

The caucus of the board on the next evening, Sunday the 25th, was a stormy affair. While an agreement was reached, it came only after a bitter debate which threatened at one point to disrupt the administration. Money problems were kept out of this debate, but they were present as undercurrents in what were ostensibly disputes on higher levels. Boxton, as a member of previous boards, had been strongly on record for years against a competitive telephone system, and rebelliously refused to vote for it. McGushin was still honestly advocating the doctrine of public ownership, and also opposed the dial telephone as a labor-saving device. McGushin and Rea were being kept in ignorance of the fact that money was involved on either side of the question. Finally, after stern demands from Ruef and Schmitz, it was agreed that an ordinance for the sale of the new franchise should be passed to print without dissenting votes, but that Boxton would absent himself, and that McGushin would be excused from voting. This procedure was followed at the regular public meeting of the board the next day.

The telephone ordinance received final passage on Monday, March 5, 1906, after the expiration of the legal period of one week following the day it was passed to print. It provided that a fifty-year franchise for a competing system be sold to the highest bidder at the meeting of the board on Monday, April 23. There were five supervisors who did not vote for the ordinance on final passage: Boxton, Rea, Sanderson, and Walsh voted against it, and McGushin was again excused from voting.

Under the circumstances, Ruef was not particularly surprised when he received an outraged call from Theodore V. Halsey. Moreover, he took a certain amount of satisfaction in Halsey's predicament, which was the result of an attempt to circumvent Ruef's own position, and in effect to buy the supervisors away from him. According to Ruef's account of this interview, Halsey protested that he had been "double-crossed."

"You don't mean to tell me," Ruef asked, "that your company paid those supervisors money for their votes?"

"Certainly," said Halsey, "and you know it."

Halsey insisted that he had thought he had Ruef's friendship all along and implied that his $1,200 monthly attorney's fee should have been sufficient insurance of it. Ruef replied that Halsey had made a series of mistakes. He had never taken Ruef into his confidence; he had tried to buy supervisors; and he had tampered with their loyalty to the administration. Nevertheless, Ruef made a guarded promise to advise the supervisors who had received money from Halsey to give approximately half of it back.

Shortly after the final passage of the telephone ordinance, Ruef received the $100,000 balance of his total fee of $125,000, just as Detwiler had agreed. At Gallagher's office, "in the dim light of his drawn shades," Ruef counted out $62,000 for Gallagher to distribute among the supervisors. But the question of amounts to be paid to particular individuals raised complicated questions of mathematics, not to mention ethical problems. Thirteen members had voted for final passage of the ordinance. Eight of these, however, had voted for it after receiving money from Halsey to vote against it. Of this Pacific States money, Ruef suggested that these supervisors should retain $2,500 each, and give the rest back. If the Home money were now divided equally among the thirteen who had voted for the Home franchise, then the eight who had been temporarily disloyal to the administration would have $2,500 more than the five who had been loyal throughout. This would have been manifestly inequitable. Instead, Gallagher apportioned the $62,000 of Home money according to a list which, in tabular form, would have appeared as follows:

Gallagher	$10,000
4 Other supervisors who voted for the Home franchise and received no Pacific States money (Davis, Duffey, Harrigan, Kelly), $6,000 each	24,000
8 Supervisors who voted for the Home franchise in spite of having received Pacific States money (Coffey, Coleman, Furey, Lonergan, Mamlock, Nicholas, Phillips, Wilson), $3,500 each	28,000
3 Supervisors who voted against the Home franchise and received Pacific States money (Boxton, Sanderson, Walsh)	nothing
2 Supervisors who voted honestly against the Home franchise (McGushin, Rea)	nothing
Total, 18	$62,000

By this plan, each of the thirteen voters for the Home company would have a total of $6,000, except Gallagher who received more. But in eight cases the $6,000 would include only $3,500 of Home money, along with $2,500 from Halsey. Thus the Pacific States company had furnished part of the bribe money paid for votes which practically ensured a franchise for its competitor. The humor of this situation was not lost upon Ruef, who was delighted to have taught Halsey so ingenious a lesson. It is doubtful that more than two of the supervisors who had received Pacific States money from Halsey ever returned any part of it.

According to his memoirs, Ruef gave $30,000 of his Detwiler fee to Schmitz. This left a balance of $33,000 of the $125,000 of Home money for Ruef himself.

Of the inner history of these events, of course, the public had as yet no knowledge. Nevertheless, the board's passage of a new telephone franchise after only two weeks' deliberation became the subject of a considerable amount of public criticism. The *Examiner* went so far as to publish a front-page article under a headline "Whispers of Bribery are in Air." The people, said the *Examiner*, had previously given little attention to the Home company's demands, and that little only because Pacific States company service was "of the very worst." Now, the public suddenly found itself confronted with a fifty-year franchise, which

> must defer for half a century the proposed municipal ownership of a telephone system; . . . people are asking each other how it comes that such a project gains the support of men who were elected to office upon a platform pledging them to . . . municipal ownership.
>
> Adverse comment upon the attitude of the Supervisors in this matter has run so high that there have been whispers of bribery, of sums alleged to have been paid by the Home Telephone Company to gain its ends. There is, of course, no substantiation of any such rumors; but, for all that, the general feeling is that in the indecent haste which characterized the proceedings of last Monday week the Board of Supervisors acted just as a body of men against whom the gravest charges might have been made, would have acted.

Only thus in tortured subjunctives, however, could such guesswork be publicly expressed.

CHAPTER IX

Cable cars and trolleys

THE ordinance of 1906 permitting the street railway system to convert most of its remaining cable car lines to overhead trolleys was the occasion for the largest of all the "attorney's fees" which Ruef received, and for the largest bribery payment he made to the Union Labor supervisors.

In 1902 nearly all of the street railways in the city had been purchased by a syndicate of eastern investors, and consolidated into a new corporation known as the United Railroads of San Francisco. The most important of the new investors was Patrick Calhoun, of Atlanta and Wall Street. This grandson of John C. Calhoun was an outstanding, energetic corporation lawyer and capitalist, specializing in the reorganization and consolidation of railroads, in which he had already achieved fortune as well as fame.

It was appropriate that Patrick Calhoun should have risen to prominence as a leader in the consolidation of southern railroads. His famous grandfather, who resigned the vice-presidency of the United States to assume the leadership of the South as a conscious minority, had been keenly aware of the importance of a railroad network not only for the South's commercial prosperity but for its military security and for its independence of northern control. It was somewhat ironic that the grandson of John C. Calhoun should have become, in 1894, a leading instrument in the consolidation of the great Southern Railroad system by J. P. Morgan and Company of New York. But this is less surprising in view of the fact that long before the 'nineties northern capital had made a well established practice of using historic southern names for similar purposes.

As a reward for his services to Morgan and Company as general counsel of most of the lines which were merged into the Southern Railroad, Calhoun had received not only a very profitable return on his own shares of stock in that enterprise, but also a very favorable introduction to the highest circles of the New York financial world. He had established an office and a residence in New York, and put his money, reputation, and talents into several fields of investment in different parts of the country. His acquisition of control of the street railway system of San Francisco in 1902 was only one of a long series of his ventures during the same period. These included an oil company in Texas; an investment company and cotton mills in the southeast; a large real estate development in Cleveland; and the consolidation and development of the street railways of Pittsburgh, Baltimore, and St. Louis as well as those of San Francisco.

Calhoun's appearance and manner were those of an aggressive and forceful man of affairs, although he was physically of "plump and comfortable" proportions, being six feet tall and weighing more than two hundred pounds. His eyes were as commanding as those of his grandfather, but in a different way. They were not fiery, but rather cold and steel-like, of a very pale blue in color, and with "a faculty of looking *through* whatever their glance rests upon, be it a man, a railroad, a plan of battle, a tangled legal problem, or a complicated corporation report." This, combined with the fact that his mouth was habitually turned down at the corners and almost covered by his drooping white mustache, made Patrick Calhoun appear somewhat stern and humorless. His experiences in San Francisco were destined to emphasize rather than to soften these qualities.

It was almost universal gossip in San Francisco that the owners of the previous street railways companies, notably Henry E. Huntington, had forced the eastern capitalists to pay an exorbitant price. Calhoun did not think so at the time, because he expected the population of the city to double within one or two decades, and the value of its street railways to double with it. The capitalization of the new corporate structure was based on this assumption. Theoretically, the total value of the properties in the spring of 1902 was about thirty-nine million dollars, including the stocks and bonds of the previous companies. The new United Railroads of San Francisco, however, was capitalized not at thirty-nine million but at seventy-five million dollars: twenty millions of preferred stock, twenty of common, and thirty-five millions in bonds.

The twenty million dollars' worth of common stock in the United Railroads was in effect a bonus to Calhoun and his associates for their enterprise and risk. It was, of course, merely a "discounting" of the future; that is, an estimation of the present value of anticipated revenues. The common stock would be of no value unless actual returns brought in more than enough to pay dividends on the preferred stock and interest on the bonds— until, in other words, the actual value of the properties began to increase as much as the promoters hoped it would.

These were merely the accepted methods of the times in the financing of railroad and other industrial consolidations. There were many precedents in the history of both steam and street railroads, including Calhoun's own experiences in the South, which led him to expect equal success in the San Francisco venture. In the 'eighties and 'nineties a syndicate composed of Thomas Fortune Ryan, P. A. B. Widener, and others had vastly enhanced their fortunes by gaining control of the street railroads in New York, Philadelphia, and nearly a hundred lesser cities. Charles T. Yerkes had grown enormously wealthy by developing the street railroads of Chicago, in a pyrotechnic career which Theodore Dreiser later novelized in *The Financier* and *The Titan*. These great traction magnates had operated by means of the monopolistic consolidation of networks of valuable franchises —many of them obtained by bribery—and by generously watering the new stock. But Calhoun's group failed to realize that the companies it was buying in San Francisco in 1902 had already been generously overcapitalized. And at that time, of course, no one could have foreseen either the earthquake or the graft prosecution.

At the outset, Calhoun did not suppose that he would be forced to neglect his other enterprises to the extent of taking personal charge of the San Francisco streetcar system. But the company was soon confronted with a series of very difficult problems. The most immediate of these was the result of the organization of a carmen's union which threatened a substantial increase in the company's labor costs. It was the labor problem which finally forced Calhoun to take the presidency of the United

Railroads himself, and to spend several months of each year in San Francisco.

During the 'nineties Henry E. Huntington and the other San Francisco streetcar magnates had dealt firmly with their labor problems through the policy of discharging any man suspected

PATRICK CALHOUN
A drawing from *Men Who Made San Francisco.*

of trying to organize a union. But in the latter part of 1901 the carmen took courage from two circumstances. The ownership of the streetcar system was about to change hands, and a labor mayor had been elected. The carmen organized, and the new owners decided that it would be bad public policy to announce a strong stand against labor as one of their first public actions.

During 1902 and 1903, in bargaining with the new United Railroads, the carmen won substantial wage increases. They received important help from the Schmitz administration, notably the mayor's refusal to offer police protection for strikebreakers.

By this time Calhoun was well aware that he and his associates had paid too high a price for the San Francisco street railroads, and that they would be hard pressed to show anything like the expected profits on their inflated capitalization. Calhoun felt that any further increase in labor costs must be prevented, and that the management and operation of the San Francisco lines must be drastically reorganized and modernized.

Consolidation of management and rolling stock had already made it possible to cut some of the expenses of operation. But "consolidation" of so miscellaneous a jumble was neither so easy nor so profitable as Calhoun had originally supposed. In the 234 miles of track there were then 56 miles of cable, 166 of overhead trolley, four miles for horse cars, and eight miles of equally ancient steam railroad. Each of these four methods of propulsion used a different gauge of track. Of rolling stock there were 376 cable cars, 414 trolleys, 65 "steam dummy" cars containing their own small steam engines, and ten horse cars. In San Francisco, as in American cities generally, the history of street railways had been a motley pageant of different methods and eras of transportation overlapping each other. Horse car and steam railroad companies had flourished in the eighteen-sixties, and some of them had been granted fifty-year franchises. During the 'seventies and 'eighties, following the invention of the cable car by a San Francisco manufacturer of wire rope, cable car lines had spread rapidly in most of the larger cities, until the introduction of the first commercially successful electric trolley system in Richmond, Virginia, in 1888. Since then, trolleys had been gradually replacing cables.

When the United Railroads took over the San Francisco system, it had been somewhat more than half converted to overhead trolleys. Calhoun determined to complete this conversion and thus standardize the system as soon as possible, except for a few cable lines on some of the steepest hills.

One obstacle in Calhoun's way was a powerful section of public opinion opposed to overhead trolleys. There was little opposition to electricity as such, since most other large cities had already abandoned the cable car in favor of the greater efficiency of electric power. But there was strong sentiment in San Francisco in favor of laying the electric wires in conduits where they would be less dangerous and less unsightly than if strung overhead. In the early 'nineties some of the cable car companies, who did not welcome the competition of electric railways, had fostered an agitation against the possible danger of stringing live wires above the public streets. There had been a strong moral issue in the idea that trolley promoters were ready to risk the lives of the public for the sake of greater private profit, and the newspapers and even the clergy had taken it up. This propaganda had been highly effective. Martin Kelly recalled that "in saloons and corner groceries you could hear vivid descriptions of how a trolley wire broke loose somewhere in Siberia or Patagonia and went hissing and twisting on its way, licking up a large assemblage composed mainly of women and children." The fears thus engendered had never entirely died down.

Another obstacle to any further conversion to overhead trolleys by the United Railroads was the fact that many of the franchises it had acquired from the earlier companies had specified the permissible form of motive power on particular streets as either horses or cables. This was the case with some of the most important lines in the city.

Several other franchises had omitted any specification of motive power, but in all of these cases the lines had already been converted to overhead trolleys in the 'nineties. Any further conversion would require a permissive ordinance by the board of supervisors. It was undoubtedly with this in view that Calhoun sought to obtain the good will of Ruef.

As early as 1902 the United Railroads had begun to pay Ruef a regular, secret monthly fee, for being on call in case the company should need his services as a special "consulting attorney." The official who made these payments to Ruef was the United Railroads' chief counsel, Tirey L. Ford. At the time the payments began, Ford was not only the chief counsel of the new corporation; he was still attorney general of the state of California as well, and he remained in this office for a time after accepting his new position. This had made a deep impression on Ruef's mind. Ford, in advising his private employers during the organization of their company, had determined several important legal questions, such as the interrelations of the various franchises, questions on which he himself, as attorney general of the state, might be asked to rule. Yet neither the public nor the bar association had made any criticism of the company for selecting the attorney general as its chief counsel, nor of Ford for accepting the employment. In the fact that the standards of the times considered such a situation perfectly ethical, Ruef found a ready rationalization for his own acceptance of his secret fee of $500 a month, which he regularly collected from Ford in cash in the offices of the legal department of the United Railroads. "Even in our most intimate conversations," Ruef wrote later, "Ford shrank as I did, naturally, from discussing any question of influence. Everything was on a basis of absolute legal service, but I had no misunderstanding of what was meant."

One day when Ruef called at Ford's office, Ford introduced him to Patrick Calhoun. Ruef remembered the occasion vividly. "I was, at first sight, very much impressed. . . . Mr. Ford introduced us, saying: 'This is Mr. Ruef, one of our prominent attorneys and influential men, who is our good friend and can be of much service to us.' Mr. Calhoun replied: 'Everybody has heard of Mr. Ruef. I am glad to know him and hope to know him better.' We talked of various general matters. No business of the company was touched upon. After a few minutes of entertaining speech, Mr. Calhoun withdrew to his own office. Mr. Ford and I completed our interview."

When Ruef met Calhoun thereafter, Calhoun never referred to Ruef's employment by the United Railroads, though "fully cognizant of it." Ruef noted that "presidents of corporations deal peculiarly, as do bosses. They never say anything of importance concerning their business to anyone where it is not necessary."

Ruef was already an admirer of "General" Ford, and he soon developed an equal admiration for Calhoun. "The generations of his fighting blood," Ruef wrote, "the inherited abilities of his ancestry and his own skill and eloquence made favorable impression and gained headway for him in the community." His "forceful, able presentation of his company's claims" became "a factor in the public life of the city" to a degree remarkable for so recent a resident. During the periods when Calhoun was in the East, his executive assistant Thornwell Mullally was in charge of the company's affairs in San Francisco. Mullally, a protégé of Calhoun, was a brilliant young corporation lawyer, born in the South and educated at Yale; and Ruef found him as genteel, affable, and gracious as Calhoun himself. The two men, Ruef thought, were an ideal combination for "successful work among a sentimental and warmhearted people like those of San Francisco before the fire."

In 1904 the United Railroads embarked on a "campaign of education" in favor of overhead trolleys. To show how far trolleys could improve service, Calhoun first proposed the electrification of the Sutter Street system, a particularly inefficient mixture of horse cars and cables. But among the owners of property on Sutter Street were ex-Mayor Phelan and Rudolph Spreckels. Moreover, Spreckels' home was on the Pacific Avenue part of the Sutter Street carline. While Spreckels owned carriages and automobiles and did not use the street cars himself, he felt strongly that the erection of trolley poles and wires would mar the beauty of the city and damage the value of property, not only in the vicinity of his own home, but wherever they were built. He believed that underground conduits would have neither of these disadvantages, and while he knew that they were more expensive to install he felt that San Francisco was at least as much entitled as Washington and New York to the best and most modern street railways.

In the spring of 1905 the Sutter Street Improvement Club was organized, with Rudolph Spreckels as a prominent member, and this organization went firmly on record in favor of underground conduits. Ex-Mayor Phelan was president of the Association for the Improvement and Adornment of San Francisco, which had recently employed the great architect Daniel Hudson Burnham to draw up a city plan. This body also joined the movement against Calhoun's proposal for a city-wide system of overhead trolleys.

From this time forward Calhoun did not believe for a moment that either Spreckels or Phelan could be motivated by civic consciousness alone, if at all. He explained to Ruef that the opposition to his own plans for the city was coming merely from "a group of petty, selfish, local financiers," prejudiced against him as an eastern interloper, and wishing to keep San Francisco as a feudal province for themselves. And according to the later testimony of Spreckels and Phelan, Calhoun offered both of them highly valuable inducements to cease their opposition to the overhead trolley projects. To Spreckels, who owned a large lot at the corner of Sutter and Powell, Calhoun made a proposal to tunnel the Powell Street hill and thus to make the corner of Sutter and Powell the most important transfer point in the city. To Phelan, who was interested in extensive properties in the vicinity of the proposed Golden Gate Park panhandle, Calhoun suggested indirectly that the United Railroads would give the city $200,000 for the development of parks and of this project in particular, in return for the trolley privilege. These offers were refused. Calhoun argued that conduits were impractical in San Francisco because they could not be kept free of water in the rainy season. Spreckels insisted that this problem could be solved by ordinary drainage pipes, and offered to pay the cost of constructing such pipes for an experimental conduit system. Calhoun declined.

The controversy became intense during the last weeks of 1905, and remained so until the morning of the earthquake on April 18, 1906. The newspapers were generally unfriendly to the United Railroads' petition, and the *Bulletin* in particular launched a long series of editorials and cartoons criticizing the company for "wretched service but enormous profits." Public opinion was not entirely one-sided. The Merchants' Association employed the nationally famous engineer William Barclay Parsons to make a recommendation, and he reported in favor of the overhead wire, explaining that the higher cost of conduits had prevented their installation in any city in the country outside New York and Washington, that a uniform system was desirable, and that trolleys were actually superior for San Francisco's needs. The Merchants' Association then sharply divided over the question of endorsing Parsons' report, and in fact the controversy broke up many old friendships and caused many ill-tempered arguments throughout the city. On December 9, the trolley petition was voted down by the streets committee of the outgoing Democratic board of supervisors.

Since the election of the Union Labor ticket in November, the officials of the United Railroads had greatly increased their interest in the advice of their confidential attorney, Abraham Ruef. His retainer was now increased from $500 to $1,000 per month. In February, 1906, Ford asked Ruef to come to his office, where he told him that the company wished to press the trolley matter before the new board of supervisors. Ruef replied that he himself would be in favor of granting the United Railroads' petition, but that newspaper opinion in the city was almost unanimously against it, and that the company must offer some concessions to prove the sincerity of its claim that its motive was to improve the city rather than merely to protect its own profits. He suggested that all of the new trolley poles be of an ornamental design and also fitted with street lamps, and that the company should pay for the electricity, thus relieving the city of the cost of lighting the streets concerned. Ford investigated this proposal, and at their next interview protested that the cost of lighting all the lines the company wished to electrify would be far more than the privilege was worth, and that it could afford to assume only part of this cost. He offered ornamental poles, lamps, and electricity for parts of two streets: Market from the Ferry to Valencia, and Sutter from Market to Van Ness. Ruef concurred.

As Ruef was leaving the office, Ford remarked that since Ruef's legal advice in this matter would be of extraordinary value, the company would expect to pay him, in addition to his regular monthly retainer, a special attorney's fee "commensurate with the extent of your service and the importance of the proposition." A few days later Ford mentioned the figure of $50,000. Ruef protested that the company would lose respect for an attorney who would be satisfied with so little, since comparable corporations in the East would think nothing of paying several hundred thousand dollars for comparable services. Ruef then spoke of $250,000 as a fair charge. Ford offered $150,000. Ruef and Ford finally shook hands on the compromise of $200,000, for services in reference to the trolley petition, payable when the work had been completed.

In March Calhoun announced his company's intention to present to "the proper authorities" a plan for the improvement of the city by means of a uniform overhead trolley system.

Rudolph Spreckels and James D. Phelan had been convinced for some time that the Schmitz-Ruef administration was corrupt. In January they had privately guaranteed a fund for a possible special investigation of it by William J. Burns and Francis J. Heney. They were unwilling to see the United Railroads trolley petition granted by the Union Labor supervisors without a drastic attempt to bring public pressure against it. As "a last resort," Spreckels and Phelan determined late in March to organize a competing street railway company which should disprove Calhoun's arguments that the underground conduit was impractical in San Francisco from the engineering viewpoint. Rudolph Spreckels had now reconciled himself with his father, and Claus Spreckels became one of the incorporators and subscribers of stock in the new company.

At this time Phelan was aware, as he testified later, that the project might be compared in certain respects to previous ventures of the Spreckels family into new competitive enterprises, such as the Philadelphia sugar refinery, the San Joaquin Valley Railroad, and an independent gas, light, and power company in San Francisco. It was common knowledge in the city that the Spreckelses had eventually disposed of all three of these enterprises at large profits. Phelan observed, however, that they had also accomplished the purpose of forcing entrenched monopolies to recognize the rights of the public, and he was certain that this was the sole purpose of the new company, the Municipal Street Railways of San Francisco. Its plan was to apply for a franchise to construct and operate a model conduit system on Bush Street, which might be acquired by the city at any time the city might wish.

The Municipal Street Railways of San Francisco filed articles of incorporation in California on April 17, 1906. On the next day, however, the trolley-conduit controversy, like every other human conflict in the life of the city, was catastrophically interrupted by the great earthquake.

CHAPTER X

Earthquake, fire, and emergency government

THE earthquake attacked San Francisco with satanic ingenuity. It came at 5:14 in the morning of Wednesday, April 18, 1906. San Franciscans, anxious to counteract the impression that their city could ever be destroyed again by another similar catastrophe, have always correctly insisted that the bulk of the damage was not caused by the earthquake, but by the great fire, whose recurrence could be rendered impossible by a better-planned water system. More than fifty small fires began within a few minutes after the earthquake, where gas connections were broken, electric wires crossed, chimneys damaged, stoves overturned, and jars of chemicals spilled in drug stores. Most of these fires were soon extinguished, but others spread beyond control. By the second day, the downtown section was an appalling spectacle, engulfed in one vast inferno. After watching the scene from a launch on the bay, a reporter for the *Bulletin* wrote that "the most dreadful feature of the whole panorama was the intense silence and the intense motion. . . . The colors were neither those of night nor day, but fierce, vivid, frenzied tones unimaginable outside the crater of a volcano. The background was a sickly and lurid glow like the unearthly flush on the face of a dying man."

In the twenty-eight seconds of the earthquake's duration it broke the main arterial conduits of the city's water system. Along the peninsula, one of the three pipe lines ran for a distance of six miles directly over the line of the fault, and was almost completely destroyed. The other two main pipe lines were broken at points where they crossed marshes. Within the city the pipes of the distributing system were ruptured in the whole area of filled ground on which a large part of the downtown district was built.

The extent of the destruction which the earthquake wrought almost instantaneously upon the city's water system was quite sufficient to disorganize the fire department and to make its task hopeless. Ironically, the earthquake fatally injured the fire chief. A few seconds after the initial shock, Chief Dennis T. Sullivan heard a terrific crash from his wife's adjoining bedroom. In the darkness he tore open the door, rushed through it—and fell three stories through a hole in the floor. A large ornamental tower had fallen from its place high on the roof of the neighboring California Hotel, and had crashed through the building in which the chief's quarters were located.

On the north and east, fire boats saved the wharves and such buildings as were within range of their hoses. On the west the fire was finally checked at Van Ness Avenue, where army engineers and a navy gun crew dynamited the buildings in a long strip a full block deep on the east side of the broad street. On the south the fire ended along a ragged line from 20th and Dolores in the Mission district to the bay at Townsend Street. Thus before the last flames were extinguished on the fourth day, Saturday the 21st, the fire had devastated the main part of the city over an area of nearly five square miles. In this vast lake of destruction only one or two small islands were spared. Legend has it that the Italian residents of Telegraph Hill saved their homes by using barrels of wine to wet down a strip in the path of the flames. The skeletons of the City Hall, of the Claus Spreckels Building, and of several lesser skyscrapers, built on steel frameworks, were still standing.

The responsibility for leadership in this crisis was thrust into the hands of Schmitz as mayor. It was his finest hour. He rose to the occasion with a degree of executive ability and of genius for improvisation much greater than he or anyone else had known that he possessed. In the months after the earthquake he often said that his life began on the 18th of April.

One of his first public actions was to issue his famous and drastic decree for the maintainance of order, which was printed on handbills and distributed throughout the city. This proclamation warned that "The Federal Troops, the members of the Regular Police Force and all Special Police Officers have been authorized by me to KILL any and all persons found engaged in Looting or in the Commission of Any Other Crime."

Schmitz realized that the existing agencies and personnel of the city's government could not cope with such an emergency; and in the early morning of the 18th he appointed the famous "Citizens' Committee of Fifty." This plan has since been attributed to the great lawyer Garret W. McEnerney, and also to the millionaire capitalist J. Downey Harvey. But at the time, Schmitz received full credit for the plan and for the selections. It was a list of the city's ablest lawyers, business executives, and civic leaders. The city fathers on the board of supervisors were entirely omitted from it, and many of the strongest critics and political opponents of the Schmitz administration, notably ex-Mayor James D. Phelan and Francis J. Heney, were included. Ruef's name was not on the original list, but it was added by Schmitz soon afterward.

The Committee of Fifty held its first meeting a few hours after the earthquake, at three in the afternoon of Wednesday, April 18, in the Hall of Justice at Kearny and Washington. It elected Mayor Schmitz as chairman, and authorized him "to issue orders for supplies to be given to those in need." At the same time, however, it placed control of relief finances in the hands of James D. Phelan, as chairman of a finance committee of the Relief and Red Cross funds, with power to name the other members. Phelan named a committee including J. Downey Harvey as secretary, and M. H. de Young, Frank G. Drum, William F. Herrin, Joseph S. Tobin, Garret McEnerney, Rudolph Spreckels, and several other wealthy and prominent citizens.

Before the Committee of Fifty had finished its session on Wednesday afternoon, it was apparent that the Hall of Justice would not be available for the next meeting, since flames were rapidly approaching the building. The committee adjourned to meet at ten the next morning at the Fairmont Hotel, near the crest of Nob Hill. By that time, the Fairmont itself was threatened, and the committee was forced to hold its Thursday morning meeting in the North End police station. This structure was also engulfed before the Thursday afternoon meeting, which finally assembled at 4:30 in Franklin Hall on Fillmore Street, well out into the Western Addition.

Throughout this unfolding catastrophe, Schmitz was an inspired and inspiring figure. Even an extremely unfriendly journalist, months later, in an article strongly criticizing Schmitz's whole career, remarked with reluctant admiration that the former conductor of the Columbia Theatre orchestra "ran the Committee of Fifty as he would a hurry rehearsal. . . . He swung his baton and played his new band with as much aplomb as if he had been conducting it for years. He did not stop to think what kind of music it made; he knew enough to know that there must be some kind of music to keep the audience from panic." Men who would have refused to shake his hand before, now praised him, offered him suggestions, and were often delegated to carry them out. Among the general public, hero worship of Schmitz became so strong that even those who did not actually share in this feeling paid lip service to it. Even the *Bulletin* stated early in May that Schmitz's actions since the earthquake had "merited unqualified admiration." A few days later it remarked that "the fire has burned out old enmities. . . . The *Bulletin* has seen Mayor Schmitz, former Mayor Phelan, John Partridge, Abraham Ruef and Gavin McNab forgetting factions, ignoring conflicting political interests, sitting together harmoniously in committees and giving freely to the city of the best that was in them. . . . In this spirit the *Bulletin* is coöperating and will continue to coöperate with the men who are laying the foundations of the new San Francisco." Actually, Fremont Older did not think for a moment of abandoning his secret plans for a graft prosecution. He wrote later that his dominant feeling was one of irritation that these plans would now be delayed. But for several weeks after the earthquake the *Bulletin* suspended all criticism of Schmitz.

The city took pride in a historic tradition of triumphant resurgence after all but complete destruction by fire. This had occurred so often during the gold rush years that a phoenix rising from the flames and ashes had been made one of the figures on the seal of the city and county. While a large part of the population left the city during and after the great fire of 1906, most of those who remained were bound together, for some weeks at least, by strong feelings of the comradeship of disaster. Social distinctions were temporarily swept away. Everywhere in the city outside the burned area, families of all classes cooked their meals on stoves brought out onto their sidewalks, following an order by the mayor to light no more fires in their houses. "Most of the servants have either run away or been sent away," wrote a correspondent for the Los Angeles *Times*, "and the people who get their own meals out of doors are among the best in the city. Cooking their dinners in the streets may be seen girls who have been educated at Stanford, Berkeley, Vassar and Bryn Mawr." And the same correspondent reported that the most remarkable "of all the astounding leveling feats accomplished by the fire and earthquake" had occurred in front of the mansion of Rudolph Spreckels on Pacific Avenue, where a daughter was born to Mrs. Spreckels behind some screens set up on the sidewalk. "On a similar sidewalk in the next block that same night a lost cat who had no home brought forth a litter of kittens."

During the days and nights immediately after the earthquake, Ruef shared in the city's extraordinary spirit of comradeship, and in the temporary general amnesty of personal hostilities. He performed the tasks assigned to him by the Committee of Fifty with energy and diligence, and went for many days without a change of clothes and with very little sleep. But he disliked the plan of Schmitz and Harvey, which assigned only a minor position to Ruef, and under which Schmitz was beginning to feel independent of him. He had no intention of remaining for long in a subordinate role in the emergency government, and he made this clear to the mayor privately. On May 3, Schmitz announced that the Committee of Fifty would be terminated and replaced by a "Committee of Forty on the Reconstruction of San Francisco." In the latter, Ruef was to be the dominant member of a committee on organization, that is, on the membership of subcommittees. In the earlier scheme, Ruef had been chairman of only one relatively minor subcommittee, on the permanent location of Chinatown. Under the Committee on Reconstruction, he held several key chairmanships. Several men who had originally been named to the Committee of Fifty were not reappointed—Francis J. Heney in particular.

The fact that Ruef had thus assumed the most powerful role in the Committee on Reconstruction later gave rise to many charges that he manipulated its policies in his own selfish interests, to the city's disadvantage. In particular, he was charged with the responsibility for having sabotaged the famous and idealistic "Burnham plan." This charge was not entirely fair to Ruef, and the actual circumstances must be carefully examined.

Two years earlier, the Association for the Improvement and Adornment of San Francisco had been formed, with James D. Phelan as its president. The association was founded with the idea of creating a master plan for the city, and to this end it secured the services of the Chicago architect Daniel Hudson Burnham, then regarded as the leader of the "city planning movement" in the United States. The reputation which Burnham had made in designing buildings for the magnificent "White City" at the Chicago World's Fair in 1893, and his permanent plan for the Chicago lake front, had also brought him commissions from Washington and Cleveland. Burnham came to San Francisco in September, 1904, to work in a bungalow built for this special purpose, high on a spur of Twin Peaks, with the city spread out beneath it like a map. He remained for about a month, and then sailed for Manila to execute a similar commission, leaving the details of his conception for San Francisco to be worked out by his assistant, Edward Bennett. The plan which emerged was of the "city beautiful" type, rather than a plan based on business and traffic surveys, and it gave rather slight emphasis to concepts of economic function, although it did contain the eminently sensible suggestion of subways.

When the greater part of San Francisco was leveled by the earthquake and fire only a few months after the Burnham plan was published, James D. Phelan became the leader of those who wished to seize the opportunity to build Burnham's ideal city. Ruef offered no public opposition to this sentiment. In the Committee on Reconstruction, he permitted the creation of a subcommittee on the Burnham plans, with Phelan as chairman and including the architects Willis Polk and John Galen Howard. Burnham himself came to the city in May to offer his advice. Immediately, however, strong protests arose from merchants and others who feared that the rebuilding of their places of business would be delayed by the uncertainties of Burnham's plans for relocating streets in the downtown district. His original plan had contained such radical proposals as the one recommended in its "theory of the hills": that "each hill . . . should be circumscribed at its base . . . by a circuit road" with "contour roads" at progressively higher levels. In May of 1906 such ideas had to be abandoned. Majority opinion was overwhelmingly opposed to any "impractical" or aesthetic considerations. Among the ruins, "adornment" seemed only a grim joke to all but the most idealistic citizens.

In these circumstances, the subcommittee issued a drastically modified Burnham plan calling mainly for a civic center, for a new inclined approach to Nob Hill, for the widening of streets, and for one or two new boulevards. The subcommittee concluded its report with an eloquent but futile warning: "The City of London, after its great fire, rejected the plans of Sir Christopher Wren, according to the history of that time, on account of 'jealousies among the people,' and since then the City of London has not only regretted its failure to take advantage of the occasion, but has paid enormous sums to effect the very same results."

Burnham himself showed his awareness of the prevailing opinion when he said in an interview that "the public will be surprised to learn how few and practical are the changes recommended." This statement represented a decided compromise with his own famous slogan: "Make no small plans."

Some years afterward, the Civic Center did emerge as one major project salvaged from the Burnham plan. But in 1906 practically the only recommendations of Burnham which were put into effect were those approved by the subcommittee on the widening and grading of streets, of which Ruef was chairman. And in many cases the widening of streets was effected not by pushing back the permissible lines of the storefronts, but simply by narrowing the sidewalks.

As for the question of the degree of Ruef's responsibility for the city's failure to make any substantial use of the Burnham plan in its reconstruction, it must be emphasized that the businessmen were overwhelmingly against it, and that this opinion was generally shared by the newspapers. The *Bulletin*, for example, expressed its views on May 1 in an editorial headlined "Dreams Will Not Rebuild San Francisco." "We cannot stand too heavy a tax rate," said this editorial, and "visions of the beautiful must not blind us to the real needs of the city [and] the indispensable conditions of industries." The city was still young, and must leave considerations of beauty to "a future and more opulent generation." Toward the end of May the *Bulletin* expressed regret at the discord caused by discussions of the Burnham plan, but remarked, "This is a time for action, not regrets. . . . It is desirable to have a beautiful city, but it is urgently necessary to have a city of some sort instead of a heap of ruins."

Merchants and owners of real estate in the downtown district were intensely anxious to rehabilitate their fortunes by rebuilding as soon as possible at exactly the same locations as before. Ruef could probably not have resisted this pressure even if he had wished. He did not. He was himself one of the important owners of real estate, and he shared the point of view of the majority of them. Not even the long-desired project for a permanent relocation of Chinatown could be accomplished. The Chinese owners refused to move to any less central location, and Ruef admitted in his subcommittee's report that the city had no possible legal means of forcing them to submit to its request.

Undoubtedly Ruef continued to use his political position in the months after the earthquake for the purpose of enhancing his own fortune in real estate. During this period the unburned area west of Van Ness became the center of the truncated city. Fillmore Street, previously a third-rate thoroughfare of shabby flats and small grocery stores, now became both the main commercial artery and the tenderloin of post-fire San Francisco. In this suddenly booming district, with space at a premium and rents exorbitant, Ruef acted as agent in securing emergency locations for the various city government offices. They had to be scattered over the district, as he admitted, in "spectacular disarray." The members of the board of supervisors held their first meeting after the fire in Supervisor McGushin's saloon on Hayes Street near Laguna. Later they moved to Mowry's Hall, a modest structure at Laguna and Grove. Police headquarters were in a bakery at Bush and Fillmore. Ruef's own law office, in some respects the most important office of actual government in the city, was located at first in two rooms, formerly a kitchen and bathroom, in a flat on Pine Street. Later, however, Ruef managed to establish quarters in a hastily erected three-story frame building at the corner of Fillmore and Bush. Here, as the *Call* remarked, Ruef had the most commodious law offices in town, with six sunny rooms, twice as many as he had had in his building downtown at Kearny and California. The new building also housed a bank and a French restaurant, in both of which, the *Call* alleged, Ruef now owned a substantial interest. According to the *Call's* account, the erection of this structure had originally been begun by two French restaurant keepers, who had been forbidden to proceed with it, under an emergency proclamation of the mayor against frame buildings of more than one story; but this order was set aside after Ruef was employed as attorney, and after he joined the original promoters in organizing the Fillmore Street Building Company, to which he was admitted as a stockholder.

Other charges that Ruef made improper use of his power at this time grew out of certain proposals which he advocated before the special session of the state legislature in June. The great fire had created various extraordinary problems, such as the burning of the records of property titles, from which the city sought relief by changes in state laws. In the Committee on Reconstruction, Ruef had secured the appointment of Tirey L. Ford as chairman of the subcommittee on proposed state legislation, and also his own appointment as chairman of the important subcommittee on proposed amendments to the city charter. Before the special session at Sacramento, Ruef and Ford advocated changes which would have removed all state supervision over the city in matters of relocating streets and modifying the terms of franchises, and would have placed final authority, for a period of time, in the hands of the mayor and the board of supervisors. The legislature declined to approve these particular proposals, and the San Francisco *Bulletin* asserted that the city had thus escaped "a worse evil than earthquake and fire." The *Bulletin* charged that the scheme had been planned with remarkable "audacity . . . by a crafty brain," and that if it had succeeded, "a place on the Board of Supervisors would be worth a million dollars a year to a boodler."

Undoubtedly there was some justice in the *Call's* assertion a few weeks later that Ruef's plans for a new San Francisco were influenced by his "plans for a greater Ruef."

CHAPTER XI

Business as usual

IN WRITING his memoirs, in 1912, Ruef was at pains to deny
that he had taken advantage of the conditions following the earthquake and fire to originate any new major projects for receiving
money. It was entirely unfair to him, he insisted, to charge that
any of his major "deals" had been devised "amid the ashes and
the mourning."

There were, however, four specific projects which Ruef nego-
tiated after the fire. It was true that all of them had been conceived before the disaster. The Home Telephone franchise and
the United Railroads trolley ordinance were successfully completed soon afterward. The Parkside project remained unsuccessful until more than two years later, when the franchise was
finally granted on its own merits by a different administration.
There was another scheme which, had it been successful, would
have been the largest of all. This was the proposal of the Bay
Cities Water Company. Ruef had made plans for all four of
these projects before the great catastrophe. But he did not drop
any of them because of it.

The ordinance providing for a new telephone franchise in
San Francisco, passed on March 5, had fixed the date for the final
bidding and sale at Monday, April 23, which was only the fifth
day after the earthquake. On the morning of that day, Ruef
wrote, he was "still in the greasy, dishevelled attire which had
served him through five days of terrible experience," and had
forgotten all about the telephone matter, when Robert Frick,
one of the Home Telephone Company's attorneys, sought him
out at the headquarters of the Committee of Fifty. Frick inquired anxiously whether the board of supervisors would meet

that afternoon, to receive bids and conclude the sale of the telephone franchise as the ordinance provided.

The board of supervisors had received very little attention from anyone since Wednesday, the day of the earthquake, when the Committee of Fifty had been organized and had assumed all of the special functions of government which the emergency required. In the meantime the regular meeting place of the supervisors in the city hall had been destroyed, and for several days the members of the board had concerned themselves with their individual problems. They did not meet until Sunday, when a few of them gathered in Supervisor McGushin's saloon, now closed like all such establishments by a proclamation of the mayor against the dispensing of liquor. After this meeting on Sunday Gallagher reported to Ruef that some of the members resented the manner in which they had been pushed aside, and that they were determined not to abdicate completely in favor of the Committee of Fifty. Ruef assured Gallagher that the committee was intended only for urgent relief and rehabilitation work requiring "the united coöperation of everybody, and not merely official action." Ruef also engaged Mowry's Hall, in the Western Addition, as a regular meeting place for the board beginning on Monday afternoon.

When Frick reminded him on Monday morning that the telephone franchise was scheduled for sale that day, Ruef at first advised its postponement on the ground of doubts of its legality. The ordinance had specified the place of sale as the board's regular meeting room, which was now destroyed. The California law required competitive bidding, and potential bidders would not have adequate notice of the change in the place where they could submit their bids. But on behalf of the Home Telephone Company, Frick insisted that the sale should proceed that afternoon, and that his corporate client would take its chances in the courts afterward. Ruef finally consented. Frick himself attended to the posting of notices of the change of the meeting place. About noon he made his way to the ruins of the city hall, where some of its embers were still smoldering. There he set up a small sign bearing the notice that bids for a telephone franchise would be received by the board of supervisors at Mowry's Hall at two o'clock of the same day.

The reason for Frick's anxiety and for his opposition to any delay was that shortly before the earthquake a strong competitor for the new franchise had appeared in the form of the United States Independent Telephone Company. This was one of the many enterprises of Adolphus Busch, the St. Louis brewer and capitalist, and apparently Busch's agents had serious intentions of outbidding the Home Telephone Company for the new franchise in San Francisco.

If the United States Independent Telephone representatives had been as alert and enterprising as Frick, they could have entered into the bidding at Mowry's Hall on the legal day of sale. But they did not appear. The franchise was awarded to the Home Telephone Company for its bid of $25,000, which was the only one submitted. Originally Detwiler had agreed with Ruef on $100,000. Having secured the franchise for only $25,000, the Home company contributed $75,000 to the emergency relief fund. Later the United States Independent Company, in unsuccessfully contesting the award of the franchise, claimed that it would have been willing to bid as much as $1,000,000. Undoubtedly the real value of the privilege had actually been increased by the disaster, which had destroyed most of the system of the incumbent Pacific States company in San Francisco, thus placing its new competitor in a much more nearly equal position.

The final sale of the franchise for a new telephone system, five days after the earthquake, was merely the completion of a matter which had been determined in principle several weeks before. The Home Telephone money had been paid to Ruef, and part of it was given by Ruef to the supervisors, in March. The United Railroads' overhead trolley matter, however, was in a much less advanced stage. In February, Tirey L. Ford, chief counsel of the railroad, had reached a preliminary agreement with Ruef on an attorney's fee of $200,000, payable when the "work" should be "completed." In March, Patrick Calhoun, the president of the railroad, had broken off negotiations with the groups advocating the underground electric conduit, and had publicly announced his company's intention of applying to the board of supervisors for the privilege of converting its cable lines to overhead trolleys. But at the time of the earthquake this had not yet been formally proposed, no money had been paid, and Ruef had not yet mentioned the subject to his leader of the board, Supervisor Gallagher.

The earthquake and fire strengthened the resolution of the United Railroads officials to proceed with the trolley matter. The city was in desperate need of a resumption of street rail transportation at the earliest possible time. Trolleys were the method which could be put into operation most quickly. Underground electric conduits, apart from their greater cost, would require a much greater length of time to construct. As for the old cable roadbeds, there was conflicting testimony on the extent to which they had been damaged, but spokesmen for the United Railroads insisted that many of the slots had actually melted shut under the heat of the fire, and that many more were so twisted and warped as to be practically irreparable.

A few days after the earthquake, Ford called at the little flat on Pine Street, where Ruef had established his emergency quarters. The public part of Ruef's office, formerly a kitchen, was crowded, and Ford and Ruef stepped into the private office, formerly a bathroom. Ford did not discuss business matters, Ruef recalled later. He "had called merely to see how nearly alive I might be, and to advise me that the United Railroads was furnishing the best lunch in the city, free, at its carhouse at Turk and Fillmore." A decent meal was extremely rare in San Francisco, and Ruef accepted Ford's invitation with delight. A private car had been fitted up as a dining salon for the company's officials and their guests. Here, and later at a nearby residence even more comfortably equipped for the same purpose, Ruef became accustomed to having his midday meal, often with some of the supervisors who had also been invited. But no mention of the trolley question ever intruded itself into the pleasant hospitality and spirited conversation of these luncheons. "We might all have been as disinterested," Ruef wrote, "as denizens of Mars."

During this period, Ruef, Ford, Mullally, and Calhoun were working together on the most cordial and comradely terms in the reconstruction of the city. Mullally was chairman of the subcommittee on resumption of transportation, in the Committee on Reconstruction, and he and Ruef were often seen hurrying about the city in Mullally's automobile. Ford and Ruef served together on the subcommittees on the judiciary, and on emergency legislation to be proposed to the state. In their capacities as general and special counsel, respectively, for the United Railroads, Ford and Ruef also discussed the details of a trolley privilege ordinance to be submitted to the board of supervisors. But they were careful never to mention the idea that any part of Ruef's prospective fee might be paid to any member of the board. Moreover, the business of the law department of the United Railroads was carefully segregated from all other matters. Ford was the only representative of the company who ever mentioned the subject of Ruef's employment as attorney. Only once, as Ruef recalled, did Calhoun ever forget himself to the extent of hinting at it. While discussing the city's urgent need for transportation, Calhoun remarked to Ruef, "I understand General Ford has had a talk with you about this." Ruef gave him a startled glance, whereupon Calhoun recollected himself, and hastily changed the subject.

As soon as the fire had died down, the United Railroads began to concentrate its efforts on restoring service over a few of its trolley lines which could be most hastily repaired. On the morning of April 27 the first streetcar to run for any distance since the earthquake was ready to make a token trip. Operated by the mayor himself, and carrying officials of the United Railroads, the supervisors, and other distinguished guests, the trolley car made its way without stopping, from the Turk and Fillmore carbarn along Fillmore to Pacific Avenue, along Sixteenth to Mission, down Mission to Fifth, around a block to Market, and back by the same route. Its dramatic appearance, a symbol of the gradual renewal of the flow of life in the city, brought hearty cheers wherever it passed. Men jumped on the steps and rode a few feet, for the honor and thrill of having traveled on it. Mullally and Calhoun announced that with trolleys they could have several more lines running in a few days, and the entire system within a few weeks. In the meantime, the United Railroads had done much to earn the city's good will. It had made the first large contribution to the relief fund. It had opened its carbarns as shelters, and distributed food and clothing to the needy. It had kept all its carmen on full pay, and tendered their services to the city as special police and street cleaners.

Public opinion was now undoubtedly in favor of trolleys for the time being, and was giving little thought to the more distant future. The *Bulletin,* seldom noted for its friendliness either to the United Railroads or to the administration, remarked that the needs of the emergency had converted many opponents of the overhead trolley wire. When an ordinance permitting the United Railroads to equip its entire system with trolleys was introduced in the board of supervisors on May 14, passed to print, and thus scheduled for final passage a week later, public opposition came from only one source, the *Examiner*. From a temporary shack on the waterfront, Hearst himself began to direct a slashing attack on the proposed ordinance, and on the supervisors. The issue of May 15 carried the banner headline, UNITED RAILROADS WOULD TRY TO LOOT THE STRICKEN CITY! This article derided a statement by Mayor Schmitz, which indeed he soon retracted, that the trolley privilege was a temporary emergency measure. The *Examiner* pointed out that everything in the language of the ordinance pointed to permanency. The electrical equipment was to be "of the first class in every particular." Along Market from the Ferry Building to Valencia and along Sutter to Van Ness there were to be "highly ornamental poles," from which the United Railroads was also to furnish light for the streets. An editorial in the *Examiner's* next issue was headlined, SNEAK THIEVES AMID THE RUINS AND SENTRIES WHO TURN THEIR BACKS. Admitting that trolleys were necessary as an emergency expedient, the *Examiner* insisted that the city wanted underground conduits as its permanent system. "If the Supervisors are honest in this matter they can go about the solution of this problem in the right and simple way," by a short-term license. A permanent grant would be "the wrong way—a way so wrong that it smacks and smells of bribery and of a ghoulish effort to steal from the city in her time of need." Should the supervisors aid and abet this theft, "the people will be warranted in setting up their effigies in lasting bronze, a group of everlasting infamy, with the inscription: THESE MEN LOOTED SAN FRANCISCO AT THE TIME OF THE GREAT FIRE OF 1906."

The fact that the *Examiner* was alone among the major newspapers in its strong public opposition to the trolley ordinance encouraged Ruef to proceed with its passage. When one representative of a group who preferred conduits tried to dissuade him by arguing that the *Examiner* could eventually bring about his political ruin, Ruef replied, "To Hell with the *Examiner*, no public man can afford to swallow that paper. This thing will go through on Monday. It is all settled." The ordinance received final passage by unanimous vote on Monday, May 21. Gallagher, in a speech at the meeting of the board, and Schmitz, in signing the ordinance the next day, pointed out that the city had no legal power to compel the United Railroads to install underground conduits when the corporation had refused to do so.

The *Examiner* now intensified its daily denunciations. SCHMITZ DELIVERS THE CITY'S STREETS TO THE LOOTERS! said one headline. A cartoon portrayed Ruef as a grinning spider weaving a cobweb of trolley wires over the ruins. And an editorial on the same page made a kind of last appeal to Schmitz, whom the *Examiner* had often courted, to "become what the vast majority of the people of San Francisco supposed him to be—a workingman who sympathized with workingmen and their needs, an honest man and an honest Mayor. . . . Let him cut loose from Abe Ruef and the corporations that make merchandise of the city's misery."

The positions taken by the *Examiner* and the *Bulletin* on this question showed a curious realignment. Hearst's *Examiner* had been relatively friendly to the Union Labor administration from 1901 to 1905, when the *Bulletin*, headed by Older and Crothers, had been attacking the administration constantly. Now, after the earthquake, although Older was continuing to work secretly for a graft investigation, the *Bulletin* was publicly calling for unity. Moreover, the *Bulletin* criticized its competitor for creating disharmony while the city was trying to recover from the disaster. Why, asked the *Bulletin*, had the *Examiner* waited until now to oppose trolleys and attack the administration? The answer, in the *Bulletin's* editorial opinion, was that until the earthquake the *Examiner* had feared to lose circulation in the districts where the followers of Schmitz and Ruef were most numerous, and these districts were now burned out. But this did not account for the *Examiner's* strong accusations of bribery in the telephone franchise, which were made in March, before the earthquake. The fact was that the *Examiner* had been strongly critical of public utility corporations for months. Hearst had run for mayor of New York in November, 1905, on a municipal-ownership ticket. Another aspect of the *Examiner's* attacks on the Schmitz administration in San Francisco, in 1906, was the evident fact that by that time Hearst had practically abandoned his earlier hopes of winning Schmitz's political allegiance away from Ruef.

As for the allegiance of the San Francisco workingmen in general, the *Examiner's* attacks on the administration did begin to make some headway. The Labor Council passed resolutions, supported by Andrew Furuseth and Walter Macarthur, censuring the Union Labor officeholders for "giving away the rights of the people," and for serving the interests of Calhoun and the United Railroads instead of those of the workingmen who had elected them to office.

In the trolley matter, as in the case of the telephone franchise, the *Examiner's* speculations about bribery had been more accurate than it knew. While Gallagher's later recollections varied somewhat as to the exact time, it is certain that Ruef instructed him to sound the feelings of the supervisors about the trolley privilege at some time before the ordinance was introduced for passage to print, on May 14. Most of the supervisors later testified that they would probably have been willing to vote for the measure without any payment for their votes. But during the week after the ordinance had been passed to print, and while its final passage was still pending, several of the members let Gallagher know that they felt their votes would be worth a substantial amount. Wilson especially mentioned the opposition of the *Examiner,* and suggested that the supervisors should be compensated for the violent criticism which they were receiving in the *Examiner's* columns.

Ruef's proposal to Gallagher was to allot $5,000 to each member of the board. All eighteen of the members were willing to vote for the measure. McGushin now felt that his convictions in favor of municipal ownership of public utilities had been outdated by the fire, and he was willing to accept money for his vote. One member, Rea, had received no money since his demonstration of outraged honesty at the time of the gas rate payments, and would have resented and refused any offer of payment for his vote on the trolley question. This left seventeen supervisors at $5,000, or a total of $85,000, and this was the sum Ruef eventually turned over to Gallagher. When Gallagher offered $5,000 to Wilson, the latter felt that his services as an intermediary between Gallagher and other members were worth at least $10,000. Gallagher agreed, and decided also to retain $15,000 for himself. This reduced to $4,000 the amount remaining for each of the other members of the board—fifteen exclusive of

Rea—and this was the amount which Gallagher eventually paid them. The process took three months' time, and considerable ingenuity.

On May 22, the day after the trolley ordinance was finally passed, President Calhoun of the United Railroads arranged to have $200,000 transfered by telegram from the East, through the courtesy of the Treasurer of the United States, in the form of a deposit to Calhoun's credit at the United States Mint in San Francisco. The banks of San Francisco were still closed, but the Treasury Department had undertaken to handle such transfers of money for relief and similar emergency purposes. On May 24, the day Mayor Schmitz officially signed the ordinance, Tirey L. Ford presented at the mint a written order from Calhoun to pay Ford $50,000 of the $200,000. Only gold was available for payment by the mint, and the $50,000 in gold was excessively heavy and bulky. Since the relief committee headquarters were in the same building, the gold was taken there and exchanged for currency. The currency available consisted of bills of small denominations, received by the relief committee from thousands of contributors all over the country. In this form the $50,000 was still somewhat bulky. It was taken away by Ford and by William M. Abbott, another member of the law department of the United Railroads.

On the 25th, according to Ruef's memoirs, Ford asked Ruef to call at the temporary offices of the United Railroads at Oak and Broderick streets, to pick up the packaged currency. Ruef had no place to store valuables in his own temporary office in the Pine Street flat, and he was in the habit of carrying valuable papers to and from his offices in cardboard shirtboxes, thriftily procured from the neighboring haberdashery establishment of his cousin Hirsch. On the afternoon of May 25, Ruef obtained a box, and ordered his chauffeur to drive him to the United Railroads offices. Ruef realized that his automobile might be recognized by almost any passerby. Automobiles were still expensive and rare enough so that the man in the street could often identify a particular one with its owner, and Ruef's vehicle, popularly known as the "green lizard," was familiar to almost everyone in the city, "because of its ubiquity and its peculiarly vivid green color." Nevertheless, Ruef ordered his chauffeur to park immediately in front of the United Railroads offices. For several weeks he had called on Ford so often on reconstruction matters, that he had no reason to suppose that this particular visit would ever attract comment. Ford, in handing Ruef the packaged money, apologized for its bulk. Ruef laughed, and replied that this automobile could carry much more.

Ford drew the balance of Calhoun's $200,000 in two installments, one of $50,000 late in July, and one of $100,000 on the 23d of August. At these times Ford was able to exchange gold for bills of large denominations at the U. S. Subtreasury, and thus to turn the money over to Ruef in more convenient form. Ruef also paid the supervisors' share of the trolley money to Gallagher in two installments, one of $45,000 late in July, and another of $40,000 some time in August.

Toward the end of August, according to his memoirs, Ruef paid Schmitz a total of $50,000 of the trolley money, in large bills, at the mayor's home. Ruef did not tell either Gallagher or Schmitz the total amount of his own fee. Gallagher later heard rumors that it had been larger than he had supposed, and he once approached Tirey L. Ford, "on a pumping expedition," to try to discover the exact amount. But Ford would not say a word on the subject.

Like the telephone franchise and the trolley privilege, the Parkside matter had been awaiting settlement at the time of the earthquake on April 18, 1906. Gus H. Umbsen, agent for the sale of lots in the Parkside tract, had arranged the confidential employment of Ruef as attorney for the Parkside Realty Company, in February. By authority of the president of the company, J. E. Green, and by some complicated bookkeeping, Umbsen had then obtained $30,000 in thousand-dollar bills, which he was holding for payment of Ruef's fee. During this period Umbsen began to suffer increasingly from nervousness and insomnia, to such an extent that he was forced to leave San Francisco on March 17 for several weeks' vacation and rest in Hawaii. On March 26, the board of supervisors gave final passage to a resolution providing for the sale, on May 7, of a franchise for a street railroad along 20th Avenue, which would make possible the successful development of the Parkside tract by connecting it with the nearest United Railroads carline about a mile to the north, at the southern boundary of Golden Gate Park.

The great fire stimulated the desires of the Parkside promoters to hasten the completion of their project. The destruction of so much of the older part of San Francisco led many thousands of former residents of the burned areas to look for sites for new homes in the surrounding districts of the bay region. If Parkside could be opened soon enough, many people could be persuaded to build homes in this new district of San Francisco, rather than in neighboring counties. The executives of the Parkside company became discontented with one aspect of the franchise which they were to have the opportunity to purchase on May 7. The route specified for the proposed street railway, 20th Avenue, was still only a surveyor's line over the sand dunes. On the other hand, 19th Avenue was already graded and macadamized. Many months could be saved in the construction of the railway if the franchise could be shifted from 20th Avenue to 19th.

Gus Umbsen returned from Hawaii on April 25, a week after the earthquake, and began to urge upon Ruef the change which the Parkside company desired. Ruef pointed out a legal difficulty. Because 19th Avenue was a boulevard, a franchise for a railway on a street so designated would violate the city charter. But the designation of any particular street as a boulevard could be revoked by a city ordinance, and the Parkside executives hoped that they could persuade Ruef to favor this plan. Up to this time no money had been paid to him. He had asked for $15,000, or half of the agreed fee, when the resolution for sale of a franchise was passed in March. But President Green had then refused to authorize Umbsen to pay Ruef any part of the fee until a franchise had actually been purchased. Instead of submitting a bid for the original 20th Avenue franchise on the legal date of May 7, the Parkside officials allowed this privilege to lapse, and Umbsen continued to press Ruef for a franchise on 19th Avenue.

At this point, Ruef was somewhat irritated. He recalled that the Parkside promoters had originally purchased from himself and others, secretly and through third parties, lots which they now hoped to sell for at least five times the purchase price. He demanded that Umbsen pay him his fee before he would proceed any further. After a talk with Green, Umbsen made a $15,000 down-payment to Ruef on May 23, and then arranged a series of luncheon meetings with Ruef, President J. E. Green, and Vice-president John O'Brien of the Parkside company, at Umbsen's home. This was a splendid residence near the Presidio, more than a mile west of the limits of the fire. There, as Ruef put it, "the flash of crystal and the glint of the silver service, the spotless napery, the quiet seclusion from the turmoil of the reviving city, were alluring. The arguments of Umbsen became convincing. I saw a way in which the problem could be solved." The Parkside company might have 19th Avenue for a carline, he suggested, if they would then assume the expense of grading and paving 20th Avenue as a boulevard. After an investigation of the cost, and with some reluctance, Green and O'Brien consented. At one of the luncheons, they stepped into the next room. Left alone with Umbsen, Ruef asked for a $10,000 additional fee, bringing to $25,000 the amount still due him. Umbsen stepped out to confer with Green and O'Brien, and returned to convey their assent to Ruef.

Ruef drafted the proposed new franchise ordinance, and the necessary supplementary agreements, in cautious conferences with a representative of the Parkside company's regular attorneys. After the fire the distinguished firm of Morrison and Cope had taken in a new partner, William I. Brobeck, formerly a law clerk in their office. The firm now delegated all of its Parkside business to Brobeck. Ruef did not confer about it with Morrison or Cope. Judge Cope later explained that the firm left all matters of franchises to Brobeck because he had once served in the city attorney's office and had thus acquired special knowledge of the subject.

Ruef was a busy man during the spring and summer of 1906, and the advent of the graft prosecution was to make him even busier in the fall. The completion of the Parkside matter continued to be delayed for month after month until it became impossible to accomplish it during Ruef's period of power. Umbsen and Ruef continued to maintain friendly relations; and Umbsen accepted appointment as a police commissioner. But he paid no more money to Ruef after the first $15,000. None of the Parkside money was ever passed on to the board of supervisors. In March, when the original Parkside resolution was passed, Ruef had informed most of the members through Gallagher that they would receive $750 each when the franchise was finally sold. In the fall, when a new resolution for 20th Avenue was being prepared, and Ruef had received the promise of a supplementary fee, the supervisors, except Rea, were led to expect $1,000 each. But this resolution was never pushed through to final passage. Gallagher received, and reported to Ruef, many inquiries, complaints, and importunings from several members of the board. But none of the Parkside money ever passed beyond Ruef.

Of all the profit-sharing schemes in which Ruef participated, the most important, if it had succeeded, would have been the design of the Bay Cities Water Company. This corporation, headed by William S. Tevis, wished to sell the city a water supply in the Sierra for $10,500,000, of which Ruef would have received no less than one million dollars as special attorney for the company.

Until the twentieth century was well advanced, San Francisco remained dependent for its water upon nearby lakes and reservoirs owned by the venerable Spring Valley Water Company. This enterprise had long since begun to attract a great deal of public criticism. As early as the 1870's the city had made serious efforts to buy the Spring Valley system, but there were various difficulties, including failure to agree upon a price. In the 'eighties and 'nineties the Spring Valley company's rates were fixed annually by the board of supervisors, and it was widely believed that the members were often bribed to set the rates higher than they should have been. By the turn of the century, it was the opinion of almost everyone except its stockholders that the Spring Valley company's facilities could never be adequate for the city's ultimate needs, and that the city itself should acquire a water supply in the Sierra Nevada.

In 1900, City Engineer C. E. Grunsky began an investigation of possible sources, and in the following year he recommended that the city secure the right to store and use the waters of the Tuolumne River—in the northern part of Yosemite National Park—by means of dams and reservoirs at Lake Eleanor and in Hetch Hetchy Valley. Yosemite National Park was under the jurisdiction of the Department of the Interior, and since there was no provision in the Department's regulations under which a municipality could file on a reservoir site, it was decided that Mayor James D. Phelan, as an individual, should file notice of appropriation of the Tuolumne waters, and then transfer all his prospective rights to the city.

This was the beginning of a long controversy, both in San Francisco and in Washington. Nature lovers strove to save the primitive beauty of Lake Eleanor and Hetch Hetchy Valley, while advocates of the municipal water project denied that these places would be less beautiful when serving as reservoirs. The Spring Valley Water Company sent engineers to Washington armed with voluminous statistics to prove that San Francisco did not need the additional supply. And the farmers of the Modesto and Turlock irrigation districts, with the encouragement of agents of the Spring Valley company, protested that their irrigation projects would be drastically curtailed if the city were permitted to impound the Tuolumne waters. In 1903, Secretary of the Interior E. A. Hitchcock refused to grant the city's application without a special act of Congress, since an existing law required him to preserve "the natural curiosities" of the park "in their natural condition." Bills introduced in Congress were unsuccessful. Congressman Needham, in whose district the Modesto and Turlock irrigation districts were situated, was a member of the House Committee on Public Lands.

In the meantime, the Bay Cities Water Company was organized, in 1902, and acquired control of certain water rights near Lake Tahoe, on the South Fork of the American River and the North Fork of the Cosumnes River. The president and main stockholder of the Bay Cities company, William S. Tevis, was a wealthy San Francisco capitalist. He had inherited an estate estimated at $20,000,000 from his father, Lloyd Tevis, whose partnership with James B. Haggin in the land and cattle business in western states had rivaled the vast holdings of Henry Miller in the 'seventies and 'eighties.

The Bay Cities Water Company first attempted to sell its rights and properties to the city of Oakland, but in this it was unsuccessful, and it then turned its main hopes to San Francisco. In January 1906, shortly after the Union Labor board of supervisors took office, William S. Tevis had a series of conversations with Ruef. Tevis explained that his company held the options to purchase lands and rights on which it proposed to construct a water system which it would sell to the city for ten and a half million dollars. He estimated that the capital outlay by the company for lands, rights of way, improvements, and other expenses would eventually total seven and a half millions. Of the three million dollars of estimated profit, he offered a third, or one million, to Ruef. On the promise of a million dollars as a fee if he were successful, Ruef undertook to work for the project as confidential attorney for the Bay Cities Water Company. He informed Mayor Schmitz, Supervisor Gallagher, and Supervisor Jennings J. Phillips, chairman of the water committee of the board, that he wished the Bay Cities proposal to be adopted. Ruef also told Gallagher and Phillips, several times during 1906, that there would be far more money for the supervisors in this matter than in any other project during their term. Ruef's plan was to pay half of the million dollars to the supervisors, including $75,000 for Gallagher and $25,000 for each of the seventeen others. Schmitz was to receive a quarter of a million, and Ruef was to retain a quarter of a million for himself.

On January 29, 1906, the board of supervisors officially abandoned the city's claim to the waters of the Tuolumne, by adopting a resolution to "waste no further time and money" in attempts to secure the approval of the federal government; and in March the board invited alternative proposals. One of the effects of the great fire in April was to intensify the public sentiment in favor of the city's acquiring ownership of some large new supply of water. There was widespread belief that the inadequacy of the Spring Valley Company's system was chiefly responsible for the loss of control of the fire. On Ruef's advice, the board of supervisors had organized a special committee on water supply with Supervisor Jennings Phillips as chairman. On July 23, 1906, this committee presented a detailed report which had in fact been written entirely by Ruef and handed by him to Phillips that morning. The report said that the special committee had received and considered fourteen different proposals of sites for water supplies in various parts of the Sierra and the central valley. Of these it recommended five, including the Bay Cities project, for further investigation by a special board of engineers to be appointed by the mayor. Ruef had explained to Phillips that four of the five proposals were included only as window dressing, and that the Bay Cities plan was the only one of the five which any engineer could possibly approve.

The supervisors adopted this report, and the mayor appointed a board of three highly competent engineers to make the proposed investigation. These three were A. M. Hunt, Major C. H. McKinstry of the Army Engineer Corps, and Professor Charles D. Marx of Stanford University. They were by no means satisfied with the circumstances of their assignment and the limitations placed upon it. Professor Marx held a conversation with the special committee on water supply, at which Ruef was present and did all the talking. Finally the three engineers asked for a year's time and $100,000 for expenses. On September 24, the special committee submitted a second report, again prepared by Ruef, condemning the proposed delay and expense as impractical, and recommending that the engineers be asked to pass upon the Bay Cities project alone. The three engineers then resigned in high dudgeon, and sent their protests to the newspapers.

In the meantime ex-Mayor James D. Phelan, who took a strong personal interest in the fate of the Tuolumne–Lake Eleanor–Hetch Hetchy plan, had issued a series of angry statements denouncing the motives of the administration. Fremont Older had always supported both Phelan and the Tuolumne project, and on September 29 the *Bulletin* published an editorial plea "To Mr. Will Tevis, . . . From An Afflicted City." This editorial said that the Tuolumne reservoir sites could be had for nothing as compared with the Bay Cities price of ten and a half million dollars. "Mr. Tevis," said the *Bulletin,* "you know that only by one means—BRIBERY—can it be brought about that the Hetch Hetchy project shall be abandoned by the city and your scheme taken up in its lieu."

On October 8, 1906, the board of supervisors took official notice of "newspaper and personal criticism" of the Bay Cities project and gave the privilege of the floor to William S. Tevis. In a forceful address to the board, Tevis charged "Mr. Phelan and his associates" with responsibility "for the destruction of the greater part of our fair city," through their "obstinacy" in clinging to the "famous and illusory Tuolumne or Hetch Hetchy supply." It was clear, said Tevis, that that supply could never be procured from the federal government, and that even if it could, after years of delay, it would actually prove less economical than the Bay Cities company's supply, "the waters of the famous Lake Tahoe Region, known the world over for their crystal and virgin purity." Moreover the city could never actually own the lands in Yosemite National Park, and would have water rights only under a revocable permit.

Tevis made a general denial that any prospects remained for the city to secure the Tuolumne rights from the federal government if it should still try to do so. Actually these prospects, while still speculative, were by no means hopeless, and were indeed slightly improved. President Roosevelt had taken an interest in the matter, and in 1905 the United States Attorney General had conveyed to the President the opinion that the Secretary of the Interior *would* have the authority to grant the San Francisco application if he chose. Actually, however, it was doubtful that the federal government would give its approval as long as Hitchcock remained Secretary of the Interior, and as long as Congressman Needham retained his position in the House Committee on Public Lands.

Tevis' speech to the board of supervisors on October 8, 1906, was followed by a supplemental report of the special committee on water supply, more detailed than its predecessors, and also written entirely by Ruef. It maintained that Phelan was in a conspiracy with the Spring Valley Water Company to prevent San Francisco from acquiring *any* supply of its own, by keeping the city waiting interminably for the Tuolumne rights which would never materialize. It charged that this conspiracy was also the source of many attacks on the Union Labor administration, and clearly referred to the "hysterical and wild denunciations" made by Francis J. Heney in the election of 1905 as having been the result of retainers to Heney from the Spring Valley Water Company. The report also argued that the Tuolumne waters would eventually be insufficient; and that the steadily increasing summer population of Yosemite National Park would pollute these waters.

The board of supervisors unanimously adopted this report, and thus served notice of its desire to have the question of the Bay Cities purchase submitted to the voters. But subsequent events were to make this impractical.

CHAPTER XII

Ruef's star reaches its zenith

RUEF and Schmitz enjoyed a period of very high prestige in San Francisco, beginning with the sweeping Union Labor victory in the election of November, 1905, and continuing through the summer of 1906. Every one of Ruef's candidates for city and county office had been elected, in spite of the fusion of the two old parties, and this phenomenal success forced even his enemies to believe that his political ability was almost magical. The public knew nothing of the details of the transactions in which he was bribing the board of supervisors during this period. While angry suspicions of bribery were voiced by the *Examiner,* in the telephone franchise in March and in the trolley matter in May, and by the *Bulletin,* in the water question in September, newspaper talk of this kind was so familiar in San Francisco that public sensivity to it was dulled. Of those who did suspect the existence of bribery, many took it for granted, as a part of politics.

Encouraged by their rise to power in the city and county, both Ruef and Schmitz were now more hopeful than ever in their ambitions for broader successes on the state and even the national scene. Ruef planned to replace George C. Perkins in the United States Senate in 1909. Schmitz's ambitions were greatly stimulated by his popularity in the crisis after the earthquake, as the inspiring leader and symbol of the city's recovery. He became convinced that he could be elected governor of California in 1906.

The incumbent governor, George C. Pardee, like almost all of his predecessors, hoped for renomination but had little chance of it. As usual, there had not been enough patronage to go around among the various groups which had supported him in 1902.

Ruef, in particular, felt that Pardee had cheated him. Pardee had been elected over Franklin K. Lane by a margin of only a few hundred votes, and he would not have been elected without Ruef's support in San Francisco.

According to Ruef, Pardee had invited him to his home in Oakland one evening soon after the election, and had there expressed deep appreciation for Ruef's services, and promised five state jobs for Ruef's followers. In his account of this conversation, some years later, Ruef recalled the time as either Thanksgiving or Christmas, 1902. "The date can be fixed by the weather records," Ruef wrote. "It started to rain before I left, and the Doctor [Pardee], not withstanding my connection with politics, had confidence enough to lend me his gold-headed umbrella." On reading this account, Pardee denied publicly and emphatically that there had ever been such a conversation, that he had ever made any promises to Ruef, or that he had ever owned a gold-headed umbrella. Ruef replied that he had not had the umbrella assayed before returning it, but that there had certainly been a conversation, and there had certainly been promises. In any case, Ruef's hopes for state patronage under Governor Pardee were disappointed, and he was resolved to oppose Pardee's renomination in 1906.

The Republican state machine under William F. Herrin and the Southern Pacific Railroad was equally resolved against supporting Pardee. The governor had attempted to establish his independence of the Southern Pacific and had assembled a state-wide political organization of his own. It was reported from New York and Washington that E. H. Harriman himself had selected James N. Gillett, Congressman from the First California District in the northwest corner of the state, as the railroad's candidate for the Republican nomination for governor of California to replace Pardee.

Even before the primaries in August, 1906, it was clear that Ruef could elect practically all of the San Francisco delegates to the state Republican convention, and that the San Francisco delegates would hold the balance of power between Pardee and Gillett. Both candidates now sought Ruef's support. Ruef was unmoved by Pardee's entreaties. But when Herrin approached him on behalf of Gillett, Ruef saw an opportunity to place Herrin under obligation to him, and so heavy an obligation that

Herrin might reward him in 1909 with the coveted seat in the United States Senate. In order to give the greatest possible emphasis to the fact that he could control the selection of a governor, Ruef planned to withhold his support from Gillett until the last moment, meanwhile giving it ostensibly to a lesser candidate, J. O. Hayes, wealthy publisher of the San Jose *Mercury*.

When Ruef announced that he would support J. O. Hayes for governor, Schmitz was disappointed and jealous. He demanded to know why he himself would not receive Ruef's support. Ruef explained to Schmitz that he hoped to make him governor in some future campaign, but that in 1906 it would be impossible. There was no state-wide Union Labor party, and Schmitz could be elected governor only by securing the Republican nomination. Ruef would give him the San Francisco delegates, but they were only about a fifth of the total in Republican state conventions. While Ruef was a prominent Republican of long standing, Schmitz's political importance was associated with the Union Labor party alone. The railroad would not support him, and he would get only a handful of delegates outside the city. Schmitz, on the other hand, argued that he would be the only Republican candidate who could win the labor vote away from a Democrat. He pointed out that Gillett's candidacy had already been publicly opposed in statements by Samuel Gompers, and by P. H. McCarthy, the head of the San Francisco Building Trades Council and now also predominant in the state Federation of Labor. But Ruef predicted, correctly, that Herrin would not be impressed by this argument.

The fact probably was that at this time Ruef did not believe that Schmitz could ever be more than mayor of San Francisco. Schmitz could never be elected governor if he renounced his Union Labor affiliation, and the Republicans would never nominate him as long as he retained it. Thus his ambition to be governor was potentially embarrassing to Ruef's own hopes of becoming a Republican senator. Moreover, Ruef had observed with disapproval Schmitz's association with the millionaires William J. Dingee and J. Downey Harvey, and with others who seemed to be telling him that he could be an important political figure independent of Ruef. Ruef and Schmitz were beginning to distrust each other, and their personal friendship was beginning to cool.

Before the primaries, Ruef, Herrin, and Schmitz held two conversations in Schmitz's home, in which they came to an agreement on the strategy of the coming gubernatorial campaign. Herrin persuaded Schmitz to agree to support Gillett. Ruef was ostensibly to support Hayes, but he agreed to swing the San Francisco delegates to Gillett at the convention if Hayes should prove to have no chance of being nominated, which everyone thought to be probable. In return for this promise, Herrin promised to offer no opposition to Ruef's ticket of San Francisco delegates in the primaries, and also to give Ruef $14,000 of the funds of the railroad's political organization, to pay campaign and election expenses.

In the primaries, on August 14, 1906, Ruef secured the election of virtually his entire ticket of San Francisco delegates to the Republican state convention. The *Bulletin,* the *Call,* and the *Chronicle* charged that this had been achieved by "colonizing" voters in precincts in the burned districts, but if this did take place it was less important than the fact that Herrin carried out his secret bargain with Ruef. Soon after the primaries, however, Schmitz complicated matters by wavering in his agreement not to run for governor. At a pre-convention caucus of the San Francisco delegates, on August 28, someone circulated a petition in favor of Schmitz's candidacy. When Ruef asked him whether he had authorized this petition, Schmitz admitted that he had. He had yielded to the importunings of friends, he said, and he realized that he had no real chance, and supposed that the petition would be unimportant. Ruef pointed out that it would leave the delegation in doubt, and thus weaken its bargaining power in the convention. Schmitz agreed to disavow the petition, and Ruef then succeeded in getting the delegates to resolve that they would vote as a unit.

According to Ruef, the "friends" of Schmitz who were urging him to run for governor were not real friends at all, but were interested only in trying to maneuver him out of the mayoralty so that they could gain political control of San Francisco themselves. Whatever their real attitude toward Schmitz, it is certain that these men were not loyal to Ruef. The leaders of this group were four ambitious and discontented followers of the Schmitz administration. Frank Maestretti was a ward politician who had allied himself with Schmitz and Ruef; he was now president of the board of public works, and hoped eventually to be boss of San Francisco. Dr. Joseph F. Poheim was president of the police commission. Golden Moritz Roy, a jeweler who was active in politics, felt that his campaign services to Schmitz had not been adequately rewarded. At this time he was successfully concealing the fact that he had changed his name to Golden Moritz Roy from his original name of Moritz Roy Golden, after fleeing from charges of forgery in Oklahoma some years earlier. The fourth member of this group was R. H. Countryman, a San Francisco lawyer and politician who wished to succeed Schmitz as mayor.

According to Ruef, Maestretti, Poheim, Roy, and Countryman, had gone so far as to form a secret society called the "Sovereigns of America," holding weekly meetings in a lodge hall, with an elaborate ritual, and with costumes of blood-red and black. Ruef wrote in his memoirs that he had discovered the existence of this secret organization from some of his more loyal followers, who had joined it under the impression that it was formed in his interests and with his approval. He had then assigned two trusted men to report to him on the activities of the organizers of the secret order. Receiving definite evidence of their disloyalty, he decided to remove Poheim and Maestretti from the administration. Poheim had received public criticism for establishing a saloon glassware business which would profit from his official power over saloon license renewals as president of the police commission. On this pretext, Ruef forced Poheim to resign early in July 1906. Maestretti refused to resign as president of the board of public works, and Schmitz was reluctant to order his removal. Ruef knew that it was "not politic" for an organization to "remove important limbs" too hurriedly. Maestretti's removal was delayed, but his relations with Ruef were embittered, and he increased his efforts to turn Schmitz against Ruef.

The Republican state convention of 1906 was scheduled for the first week in September at the beach resort town of Santa Cruz, about sixty miles south of San Francisco. Ruef planned to take the train to Santa Cruz late in the evening of Sunday, September 2. It was his birthday, and he had arranged a dinner party at his home, with his parents, his sisters, and a few friends for the late afternoon. But on Sunday morning in response to a telephone call from Schmitz, Ruef walked over to the mayor's home, about a block from his own. There Schmitz told him that he had decided to announce his candidacy for the Republican nomination for governor. Maestretti, Roy, and Countryman, Schmitz explained, had convinced him that he could be nominated and elected. Ruef spent all of the afternoon, missing his birthday dinner, in earnest argument with Schmitz. There was barely time to catch the train to Santa Cruz when he finally succeeded in persuading the mayor to remain in San Francisco, and to promise not to authorize the presentation of his name to the convention.

By Monday, September 3, the Sea Beach Hotel at Santa Cruz was a hive of activity. Many of the most important figures in the California Republican party had reserved rooms there, and the corridors and verandas of the rambling resort were full of newspaper reporters, photographers, and cartoonists. With Ruef supporting J. O. Hayes, it was clear that neither Gillett nor Pardee could get a majority. Candidates for lesser offices, from various parts of the state, sought to trade the support of their little blocs of delegates for promises of support for themselves. Pardee again importuned Ruef, and while Ruef was adamant, Pardee took advantage of the opportunity to be photographed in friendly and intimate conversation with the San Francisco boss, in the hope of giving the impression that he might yet win the crucial support of the San Francisco delegates. Ruef persuaded J. O. Hayes to agree to the withdrawal of his candidacy at the last moment, the time to be at Ruef's discretion.

The nomination for governor was scheduled for Thursday, September 6. On Wednesday evening, Ruef learned with disgust that Schmitz had again broken his promise, and was on his way to Santa Cruz. He arrived about midnight, and came to Ruef's rooms accompanied by Maestretti, Roy, and other members of the group who had again succeeded in persuading him to seek the nomination. His friends assured him, he explained to Ruef, that the convention would be deadlocked between Pardee and Gillett. Why should he not be the compromise candidate?

Ruef lost his temper. He denounced Maestretti and Roy, and told Schmitz that they were trying to make a fool of him. Angered by this, Schmitz blurted out that Ruef had accepted $14,000 from Herrin to throw the San Francisco votes to Gillett. Ruef ordered the others out of his rooms, and then, alone with Schmitz, explained the foolishness of this disclosure. In support of his argument, that Schmitz's supposed friends were actually enemies of Schmitz as well as of himself, Ruef predicted that they would tell Herrin of Schmitz's indiscretion before morning, thus revealing that they wished to injure Schmitz as well as Ruef.

The convention was being held in a large, gaily decorated tent. The headquarters of the San Francisco delegation were in a smaller tent not far away, and there, in a caucus on Thursday morning, Ruef instructed the delegates to vote for Gillett. With a cheer they voted to comply, and adjourned to the main tent for the colorful spectacle of the gubernatorial nomination proceedings. In the galleries of raised seats around the convention "floor," an enthusiastic audience of ladies of Santa Cruz and seaside visitors lent a holiday touch to the atmosphere. When the nominating speeches were about to begin, Schmitz made a carefully timed entrance, expecting to receive a spontaneous ovation as the brave mayor of a dauntless city. But when he appeared and was escorted to a seat on the platform, only the San Francisco delegation burst into cheers. The applause from the rest of the convention was only mild and polite. Schmitz was somewhat crestfallen, and according to Ruef this finally convinced him that he could not have been the convention's choice. The nominating speech for James N. Gillett was then delivered by the San Francisco lawyer and politician George Knight, veteran party orator of many a state and national Republican convention. In the days before public address systems, when most convention speakers began their remarks the audience often cried "Louder!" but it was said of Knight that when he began to speak the audience often cried "Not so loud!"

The votes of the San Francisco delegates, delivered by Ruef, gave the nomination to Gillett on the first ballot. Ruef had established himself as the key figure of the California Republican party, and Gillett and his campaign managers, the leaders of the Southern Pacific machine, were unrestained in their expressions of gratitude.

The climax of Ruef's triumph came that evening, when he and Gillett were the guests of honor at a dinner party given by Major Frank McLaughlin, wealthy chairman of the Republican state central committee, in McLaughlin's magnificent home in Santa Cruz. Many of the members of the party's inner circle were present, and it occurred to the host that he would like to have a photograph "of his radiant table and his distinguished guests," as Ruef put it, to keep as a souvenir. He summoned a photographer, who took a picture which later became famous. Ruef was seated in the place of honor beside his host, at the center of the table. The others were standing. Behind Ruef was the future governor, James N. Gillett, his hand resting affectionately on Ruef's shoulder. The others from left to right were Judge Frederick W. Henshaw, who had been renominated as a justice of the state supreme court; Rudolph Herold, a Southern Pacific politician; J. W. McKinley, head of the railroad's law department at Los Angeles and chairman of the convention; George Hatton, a lobbyist; Walter F. Parker, boss for the railroad in Southern California; Warren R. Porter, the railroad's nominee for lieutenant governor; Judge Frank H. Kerrigan of the court of appeals; and Congressman J. R. Knowland of Oakland. Later, opposition newspapers were to caption this photograph "Herrin's Cabinet," and "The Shame of California." For the time being, however, Ruef could enjoy it as an unalloyed triumph.

As Ruef traveled back to San Francisco from the Santa Cruz convention, he had never felt more secure in his power, or more confident of his future. Although he had heard a report several months earlier that Older was trying to enlist Burns and Heney in a secret investigation, Ruef did not believe that anything would come of it. He did not know that agents of William J. Burns had been shadowing him for four months, and that Burns himself was on his way to San Francisco from Washington.

CHAPTER XIII

The prosecution begins

THE plans for what was to become the famous San Francisco graft prosecution had been tentatively agreed upon as early as January, 1906. Francis J. Heney, Rudolph Spreckels, Fremont Older, and James D. Phelan had met in a quiet luncheon conference at the University Club. Spreckels had promised financial support, and Heney had agreed to act as special prosecutor. Spreckels had raised the question of Heney's fee, and Heney had said that all of the special fund of $100,000 would probably be needed for other expenses. He offered to contribute his time to match Spreckels' money. It would be a service, he explained, which he felt that he owed to the city where he had been born and spent his boyhood; and it would be a service to his country, to reveal in San Francisco the condition which had recently been exposed in St. Louis, Philadelphia, and Minneapolis—"such a condition of corruption as must inevitably lead to the destruction of the republic" if it were not checked.

In the hope of persuading President Roosevelt to lend Heney and detective William J. Burns to San Francisco, Older then sought to discover evidence that Ruef's corruption might have a federal aspect. He assigned two *Bulletin* reporters to investigate the rumors that women were being brought from China to the white slave market in San Francisco's Chinatown, in violation of the federal immigration laws. Older's men discovered that such women, worth $3,000 in the "slave market," were being imported under the misrepresentation that they were the wives of American citizens of Chinese ancestry. It was necessary only to find a notary who would make a fraudulent marriage affidavit for a Chinese girl and her "husband." While no connection of Ruef with this traffic was ever to be established, Older was able to obtain evidence that the traffic did exist, and in February he made a second trip to Washington to present his evidence to the President. Roosevelt forwarded a copy of the report to Heney and Burns, and promised to release them from their duties in the Oregon land cases whenever circumstances would permit. But Heney was unable to free himself from the Oregon cases immediately, and during the next several months he had to make extended trips to Portland and to Washington, D. C. He left for Washington in March, and he did not return to San Francisco until after the earthquake.

One day in May, Heney and Older made their way through the ruins of the downtown district for another conference with Rudolph Spreckels. Spreckels had recently been elected president of the First National Bank, and they found him, as Older recalled, "in the little temporary office, roughly made of boards, which he had built amid the ruins of his bank on Sansome Street, surrounded by miles of burned brick and tangled steel girders." At this time Spreckels was about to resign from the Committee on Reconstruction in disgust at the manner in which it had been captured by Ruef, and he was more eager than ever for Heney and Burns to proceed with a graft investigation. He had now finally given up the idea of forming a committee of prominent citizens to support the prosecution, but he was ready to guarantee the full $100,000 expense fund himself. After this interview Older returned to the *Bulletin's* temporary quarters on the roof of an ice plant at the foot of Telegraph Hill, filled with secret exultation. "After five years of hard work on the trail of Ruef and Schmitz," he wrote, "I felt that at last the real fight was beginning."

William J. Burns was now employed as a private detective on an annual salary to be paid by Rudolph Spreckels as long as the San Francisco investigation should continue. The salaries and expenses of Burns' private agents, who were later to become a small army, were also to be paid out of the fund which Spreckels guaranteed. Burns himself did not begin work until September, but the first of his agents was assigned as early as May 25. Throughout the graft prosecution, Burns was to remain a private detective, on leave from the United States Secret Service, and without any official connection with the office of the district attorney of San Francisco. There would have been no hope for the success of the prosecution, however, unless it could secure the official coöperation of District Attorney William H. Langdon.

For this reason, the organizers of the prosecution were watching Langdon's activities and policies with intense interest, although they did not yet tell him of their own plans. Fortunately for the prosecution, the nomination of Langdon for district attorney was to prove one of the most costly mistakes of Ruef's life. Within a few weeks after he took office, early in 1906, Langdon gave evidence that he would not coöperate with the rest of the administration. Suddenly and without notice, he began a series of raids on gambling establishments which had previously been protected by the police. Next he undertook a campaign against slot machines, even though the police commission had recently begun to issue licenses for them. Many saloon and cigar store proprietors had petitioned the administration to permit them to install these devices on the ground that they would stimulate trade, although they were aware, as the public often was not, that the machines contained hidden regulating levers which could be adjusted to pay a very high percentage to the house. In January, a representative of the Schultz Scale Company, manufacturers of slot machines, approached Fred Hilbert, Schmitz's personal representative in various matters involving police protection, with an offer to share the profits if the machines of this particular company were allowed to operate. On January 24, the police commission, at the request of Schmitz and Ruef, revoked its long-standing resolution against slot machines, and about 800 of them were soon installed in various saloons and cigar stores. In February, in spite of the action of the police commission, Langdon suddenly announced that anyone who had the machines on his premises would be arrested by order of the district attorney's office, for violating a state law.

Ruef did not appear to take these actions of Langdon very seriously. He assumed that Langdon had political ambitions, and was trying to advance them through a crusade against gambling, in the manner of William Travers Jerome in New York. Ruef confined himself to a mild and good-humored reproof, expressed in a published interview with Rev. William Rader:

My personal view is that this city, no city can be put into a strait-jacket. Neither should it be run wide open. We must look at these things in a sensible way. Men are not alike. I know nothing whatever about the temptations of gambling, never played cards or played the races. . . . Others are given to these things. I haven't been in a theater for ten years. How can I go when I find twenty-five or thirty people waiting to see me when I go to dinner?

I cannot see any difference, however, between the poker games at the Pacific Union Club and the gambling in a saloon, or the playing of a slot machine.

There is some evidence that Ruef heard of the plans of Spreckels, Older, Heney, and Burns about this time. He later claimed to have learned early in 1906 "that Heney and Burns were after me." Older heard a grapevine report early in the year that a state supreme court justice, probably Henshaw, had learned the secret and had told Ruef. But if Ruef actually knew of the existence of the project, he did not seem to think very highly of its chances for success. Certainly he did not cease to take heavy though carefully calculated risks.

Ruef and Schmitz continued to enjoy high prestige in the eyes of the majority of the public throughout almost all of the summer. But about the middle of September, a combination of circumstances gave rise to public discontent with the administration.

A serious crime wave began to get beyond the control of the police. The newspapers carried daily reports of merchants and others being slugged and robbed in broad daylight, and at night no one was safe in the still-unlighted area of the former downtown district. The city's distressed finances had actually compelled a reduction in the size of the regular police force, while rumors of a thieves' paradise had increased the number of criminals by attracting newcomers from all over the country. For a time after the fire, looting of the ruins had been rigidly controlled by Schmitz's edict, with the aid of national guardsmen, but after the troops had withdrawn, the vigilance of the police had gradually relaxed. It was hard for the police, on seeing men digging in the ruins, to distinguish between looters and the actual owners or their employees.

Along with these mitigating circumstances, there was an undoubted increase in corruption in the police department. Chief Jeremiah Dinan, since his elevation from the rank of sergeant in March, 1905, had followed a policy of compromise with criminal elements, ostensibly in order to moderate their activities. According to one story, for example, early in 1906 a Scottish traveling salesman had been drugged in a house of prostitution and robbed of his watch, his diamond pin, his letter of credit, and $2,500 in currency. When the victim brought his complaint to Chief Dinan, the chief made a telephone call to an attorney who represented several such establishments. Within half an hour, the watch, the diamond pin, and the letter of credit, but not the money, were returned. At Dinan's advice, the victim accepted the compromise, since publicity would have ruined him. It was also reported that during the summer of 1906 the police not only abandoned attempts to prevent looting, but began to levy blackmail upon looters and junk dealers.

The appearance of sudden wealth on the part of some of the Union Labor supervisors also began to attract unfavorable comment. McGushin opened a handsomely appointed new saloon in an expensive location at Fulton and Van Ness. A journalist observed that "Men, who in private life had earned less than $100 a month, and as supervisors were receiving only that amount, gave evidence of being generously supplied with funds. Supervisor Coffey, a hack driver, took a trip to Chicago. Lonergan, driver of a delivery wagon, announced plans for a tour of Ireland with his wife and children." On October 1, Mayor Schmitz left the city for a trip to Europe, leaving Supervisor Gallagher as acting mayor. His announced purpose was that of persuading certain German insurance companies to give up their claim that they were not fully liable for fire losses resulting from the earthquake in San Francisco. Ruef advised against the trip. He suspected that the role of "the man of the hour" which Schmitz had played since the disaster had given him a highly exaggerated opinion of himself, and that the mayor expected to be received in Europe "as one of the crowned heads. He thought his fame would spread throughout the world and he hoped to be lionized abroad and, incidentally, gain social prestige." There was soon unfavorable reaction in San Francisco to reports that the mayor had occupied one of the finest suites at the Waldorf Astoria in New York, and then that he was touring Europe "like a newly created Nevada millionaire." Wild guesses began to be circulated by persons who claimed to know of specific briberies, and their exact amounts.

On October 10, a group of businessmen, the Potrero Commercial and Manufacturers' Association, held a meeting and proposed a plan for the organization of a "committee of safety," with 100 members, to "devise means of ridding the city of crime and corruption." This plan, it was announced, was to be ratified by the citizens in general at a mass meeting in Union Square on October 13.

The particular grievance of the Potrero Commercial and Manufacturers' Association was the result of a new ordinance governing the building of spur tracks, which the board of supervisors had passed a few days before. In most eastern cities the various railroads freely interchanged freight cars over the spur tracks built from the main lines to private warehouses, but in San Francisco the Southern Pacific had never permitted the use of its spur tracks by cars of the Western Pacific or the Santa Fe. After the fire many large wholesalers had established their warehouses in the new Potrero district. During the summer the Union Labor supervisors granted franchises for several new spur tracks in this section, even though the teamsters' union, as usual, was bitterly opposed. The wholesalers, as part of a drive to force lower freight rates through freer competition, asked the supervisors for an ordinance requiring that all future spur tracks be open to the freight cars of any railroad. The political agent of the Southern Pacific, Jere Burke, opposed this ordinance, and on receiving instructions from Ruef the supervisors passed it with amendments which defeated its purpose. The merchants then began to talk angrily of a citizens' committee to break the hold of "Abe Ruef and the Southern Pacific" on San Francisco.

Apparently the main purpose of the leaders of the Potrero Commercial and Manufacturers' Association in calling a citizens' mass meeting for October 13 was to bring pressure on Ruef to change his mind in the matter of their special grievance, the spur tracks. Beyond that, their intentions were uncertain; and they were thoroughly frightened by the size and the noisiness of the crowd which packed Union Square on the announced date, a Saturday afternoon. To assemble a meeting with something of vigilantism in the air, at a time when men's nervous emotions had been intensified by the difficulties of life since the fire, was a dangerous expedient. Moreover, these various groups of angry men were at cross purposes. Workingmen feared that merchants and other employers would dominate the proposed movement. Walter Macarthur and George Benham complained that the San Francisco Labor Council would have only two representatives in the citizens' committee, while several businessmen's groups would each have the same number. Another discordant element in the crowd was composed of political followers of Ruef and Schmitz.

The chairman of the meeting, W. A. Doble, explained that it had been called only to approve or disapprove a set of resolutions proposed by the Potrero Commercial and Manufacturers' Association. The resolutions were then hastily read by E. R. Lilienthal, a prominent wholesale liquor dealer. They were surprisingly mild, and spoke not of municipal corruption but only of "many problems" and of a need for civic unity and cooperation in solving them. There was to be a committee of 100, with very vague duties. Twenty local organizations were to appoint two members each, and the remaining sixty were to be appointed by Doble, as chairman of the meeting. When Lilienthal had read the resolutions and moved their adoption, chairman Doble called for the "ayes." Then, without calling for "nays," he proclaimed that the "ayes" had it; and amid cries of "Let's have the 'nays,'" he declared the meeting adjourned. Acting Mayor Gallagher now stepped forward. "I would suggest," he said, "that you disperse to your respective homes." Few obeyed this suggestion, and the proceedings became somewhat chaotic. There was a series of speeches, but since the meeting was officially adjourned and no longer had a chairman, some of the speeches were given nearly simultaneously. At the height of the confusion, Ruef appeared on the platform.

As soon as he had heard of the plans for the Union Square meeting, Ruef had made plans to capture it, and he did so now with remarkable success. At the beginning of his speech he was interrupted by jeers. According to the *Call,* when he said, "I am here as a representative of property . . . ," someone shouted "Tell us where you got it!" But Ruef had always been a master at turning jeers from an audience to his own advantage with quips which caught the whim of the crowd; and as his speech progressed there was applause, first from his claque, then from others.

The position of being his own Marc Antony occurred to Ruef as he spoke, and he parodied Antony's funeral oration, referring repeatedly to his own enemies as "honorable men." He was not as modest as his model. "Marc Antony never gave Caesar so handsome a character as Ruef gave himself," the *Call* reported. "Ruef explained that his presence at the meeting was due to his single-minded devotion to the city, that he had given attention to politics to his own financial loss, and that he stood ready to coöperate with any public movement calculated to rid the city of the lawless element." He concluded: "I came here not as a reviled boss but as an American citizen, to assist honorably in whatever way I could in securing conditions better than now exist, conditions not so much the result of bad administration, as a consequence of a great disaster by which the harpies of the world have been attracted to San Francisco." When the meeting finally ended, said the *Call*, "the entire movement was as loyal an ally of the Ruef machine as the Board of Supervisors."

To Spreckels, Heney, Burns, and Older the Union Square meeting brought no satisfaction and some alarm. They feared that the committee of 100 and its proposed "investigation" would supersede their own plans, and that it might even have been designed for this purpose. Rudolph Spreckels had been invited to take part in it, but he had declined on the ground that it seemed to be a capitalistic class movement inimical to labor. The resolutions and the scheme of organization had been drawn up by Samuel Shortridge as attorney for the Potrero Commercial and Manufacturers' Association. Shortridge was a friend of Ruef, and later served as his attorney. Spreckels and Heney now decided that it was time to preëmpt the field of "investigation," lest it be appropriated by the citizens' committee, which appeared to be sympathetic to Ruef. They decided to reveal their plans to District Attorney Langdon, and to ask him to appoint Heney as an assistant district attorney of San Francisco.

In September, Langdon had been nominated for governor by the Independence League, a political movement inspired by William Randolph Hearst, and advocating public ownership of public utilities. Hearst was running for governor of New York

on the Independence League and Democratic tickets, and he had
selected Langdon as his California candidate because of the
reputation as a reformer which the San Francisco district attorney had made in his raids on gambling establishments. For the
positions of president of the Independence League in California,
and manager of Langdon's campaign for governor, Hearst had
selected Joseph J. Dwyer, a lawyer who had taken a leading part
in the San Francisco reform movement of the early 'nineties.
Dwyer had also been selected by Francis J. Heney as an associate
in the law firm of Francis J. Heney and Charles Cobb, which
Heney had organized a few months earlier for the purpose of
having partners in San Francisco to aid him in planning the
graft prosecution, and to advise Spreckels and Burns when
Heney had to be in Portland on federal business. Thus Dwyer
was a member of the inner circle of the graft prosecution, and
also in an ideal position to approach Langdon with a request
to coöperate with it.

At the time of the Union Square meeting, Langdon was stump-
ing the state in his campaign for governor. Dwyer found him in
Fresno, told him of the plans of Spreckels and Heney, and asked
him to appoint Heney as one of his assistants. It was a difficult
decision for Langdon to make. He would be assuming the responsibility for a hazardous project. If it succeeded, the credit
would probably go to Heney. If it failed, the blame might fall
upon Langdon. Nevertheless, after some hesitation, Langdon
consented.

Shortly before Dwyer persuaded Langdon to make this agreement, Fremont Older accomplished a coup of almost equal importance. He persuaded Judge Thomas F. Graham, as presiding
judge of the San Francisco superior courts, to discharge the current grand jury and to announce that a new one would be impaneled. Older had had some experience with the workings of
San Francisco grand juries. He had worked closely with his
friend T. P. Andrews, foreman of the jury in 1904 and 1905, in
unsuccessful attempts to secure evidence for indictments of Ruef
and Schmitz in the French restaurant and Chinatown gambling
matters. As for the current grand jury, impaneled in April, 1906,
a majority of its members were friends of Ruef, and its secretary
was Myrtile Cerf, an accountant who was a loyal agent of both
Ruef and Schmitz in various financial matters. Older was con-

vinced that the Ruef majority had been procured by fraud. The nineteen members of a grand jury were drawn by lot from 144 names, of which twelve were submitted by each of the twelve judges of the superior court of San Francisco city-and-county. Older believed that in April, 1906, the court clerk, who drew the names on slips of paper through a hole in the top of a covered box, had been a confederate of Ruef; that he had selected the nineteen most favorable names; and that before bringing the box into the courtroom he had folded these nineteen slips together into a packet, so that his hand could find them inside the box. Older communicated his belief to Presiding Judge Graham, and told him something of the plans for a special graft prosecution. The judge was persuaded to order a new grand jury.

The San Francisco graft prosecution was formally inaugurated by a statement of District Attorney Langdon, issued on Saturday, October 20, 1906, and published in the Sunday papers the next morning.

The effect of this announcement was sensational. The *Bulletin* also revealed that William J. Burns had been employed by Spreckels as a detective. The reputation of Heney and Burns was almost that of national heroes, and it was clear to the public that this would be no ordinary investigation.

Several able lawyers were to assist Heney in the monumental labors which he was undertaking. In addition to Heney's partners, Charles Cobb and Joseph J. Dwyer, Rudolph Spreckels now engaged Hiram W. Johnson, a rising attorney who at forty had established a reputation as a genius in the courtroom.

Hiram Johnson was one of the sons of a brilliant lawyer, Grove L. Johnson of Sacramento. The father imparted much of his knowledge and skill to his sons, Hiram and Albert, who studied law in his office and began practice as his junior partners. Grove L. Johnson was a stalwart supporter of the Southern Pacific Railroad in the state legislature. He was also a very domineering parent and senior partner. His sons rebelled and formed a partnership of their own. They won several cases against their father and were not on speaking terms with him for many years. In 1902, the brothers moved to San Francisco, and soon afterward Hiram won a series of cases which established him as one of the boldest and cleverest trial lawyers in the city. Johnson combined an intuitive perception of the emotions of juries with a flair for dramatic and unexpected tactics. His abilities were a valuable complement to those of Heney. Johnson was at his best in the courtroom in the heat of a trial; Heney was at his best in the grand jury room.

On Wednesday, October 24, Heney took the oath as assistant district attorney, and proceeded to his first official action—to represent the district attorney's office at the drawing of names for the grand jury in Judge Graham's court. Before the names were drawn, Heney insisted that the contents of the jury box be spread out on a table, to make certain that none of the slips had been packeted together. The slips were then returned to the box, and eighteen names were drawn. The drawing of the nineteenth name was postponed to the session of the court on Friday, October 26, two days later. In the interim, Ruef decided on a desperate move.

CHAPTER XIV

Ruef fights to stave off disaster

Following the public announcement of the beginning of a graft prosecution, most of the Union Labor officials had made brave statements to reporters, denying all guilt and welcoming investigation of all of their activities. But Ruef had held several anxious conferences with Supervisor James L. Gallagher, now acting mayor while Schmitz was in Europe; with George Keane, clerk of the board of supervisors; and with Henry Ach, Ruef's attorney, close friend, and associate in local Republican politics. In one of these conferences Ruef pointed out that under a provision in the charter of the city and county, "any elected officer" could be suspended by the mayor and removed by the board of supervisors "for cause." Ruef informed Gallagher that it might be necessary to suspend and remove District Attorney Langdon, and as the drawing of the new grand jury neared completion, Ruef decided to resort to this drastic and daring expedient.

During the afternoon of Thursday, October 25, the supervisors were kept waiting in their meeting room for about four hours while Gallagher was in Ruef's law office, conferring with Ruef and Thomas V. Cator, an attorney and member of the board of election commissioners, who often served as an agent of William F. Herrin. Henry Ach joined the conference about five o'clock. Ruef informed Acting Mayor Gallagher that he had already decided on the suspension of Langdon, and that the only question was that of whom to appoint as acting district attorney in Langdon's place. Several possible appointments were considered, including that of Ach, who declined. Finally it was decided that Ruef himself should take the office. Ruef had already prepared a long document containing the order and specifications of causes for the suspension of Langdon, in the form of a communication from the acting mayor to the board of supervisors. Gallagher read it hastily "for typographical errors," and signed it. At 6:30 he arrived with it at the chamber of the board. There it was read aloud by Keane, and approved unanimously. The board then passed a resolution ordering Langdon to appear at its regular meeting a week later, and show cause why his suspension should not become a permanent removal.

The order removing the district attorney was an excellent illustration of Ruef's powers of invective. It included twelve specifications of neglect, dereliction and violation of duty, and use of office for ulterior purposes. It stated that Langdon had been absent from the city without leave for about thirty days, campaigning for the office of governor, at a time when a serious increase in crimes of violence had urgently required his presence in San Francisco. It stated that he had failed to prosecute for criminal libel the editors and publishers of newspapers which had published charges against the honesty of certain officials, charges which he knew to be false. Not only had he neglected to advise the police commissioners and the chief of police regarding their duties, but he had "entered into a combination and conspiracy for political purposes . . . to bring unmerited discredit upon said officials . . . thereby tending to impair and demoralize the Police Department" at a critical time. The order further charged that Langdon had conspired to defame the reputation of Mayor Schmitz, while the mayor was absent in Germany on a mission of great importance to the welfare of the city, and to force the mayor to return before this mission could be accomplished.

There were also several charges relating to the appointment of Heney as assistant district attorney. In a public speech in November, 1905, Heney had "aspersed the character and good name of a prominent citizen of this community [Ruef], and stated that he knew him to be corrupt." Haled before the grand jury, Heney had admitted that he had no evidence for these statements, "which facts were widely published at the time, and brought said Heney into obloquy and contempt." In full knowledge of these circumstances, Langdon had made Heney his assistant "in order to enable said Heney to use public office, position and power to gratify . . . his private revenge and malice."

As further evidence of Heney's unfitness, the order alleged that he "had publicly assailed the Judges of the Superior Court of the city and county as corrupt. . . ." This was a reference to the published version of Heney's extemporaneous reply to a toast following a banquet in a private club, in February, which had quoted Heney as saying: "A majority of the judges on the Superior Court bench of this city and county are crooked." Langdon well knew, the order went on, "that said Heney frequently, while intoxicated, made grave and serious charges involving the personal character of citizens of this city." The entire scheme of the prosecution, the order concluded, was a plot of certain newspaper, political, and corporation interests to control the labor market and subjugate the wage earners, and to elect Langdon governor.

Early in the evening Ruef filed his bond and his oath of office as acting district attorney, and wrote a curt letter dismissing Heney as his assistant. Ruef handed this order to his office boy for delivery to Heney, and went out to dinner. He considered taking possession of the district attorney's office that night, but decided to wait until morning. This was an error. Although Langdon himself was out of the city, Heney sent him a telegram, and Langdon hastily boarded a train. Heney, Johnson, Cobb, and Dwyer worked through the night on a motion for an injunction against Ruef, based on the argument that the district attorney was a county and not a city officer, and that the charter provision had not been intended to give the mayor the power to suspend a county officer. At five o'clock in the morning of the 26th, Heney and his associates got Superior Judge Seawell out of bed and persuaded him to sign a temporary order, restraining Ruef from taking possession of the district attorney's office. This order was soon served on Ruef at his home.

The drawing of the nineteenth name for the grand jury panel was scheduled for two o'clock that afternoon in the court of Presiding Judge Graham, and the question of whether Ruef or Heney would be permitted to represent the district attorney's office in that proceeding now assumed the proportions of a crisis in the history of the city. During the night Rudolph Spreckels had informed Fremont Older by telephone of Gallagher's suspension of Langdon and his appointment of Ruef. Early in the morning Older rushed to the *Bulletin* office to prepare an extra, calling on all good citizens to gather at the courthouse, to show their feelings to Judge Graham and to "help uphold his hands in giving us justice." More than a hundred newsboys distributed 20,000 free copies of this appeal. Since the fire the various departments of the Superior Court had been meeting in the Temple Israel, a large synagogue at California and Webster streets. Long before two o'clock the building was jammed, and a huge crowd was blocking the streets outside it. While the morning newspapers had carried the news of Ruef's appointment, and had generally denounced it as a usurpation of authority and a confession of guilt, they had not yet told of Judge Seawell's restraining order, and the overwhelming sentiment of the crowd was that of violent indignation against Ruef, and of resolution to prevent him from taking office.

Many leading business and professional men were among the several thousands who answered the *Bulletin's* call. Years afterward Older wrote: "On a bit of lawn, outside the windows of Judge Graham's chambers, a large group of influential persons gathered, silently glaring through the windows, just steadily glaring, without a sound, as though to warn: 'Don't dare!'. . . . The days of the Vigilantes, of riots and lynchings, were not so long past that any one could fail to recall them, and the temper of the crowd around the synagogue was unmistakable."

Heney later told Lincoln Steffens that "that crowd put the fear of God into that judge." Inside the building there was general confusion. Heney and his associates had been misinformed as to the room in which the session was to be held, and they had to push their way from one room to another, shouting demands for information. Sheriff O'Neil and Chief of Police Dinan were both Ruef men, and in attempting to clear the corridors of the building deputy sheriffs and policemen discriminated in favor of Ruef supporters.

When the session finally began, the nineteenth name was drawn from the jury box. Heney then announced that he wished to examine the prospective grand jurors. He stated that he intended to present charges of felony against Ruef, and that if any of the nineteen men should prove to be prejudiced against Ruef, or if any should prove not to be on the assessment roll, then any indictments found by this grand jury could later be invalidated. Ruef rose to speak in the capacity of an officer of the court. Heney objected to Ruef's being recognized as district attorney or as acting district attorney. Ruef replied that he would speak as a member of the bar. He then argued that there was no legal provision for the procedure which Heney suggested, and that if it were followed it would certainly invalidate the grand jury. The attorney general of California, Ulysses S. Webb, now addressed the court. He advised that in view of the doubtful question of law involved, the ruling should be postponed. Judge Graham followed this suggestion, and ordered a continuance until the following Monday.

As attorney general of the state, Webb would have had the power to take the prosecution of any criminal case out of the hands of any district attorney. He now issued a public statement that he would not intervene as long as Langdon and Heney were not interfered with in the performance of their duties, but that if they were, he would appoint Heney deputy attorney general of California, if necessary, in order to enable him to proceed with his investigation.

When Judge Graham's court convened on Monday, October 29, there was again a crowd in the courtroom and in the streets outside. Judge Graham announced his decision, that the district attorney might examine the grand jurors as to their qualifications, and that Langdon was the *de facto* district attorney. The news that "He's recognized Langdon!" soon traveled to the crowd outside the building, and the *Bulletin* reported that "clean-jawed men grasped each other by the hand or slapped the backs of their friends in gratification."

The court was next addressed by Samuel M. Shortridge, an able attorney and later United States senator. Though he was known to be representing Ruef, he asked to be permitted to speak in the capacity of *amicus curiae,* and although Heney suggested that the court did not need such a "friend," the permission was granted. Shortridge pointed out that the question of who was the legal district attorney was pending before Judge Seawell. The grand jury proceedings should be postponed until after Judge Seawell's decision, Shortridge advised, in order to insure that they would not be invalidated by it. Judge Graham overruled Shortridge, however, and ordered the interrogation of the grand jurors to proceed. Shortridge was allowed to participate, not as a representative of the district attorney's office, but as a "friend of the Court."

After several days of examination, in which some of the original nineteen were excused and the names of others drawn in their places, the grand jury was finally impaneled and sworn on November 9. B. P. Oliver, a real estate dealer, was designated as foreman, and gave his name to the Oliver grand jury. Shortly afterward Presiding Judge Graham, in a state of nervous exhaustion, left the city for a much-needed rest.

In the meantime, interest had shifted to the court of Judge Seawell, who was to decide the thorny question of the legality of Gallagher's order suspending Langdon. On November 16, Judge Seawell issued a final ruling that Langdon, not Ruef, was district attorney.

The new grand jury was called into session soon after it was impaneled. At this time almost the only actual evidence in Heney's possession concerned the charge that Ruef and Schmitz had conspired to extort money from a group of French restaurant keepers. This was the same charge which Older had published in the *Bulletin* and presented to the Andrews grand jury in January, 1905. The Andrews grand jury had taken no action on it, on the ground of doubt that what Ruef and Schmitz had done was extortion within the meaning of the law. Heney had had the same charge in mind in his Mechanics' Pavilion speech, just before the election in November, 1905, in which he had claimed personal knowledge that Ruef was corrupt.

Between November 10 and 15, 1906, Heney questioned most of the parties to the French restaurant matter before the new Oliver grand jury. Among the witnesses examined were ex-Police Commissioner Reagan, who had first been asked by Mayor Schmitz to hold up the renewals of the liquor licenses; ex-police commissioners Poheim, Drinkhouse, and Hutton; and French restaurant keepers Blanco, Adler, Loupe, Malfanti, and Marchand. Nathan Max Adler, proprietor of the Bay State, and Jean Loupe, of The Pup, denied that they had paid anything into the fund to employ Ruef as an attorney. Adler was later indicted for perjury, and Loupe, under the urgings of detective Burns, later corrected his testimony to avoid a similar indictment. On the testimony of the others, the grand jury filed five joint indictments against Ruef and Schmitz, on November 15, 1906. They charged extortion of $1,000 and $1,175 from Antonio Blanco, of the Poodle Dog; the same two sums from Joseph Malfanti and his partners in Delmonico's; and $1,000 from the proprietors of Marchand's. Judge Murasky, presiding in place of Judge Graham, immediately issued bench warrants for the arrest of Ruef and Schmitz. In the evening of the same day, by arrangement, Ruef surrendered himself to Sheriff O'Neal at the home of Judge Murasky, and was released on bail. Schmitz was somewhere on the Atlantic Ocean, on his way home from Europe.

Ruef protested bitterly against his indictment in the French restaurant matter, and insisted that the indictments could never be upheld in court. "The whole thing is absurd," he told a *Chronicle* reporter. "I was simply acting in the relation of attorney to a client. I took my fee for rendering legal services. I was retained by a contract as attorney by the restaurant keepers. If it is extortion for an attorney to accept a fee from his client, we all might as well go out of business. This is exactly the same charge that was made against me once before and was found baseless. I have nothing to fear."

Mayor Schmitz, on his arrival in New York, issued statements denying any guilt in the French restaurant matter and describing the prosecution as an attack by his political enemies. He pointed out that he had opposed Langdon's candidacy for governor, and said that Langdon was seeking revenge. Schmitz's friends now rallied to his support. William J. Dingee was eager to furnish bail, and at his request Justice Frederick W. Henshaw of the state supreme court inquired of Heney whether Schmitz would be arrested in New York. Schmitz was not actually arrested, however, until his train crossed the California state line. Sheriff O'Neil had appointed a special deputy, with instructions to spare Schmitz's feelings as much as possible, and to avoid all ostentation. The deputy, accompanied by Ruef and Myrtile Cerf, boarded the mayor's train at the little town of Truckee, and Schmitz surrendered to arrest. In San Francisco, several wealthy men, including Dingee, shared what they regarded as the honor of furnishing Schmitz's bail.

ABRAHAM RUEF AGED EIGHTEEN

Member of the class of 1883, University of California. Photograph from the
University of California Archives.

171

JAMES D. PHELAN

EUGENE E. SCHMITZ

The twenty-second, twenty-third, and twenty-sixth mayors of San Francisco. Reproduced from the official photographs in the City Hall.

P. H. MCCARTHY

WILLIAM F. HERRIN

MAYOR SCHMITZ AND THE UNION LABOR BOARD OF
SUPERVISORS, 1906

Note in the first row: Andrew M. Wilson, third from left; James L. Gallagher,
facing right, sixth from left; Mayor Schmitz, second from right.

RUEF ON THE STEPS OF THE COURT HOUSE

Taken during the first part of the graft prosecution. Photograph, courtesy the San Francisco *Examiner*.

RUEF DURING THE LATTER PART
OF THE GRAFT PROSECUTION

Photograph, courtesy the San Francisco *Examiner*.

SCHMITZ AT THE TIME OF HIS TRIAL

Photograph, courtesy the San Francisco *Examiner*.

"THE GRAFT HUNTERS"

Left to right: Francis J. Heney, William J. Burns, Fremont Older, Rudolph
Spreckels. From Evelyn Wells, *Fremont Older* (D. Appleton–Century Co., 1936).
Courtesy, Appleton-Century-Crofts, Inc.

RUEF AND TWO OF HIS ATTORNEYS

Left to right: Samuel M. Shortridge, Abe Ruef, Henry Ach.

Ruef and Schmitz were arraigned on December 6, 1906, before Superior Judge Frank H. Dunne, in a courtroom which had previously been a Sabbath-school room in the Temple Israel. During the reading of the first indictment Schmitz stood but Ruef remained seated, and when the reading of the second indictment was begun Schmitz also took his seat. Heney protested that it was customary for defendants to stand, and Judge Dunne ordered them to do so. The *Bulletin* quoted the judge as saying, "Let this be as any other ordinary trial. Let it be understood that these defendants are to receive no other treatment in this court than if their names were John Smith or William Jones. Let both defendants stand for the arraignment." Ruef and Schmitz did stand while the clerk read the last three indictments, but Ruef stood with his back turned to the judge. The *Chronicle* denounced Ruef for assuming "that a political boss was above the courts," and also criticized Judge Dunne for permitting this and other evidences of disrespect from Ruef and Schmitz and their attorneys.

The two defendants were represented by separate counsel, and it was now announced that they would demand separate trials. But in the meantime their attorneys began a long series of legal maneuvers by which they hoped to prevent the cases from coming to trial at all. The first of these was a motion by Henry Ach, to set aside the indictments on various technical grounds. It was claimed, for example, that one of the grand jurors, Wallace Wise, had served on a trial jury less than a year before, and was therefore not legally competent to act as a grand juror. Ach argued that the disqualification of this one member invalidated any indictments returned by the grand jury as a whole. Judge Dunne, however, refused to quash the indictments on this ground.

At this time Ruef and Schmitz and their attorneys must have had in mind the example of the Wallace grand jury of 1891. After four months of very revealing investigations of corruption, the Wallace grand jury had been invalidated by a decision of the state supreme court, declaring that there had been a technical flaw in the proceedings in which it was impaneled.

Ach's next move was an announcement that he wished to call the members of the Oliver grand jury to testify for the defendants. Several weeks were thus to be consumed in further exam-

inations of the grand jurors for bias, and Heney charged that
one of the purposes of the defense was to impede and delay the
grand jury's work on other pending indictments. Along with
the grand jurors, the defense also called Langdon, Burns, and
Spreckels into court for lengthy examinations. Langdon was
questioned in an attempt to prove that his motives in appointing Heney were improper, that he had unlawfully vilified and
abused the defendants, and that he was in a conspiracy with
Spreckels and others to ruin Schmitz and Ruef. Ach also tried
to prove that Heney, detective Burns, and foreman Oliver had
intimidated witnesses by threats of prosecution for perjury. In
questioning Spreckels, the defense sought to prove that he had
guaranteed the prosecution fund from motives of personal enmity and personal gain. Langdon and Spreckels denied vigorously that they were guided by motives other than concern for
the public welfare.

During these proceedings Hiram Johnson was of great assistance to Heney on the prosecution side. Johnson constantly
interposed objections to questions by the defense. Judge Dunne
sustained many of these objections, and there were frequent
evidences of bitter personal hostility between Judge Dunne and
several of the defense attorneys. Along with his aggressiveness,
Johnson occasionally showed a flash of biting wit. When Ach
asked whether the expression "the disaster" was being used to
refer to "the occurrences of April 18," Johnson replied, "Oh, yes.
We don't mean the indictments."

On January 22, 1907, after six weeks of hearings, Judge Dunne
denied the motion to set aside the indictments for bias, and
announced that he was ready to set the case for trial the next day.
The defense, however, was able to secure another long postponement of this eventuality, this time by filing demurrers. In other
words, the defense entered a plea which assumed the truth of the
allegations set forth in the indictments, and denied that the
actions described were crimes within the meaning of the law.
The penal code of California defined as extortion the obtaining
of money by means of a threat "to do an unlawful injury to the
. . . property of the individual threatened." The defense argued
that a license to sell property was not property; that the withholding of such a license from a house of assignation was not an *unlawful* injury; and that there was nothing illegal in the mayor's

threatening to do something which he had the legal authority to do. The prosecution opposed each of these arguments, and denounced the defense for taking refuge in absurdly legalistic and technical interpretations of the language of the indictments and of the law. After summarizing the French restaurant charges, Heney cried, "Do you mean to tell me that if those facts exist they do not mean extortion? I say then 'God save San Francisco from something worse than fire and earthquake.' " On February 18, four weeks after the demurrers were filed, Judge Dunne overruled them in an opinion which agreed with the prosecution's main arguments.

In the meantime, however, Ruef and Schmitz and their attorneys had made several other moves which still further delayed trial in the French restaurant cases. Schmitz made application to Presiding Judge Graham for a transfer of his case from the court of Judge Dunne, whom he accused of bias. Next Schmitz surrendered himself to the sheriff, and petitioned the state supreme court for a writ of habeas corpus, and also for a writ of prohibition against Judge Dunne's proceeding with the case. In the court of the presiding judge, and in the supreme court, Schmitz's attorneys went over most of the same arguments which they advanced before Judge Dunne himself.

While Schmitz was attacking Judge Dunne in the courts, Ruef carried the fight to the state legislature. Grove L. Johnson, chairman of the judiciary committee of the Assembly, introduced a bill under which a defendant in a criminal case could secure a change of venue simply by filing an affidavit of his own belief that he would not receive a fair trial in the court to which his case had been assigned. Grove L. Johnson was a wheelhorse of the Southern Pacific machine in the legislature. The fact that his own son, Hiram, was an active figure on the side of graft prosecution, did not deter the elder Johnson from sponsoring legislation that would be favorable to the defense. His feelings for his son were those of bitter enmity, and there were reports later that he had considered enlisting on the side of the defense as counsel for Ruef, in the hope of defeating and humiliating his own son in a famous court battle. Another supporter of the change of venue bill was state senator George Keane, who was also clerk of the San Francisco board of supervisors, a former private secretary to Mayor Schmitz, and a former assistant in

Ruef's law office. In the legislature of 1907, Keane also advocated a measure limiting public comment on a criminal trial, and another preventing stenographers and bookkeepers from testifying against their employers. But the efforts of Grove L. Johnson, Keane, and others, were unsuccessful, and none of these measures became law.

Early in February, 1907, Mayor Schmitz saw what he believed to be an opportunity not only to secure another long leave of absence from the city, and to delay his trial, but also to restore his damaged prestige. President Roosevelt invited the mayor and the board of education of San Francisco to come to Washington for a friendly settlement of the problem of the Japanese school children, which had led to a crisis in Japanese-American relations.

For some time most Californians, especially California labor organizations, had had sharp differences with President Roosevelt over Japanese immigration. Many Californians were agitating for a Japanese exclusion law, to which Roosevelt was strongly opposed. Chinese children in San Francisco had long been segregated in a "Chinese School." This building in Chinatown was reconstructed after the fire, and on October 11, 1906, the board of education changed its name to "Oriental Public School," and ordered the city's ninety-three Japanese school children to attend it along with the Chinese children. The Japanese government protested that this was in violation of treaty agreements between Japan and the United States, and there was even some sentiment in Japan for war over the issue. Roosevelt was angry at the San Francisco authorities, but as President he had no power whatever over an action which was quite legal under the school law of the sovereign state of California. It was in the hope of persuading the San Francisco board of education to withdraw its order voluntarily, that Roosevelt invited the board and the mayor to discuss the matter with him at the White House.

There was no objection by the district attorney's office, Judge Dunne gave his permission, and the board of supervisors granted the necessary leave of absence. Mayor Schmitz, the members of the board of education, the superintendent of schools, and an assistant city attorney left San Francisco by train on February 3 and did not return until March 6. In accepting the President's invitation to Washington, Schmitz acted against the advice of Ruef, who was as skeptical as he had been at the time of the mayor's trip to Europe. Again Ruef proved to be correct in his doubts as to the mayor's wisdom in leaving the city. Although the indicted mayor was entertained at various functions in his honor, including a reception by Samuel Gompers and a dinner by Vice-President Fairbanks, his hopes of increasing his popularity at home were not fulfilled. While his mission secured a promise that the President would work for an agreement with Japan on the exclusion of Japanese laborers, this was in return for a promise to revoke the Japanese school segregation order. In San Francisco the impression prevailed that Schmitz had allowed himself to be overawed by the "Big Stick" and had backed down.

When Schmitz returned to San Francisco, on March 6, the newspapers were full of sensational developments in Ruef's part of the fight to avoid trial before Judge Dunne. On February 18, during Schmitz's absence, Judge Dunne had overruled the demurrers, and Ruef had been forced to enter his plea. Ruef had pleaded "not guilty," and Judge Dunne had set his case for trial on March 5. On March 4, Ruef's bondsmen surrendered him into the custody of the sheriff, in order that he might apply to Superior Judge J. C. B. Hebbard for a writ of habeas corpus.

In applying for relief to Judge Hebbard, in another department of the superior court of the city and county of San Francisco, Ruef was resorting to an expedient almost as desperate as his attempt to seize the district attorney's office more than four months earlier. The case of Judge Hebbard was at once a personal tragedy and a sad commentary on the conditions which sometimes kept incompetent men on the bench for years after their incompetence had become all too apparent. The position of superior judge seldom attracted the ablest members of the bar. The salary was only $3,000 a year, and nomination and election were often dependent on the favor of a party boss. J. C. B. Hebbard was a veteran of eighteen years as a superior judge in San Francisco, owing his periodic reëlections to the Republican machine, and more recently to Ruef. He was a man of pleasant personality, and he had once been a fairly able lawyer and judge, but it was well known that for several years he had been a confirmed drunkard. There were occasional reports in the newspapers of his eccentric behavior while intoxicated—a scuffle at his club, or a maudlin eulogy delivered at the funeral of a friend, in which the judge offered to match the legendary generosity of the deceased by distributing coins from his pockets to those present. On another occasion, Judge Hebbard made public a statement to his colleagues, addressed as "Gentlemen of the Bench of the Superior Court of the City and County of San Francisco," which said in part, "This court has been criticized by the press, the public, and the leading lawyers of the bar, as incompetent. My opinion is that it is not only incompetent but incorrigible, and ought to be impossible. Personally I am in favor of a universal impeachment by the Legislature of the entire bench of San Francisco." Later, Hebbard also published a little volume of verse and prose under the title, *A Deck of Cards and a Joker, Shuffled and Dealt by J. C. B. Hebbard, Sometimes Known as Judge Hebbard* . . . . One of the poems was called "The Clock":

> Did you ever listen to the clock?
> Did you ever hear it talk?
> Did you ever in the night when you
>   were not quite right
> Hear it say as it ticked—
> "You drink
>   I think
> You drink
>   I think. . . ."

On March 4, 1907, the day before Ruef's trial was scheduled to begin in the court of Judge Dunne, the boss and his attorneys appeared in the court of Judge Hebbard in behalf of their petition for a writ of habeas corpus. Their argument was that the indictments were invalid, that Ruef was therefore being detained in violation of the federal Constitution, and that this was ground for an appeal to the federal courts. Heney and Johnson contended that Judge Dunne had already ruled on all of these points. They had no faith, however, in the ability or desire of Judge Hebbard to give a fair hearing to their side of the argument. They were convinced, in fact, that Ruef and Ach, in secret meetings with Hebbard, had prearranged the outcome. Moreover, Hebbard began to show symptoms of intoxication, and in protest against the whole proceeding, Heney and Johnson finally walked out of the courtroom. Judge Hebbard, while denying the petition for a writ of habeas corpus, permitted an appeal from this ruling to the United States Supreme Court, and used this as a basis for admitting Ruef to bail in the meantime.

After leaving Judge Hebbard's court on the afternoon of March 4, Ruef went into hiding, and the next day, when his case was called for trial in the court of Judge Dunne, he did not appear. Ruef was acting on the theory that the proceedings in Judge Hebbard's department superseded those in Judge Dunne's. Judge Dunne did not agree with this interpretation. Instead he ruled that Ruef was a fugitive from justice. On motion of Heney, he declared Ruef's bail bonds forfeited, and ordered Sheriff O'Neil to make every effort to find the defendant and bring him into court the next day. In Judge Dunne's opinion, the proceedings before Judge Hebbard had been fraudulent and without judicial weight. As for the charge that Hebbard was drunk, there was sufficient evidence that this was the case, not only on March 4 but for at least forty-eight hours afterward.

On March 6, Sheriff O'Neil appeared in court to say that his efforts to find Ruef had been unsuccessful. Heney filed an affidavit stating that O'Neil owed his office to Ruef, and was prejudiced in his favor. Judge Dunne disqualified the sheriff, and, in accordance with the law in such cases, ordered the coroner, W. J. Walsh, to arrest the defendant and bring him into court. Two days later, when Walsh had also failed to locate Ruef, Heney filed another affidavit stating that Walsh, like O'Neil, owed his office to Ruef as a political boss. Judge Dunne then disqualified Coroner Walsh, and appointed William J. Biggy as an elisor, a special officer appointed by the court to perform a duty for which the sheriff and the coroner had been disqualified.

The fact was that Heney knew where Ruef was hiding. Agents of William J. Burns had been trailing the little boss for months. Within two hours after Biggy was appointed elisor, Burns led him to the Trocadero road house, in the suburbs near the ocean, where Biggy found Ruef and placed him under arrest. Ruef insisted later that he had never been a fugitive from justice. He denied that there had been anything improper in the proceedings before Judge Hebbard. All of his attorneys had assured him, he said, that his appeal to the United States Supreme Court would bar Judge Dunne from proceeding with his trial. He had been very tired, and had wanted a few days of privacy in which he could rest and await the outcome of his appeal, and also the outcome of the change of venue bill, still pending in the legislature.

Biggy and Burns found Ruef at the Trocadero in the early evening of Friday, March 8. Elisor Biggy now faced the problem of what to do with his prisoner until Judge Dunne's court convened again on Monday, March 11. The county jail was under the jurisdiction of the sheriff, who had been disqualified. The city prison was under the jurisdiction of the police department, which was as much under Ruef's control as the sheriff's office. Biggy solved the problem by engaging an apartment in the Little St. Francis Hotel, a temporary wooden structure which had been erected beside the ruins of the old St. Francis, overlooking Union Square.

When Biggy brought Ruef into court on March 11, the boss's attorneys filed affidavits accusing Judge Dunne of prejudice. An affidavit by Ruef charged that Judge Dunne, a Democrat, was strongly in sympathy with John S. Partridge and other political opponents of Schmitz and himself; that the judge had engaged in secret interviews with Heney, to prearrange the course of proceedings in court; and that his rulings had been consistently adverse and hostile to the defense. Another affidavit, by Paul M. Nippert, stated that during September 1906, Judge Dunne, Nippert, and others had been on vacation at a resort hotel in Plumas County, and that in a discussion of political conditions in San Francisco, the judge had "said . . . that grafting was going on," and had been "extreme in his denunciation of both Eugene E. Schmitz and Abraham Ruef." Since Nippert was an official of the Aetna Indemnity Company which had furnished Ruef's bail bonds, his statement was perhaps motivated by self-interest. The next day, moreover, another witness to the conversation filed an affidavit contradicting virtually everything Nippert had said. On March 13, Judge Dunne himself filed an affidavit, denying the main allegations of Ruef and Nippert. In the meantime the judge had refused to admit Ruef to bail, and had remanded him to the custody of Elisor Biggy, in which he was to remain for many months to come. None of his appeals to higher courts eventuated in his favor.

At last, in spite of all the ingenuity of Ruef and of his attorneys, the selection of a jury began in Judge Dunne's court, on

March 13. This meant the beginning of Ruef's trial on the charge of extorting $1,175 from Joseph Malfanti and the other proprietors of Delmonico's French Restaurant. For several days, however, Burns and Heney had been hot on a trail which was to lead to far more important revelations.

CHAPTER XV

The prosecution breaks through

For nearly five months after its beginning in October, 1906, the prosecution was only moderately successful at best, and the public was beginning to wonder whether anything substantial would ever be accomplished. The strategy of delay by Ruef and Schmitz seemed to be prolonging the French restaurant case almost indefinitely. Moreover, this matter of rather petty extortion was almost the only case the prosecution had. Of the larger briberies, there was only rumor and suspicion. Ruef himself described the situation accurately in a statement to a *Call* reporter on October 28: "You saw what Tirey Ford said in the papers this morning. He denies that any money was paid to the Supervisors for the trolley franchise. The Supervisors will deny it. I will deny it. Where else are they going to find anyone to summons who could tell anything about it?"

As Heney remarked afterward, "From October, 1906, until March 8, 1907, we labored every day trying to get evidence of the graft that we all were satisfied existed in San Francisco, without getting anything. . . . For five long weary months we labored until midnight after midnight, and sometimes until two and even three o'clock in the morning struggling to work out a case."

Apart from the French restaurant charges, most of the evidence which Burns and his men could discover during November and December, 1906, concerned police protection of resorts in the Barbary Coast district. The *Bulletin* alleged that "every" prostitute in San Francisco had "contributed her mite" to Ruef and Schmitz for years. Ruef was indicted for extorting money from the "municipal crib" at 620 Jackson Street, and from another dive known as the Belvedere. Ruef and Chief of Police Jeremiah Dinan were jointly indicted for conspiracy to protect a large house of prostitution at 712 Pacific Street, and Chief Dinan was also indicted for perjury as a result of his denials before the grand jury. The chief of police was arrested by the sheriff, but he was promptly admitted to bail, and the police commission declined to remove him from office. As for graft involving the board of supervisors, the prosecution's only discovery during this period was almost ludicrously trivial. Supervisor Fred P. Nicholas was indicted for agreeing to receive a bribe of $26.10 from a furniture company, as 10 per cent commission on the city's purchase of certain desks and stools.

Burns' most promising lead was the knowledge that certain former members of the inner circle of the Ruef-Schmitz organization, especially Frank Maestretti and Golden M. Roy, were so disgruntled that they might be willing to aid the prosecution. This knowledge had first reached Burns and Heney as early as September, when *Bulletin* reporters had heard rumors of it at the Santa Cruz convention, and brought them to Older as news. Frank Maestretti, president of the board of public works and boss of the 39th Assembly District, had rebelled against Ruef's program, and advocated the nomination of Schmitz for governor. At Ruef's demand, Schmitz had reluctantly consented to Maestretti's removal from office, which was accomplished by order of Acting Mayor Gallagher on October 4, after Schmitz had left for Europe. Gallagher's letter to Maestretti charged him with responsibility for the "lamentable failure" of the board of public works to clear the streets and sidewalks of debris left by the great fire. Maestretti published an angry reply to Gallagher, describing his "alleged removal" as "part of the petty revenge instigated by yourself and an unsavory boss for the purpose of punishment of any person who refuses to prostitute himself to vicious candidates and vile methods." Maestretti also cabled a protest to Schmitz, and when the mayor did not answer, Maestretti developed as great a hatred for Schmitz as for Ruef.

Golden M. Roy was an associate of Maestretti in business and politics. Like Maestretti, Roy had been a political supporter of

Ruef and Schmitz. In the city election of 1905, for example, Roy had organized the "Schmitz Businessmen's Club." He had been a friend of Ruef for years, but more recently he had become involved in Maestretti's factional rebellion.

Older and Burns now saw the possible usefulness of these two former intimates of the administration. Older held a conversation with them which led him to believe that they might be persuaded to reveal many details of municipal graft. Older reported this possibility to Burns, Heney, and Spreckels, and when Spreckels expressed doubt that the two men could be trusted, Older replied, "Unfortunately, Rudolph, the crimes that were committed here were not known to respectable people like Bishop Nichols or our leading prelates. If we are going to get anywhere, we've got to get our information from crooks."

As soon as detective Burns met Golden M. Roy, he recognized him as Moritz Roy Golden, who had fled from Guthrie, Oklahoma, ten years before, charged with forging the name of the Secretary of the Interior on a letter purporting to appoint him as an Indian agent. Learning these facts from Burns, Fremont Older had a long article about them secretly printed in page proof in the *Bulletin* office. He sent for Roy, showed him the article and threatened to publish it unless Roy agreed to cooperate with the prosecution. Roy turned pale. Since his flight from Oklahoma, he had changed his name, and had made a successful career for himself in San Francisco. He was now the proprietor of several profitable businesses, including a jewelry store, a restaurant known as the Café Francisco, and a skating rink. Moreover, he had acquired a wife and children who knew nothing of his past, and whom he dearly loved. After thinking the matter over for a night, he promised to work secretly with Burns against the administration.

To enlist the aid of Maestretti, the prosecution counted mainly on his grievance against Ruef and Schmitz; but the prosecution also added another incentive. Three of Maestretti's political workers were serving sentences for ballot-box stuffing. Heney and Langdon promised to try to secure pardons for these men, by a recommendation from the district attorney's office to the governor, and this promise was later successfully carried out. During the latter part of 1906, Maestretti and Roy undoubtedly furnished information to Burns, but it dealt mainly with police graft. There was still no definite evidence of the briberies of the supervisors.

Burns had now decided that the only way he could get such evidence would be to trap some of the supervisors into taking a bribe, threaten them with prosecution for it, and thus try to wring full confessions from them. Burns and Roy considered and rejected various projects of this sort until late in January, when an interesting opportunity presented itself. Father Caraher, who had often crusaded against social evils in San Francisco, delivered a sermon condemning the lack of chaperonage at skating rinks, which, he said, had recently been the cause of several seductions of very young girls. Roy and Maestretti were partners in the ownership of the large and profitable Dreamland Rink. Burns now conceived an ingenious idea. He wrote a proposed city ordinance which would have forbidden the admission of young girls to skating rinks unless accompanied by their mothers—a measure which would have ruined the business of Maestretti and Roy. Burns then cast about for a way to suggest this idea to the administration. He had discovered evidence against Eddie Graney, fight promoter and owner of dubious resorts. Graney was an acquaintance of Schmitz, and by threatening to prosecute Graney, Burns induced him to take the proposed ordinance to the mayor. Graney pretended that he himself had originated the idea, as a way in which Schmitz could curry favor with the clergy, and at the same time injure Maestretti and Roy. Schmitz adopted this suggestion, and sponsored the introduction of the ordinance.

District Attorney Langdon now authorized Roy to coöperate in an attempt to trap some of the supervisors, and as the first and most likely victim, Burns and Roy chose Supervisor Thomas Lonergan. Roy invited Lonergan to meet him privately in the office at Dreamland Rink, and Lonergan did so, unaware that Burns and two of his agents were watching through holes bored in the wall. The scene had been carefully rehearsed. Roy said that it would be worth money to him to have the ordinance killed, and Lonergan agreed to accept money to help defeat it. Roy then paid him $500 in marked fifty- and hundred-dollar bills, provided by Burns.

The next move was an attempt to trap Gallagher, with an offer of $1,000. Gallagher declined to accept it, saying that Roy was an old friend of the administration, and should not be required to pay anything for such a favor. Roy urged Gallagher to take the money, pretending that he himself was merely acting as an agent for a whole group of skating rink proprietors who had contributed to a fund for this purpose. Moreover, Roy said, several other supervisors had already accepted their shares. He refused to tell which ones.

Gallagher suspected Lonergan, and he now "hurried Lonergan to Ruef much the same as [he] would have rushed a man showing the symptoms of a deadly malady to a physician." When Lonergan admitted taking money from Roy, Ruef suspected that Roy might be acting for Burns, and warned Lonergan to return the money immediately. When Lonergan tried to return it, however, Roy pretended to be highly indignant at such an accusation. He persuaded Lonergan that he could safely keep the money, and succeeded in convincing even Ruef himself that the suspicions of his complicity with Burns were groundless.

In the meantime, Supervisor Edward Walsh had accepted $500, just as Lonergan had, at the skating rink office. Next came Dr. Charles Boxton, for whom the scene of the trap was shifted to Roy's home. There Boxton accepted the money in the parlor. Burns, a private secretary of Rudolph Spreckels, and a stenographer were concealed in the darkened dining-room, watching and listening through the folding doors, left slightly ajar.

One part of Burns' original plan for trapping Lonergan had miscarried. In an elaborate scheme to clinch the evidence, Burns had directed one of his agents to go into partnership with Lonergan in a small electrical supply business, with capital secretly furnished to the agent by Rudolph Spreckels. Shortly after Lonergan received the marked money, his "partner" was to ask him to cash a check; but Lonergan, whether through cautiousness or accident, cashed the check with entirely different money. Burns then decided to "bribe" Lonergan a second time. He prepared an ordinance permitting the establishment of an oil refinery in which Roy pretended to have a financial interest. After persuading Boxton to introduce this measure, Roy offered Lonergan $500 to vote for it. On the morning of March 7, 1907, Lonergan came to Roy's home, and received the money in the parlor. This time, however, he was suspicious and worried, and immediately after he had taken the money he walked to the folding doors and began to pull them open, asking Roy what he had in the next room. The answer came from Burns, who flung the doors apart and stepped into the parlor.

"I want you to arrest this man," said Lonergan, pointing to Roy. "He bribed a Supervisor."

"Yes," replied Burns, "I saw him do it. Did you tell me to arrest him when he bribed you down at the skating rink?"

After an attempt at denial, Lonergan admitted taking the skating rink bribe. Burns urged him to make a confession of everything he knew about municipal graft, but this Lonergan at first refused to do. Burns then sent for Langdon and Heney and after the district attorney and his assistant had spent most of the afternoon in threatening to prosecute the former bakery-wagon driver for the briberies Burns had witnessed, unless he would make a general confession, Lonergan broke down. He told of the money he had received from Gallagher in the prize fight, gas rate, Home Telephone, and trolley matters; of the money promised him for the Parkside franchise and the Bay Cities Water Company purchase; and of the money he had received from Halsey of the Pacific States Telephone and Telegraph Company.

While Burns, Heney, and Langdon were inducing Lonergan to make this statement, in a bedroom on the second floor of Roy's home, their host had issued further telephone invitations to supervisors Boxton and Walsh, and to Rudolph Spreckels. Spreckels had known Boxton for several years, during which time Boxton had been his dentist. But although Spreckels added his urgings to those of Langdon, Burns, Heney, and Roy, and although these five questioned Boxton by turns until midnight, the dentist-supervisor refused to make a confession unless every other supervisor did the same. Walsh, who had been entertained too well by one of Burns' secret agents during the day, was too intoxicated to talk coherently. The next morning, however, he made a confession virtually identical with Lonergan's except in the Home Telephone matter, in which Lonergan had taken money from both sides, while Walsh had taken money only from the Pacific States company.

Heney and Langdon had obtained the confessions of Lonergan and Walsh by promising them immunity from prosecution, a tactic which Heney had used with conspicuous success in the

Oregon land fraud cases. But while the confessions of these two supervisors were an entering wedge, they were little more. They did involve Gallagher, and Halsey; but if Gallagher denied that he had paid the money, and if the other supervisors denied that they had received any similar payments from Gallagher, it would be hard to convict Gallagher, and impossible to convict any of the other members of the board, on the testimony of Lonergan and Walsh alone. Moreover, only through Gallagher was there any connection with Ruef. The prosecution decided to offer immunity to Gallagher, and entered into negotiations with him through Dr. Boxton's attorney, H. M. Owens.

Boxton, after refusing to confess, was kept under surveillance in his own home, but was permitted to speak with his attorney in private. Owens advised Boxton that if he were brought to trial on the skating rink bribery charge, he would almost certainly be convicted; that while California law gave no formal standing to an immunity contract, such an agreement would be probably valid in practice; and that if Boxton could get the district attorney's promise of immunity in return for a full confession, he would be wise to make the confession. Boxton remained reluctant to do this unless Gallagher and his other colleagues would confess also. Owens then went to Gallagher, and explained the circumstances.

In this explosive situation, Gallagher's position was complicated by the fact that he was unable to consult directly with Ruef, who was in hiding at the Trocadero until the evening of March 8, when he was confined by Elisor Biggy at the Little St. Francis. Finally, through Ruef's sister, Gallagher received Ruef's instruction. He was to "sit on the lid." But as Gallagher remarked to Andrew M. Wilson, "the lid was getting a little warm." Informed of the confessions of Lonergan and Walsh, under promise of immunity, Gallagher became anxious to know whether he could get similar terms for himself and for the other members of the board of supervisors. Owens said that he could arrange an appointment for Gallagher with Langdon or with Burns. Gallagher finally agreed to meet with Rudolph Spreckels.

The delicate negotiations between Gallagher and Spreckels were carried on in a series of three conferences on the grounds of the Presidio, the United States military reservation at the northwest corner of the San Francisco peninsula. This was soil outside the jurisdiction of the state of California, although Gallagher insisted that it was not this, but rather the relative seclusion of the place, which led him to select it. In the first meeting, Spreckels explained that the prosecution's main purpose was not to send a few politicians to prison, but to stop municipal corruption at its source; and that the prosecution believed the real source of graft to be mainly in the wealthy representatives of great corporations, who tempted politicians of small means to become their agents. To procure evidence against the greater criminals, the prosecution would be willing to grant immunity to the lesser ones. Gallagher would make no commitments or admissions in this preliminary conference, and insisted that he would not consider the proposal unless immunity were extended not only to himself but to all the other members of the board of supervisors.

In coming to a decision on the matter of granting immunity to the entire board, the prosecution considered the fact that the testimony of at least a majority of the members would be almost essential in corroborating the testimony of Lonergan and Walsh, even if the testimony of Boxton and Gallagher were added. It would be difficult to prove a motive for the bribery of only three or four of the eighteen members. Moreover, on the morning of March 14, the *Chronicle* published a story that Burns and Roy had trapped Lonergan and Boxton. This article stated that no one had yet confessed, but otherwise it was generally accurate. Heney's theory was that Ruef had given the story to the *Chronicle,* through Tirey L. Ford, in the hope of frightening the other supervisors away from the prosecution's traps. Heney also feared that Ruef might find still other means of bringing pressure on the supervisors and that unless their confessions could be secured immediately, the prosecution's entering wedge would slip away. After a conference, Heney and Langdon decided on a definite offer of immunity for all of the members of the board, and Spreckels conveyed this offer to Gallagher in a second meeting with him at the Presidio.

Gallagher then called an emergency caucus of the board of supervisors, and Boxton and Wilson joined him in urging the members to accept the district attorney's offer. Reluctantly, the members were finally persuaded to cast a unanimous affirmative vote. Gallagher carried this decision to Spreckels, and in their third conference Gallagher and Spreckels concluded what was later popularly known as "the Treaty of the Presidio." In return for full and fair confessions, and for promises of future testimony in court, all of the supervisors were to receive complete immunity. This included Andrew M. Wilson, who had resigned from the board to take the office of state railroad commissioner, to which he had been elected in the fall of 1906. George Duffey had resigned from the board of supervisors to become president of the board of public works after the removal of Maestretti, and it was agreed that Duffey should not be required to confess, lest Mayor Schmitz retaliate by removing him from his position. To the places vacated by Wilson and Duffey on the board of supervisors, the mayor had appointed O. A. Tveitmoe and J. J. O'Neil, but Tveitmoe and O'Neil were in no way involved in any of the briberies.

Not only were the supervisors to receive immunity, but they were not to be required to resign. The reason for this was that as long as these members remained in office, the prosecution would control the board of supervisors, the legislative branch of the city government, while if they resigned Mayor Schmitz would have the power to fill their places by appointment, and Schmitz and Ruef would thus regain control of the board.

Heney and Langdon now drew up a written immunity contract for each of the confessing supervisors. These documents were to be placed in the custody of Rudolph Spreckels, and District Attorney Langdon was to give his verbal promise that he would sign them when the supervisors had given satisfactory evidence that they would carry them out in full.

As soon as his colleagues had voted to agree to confess, Boxton had hastened to add his confession to those of Lonergan and Walsh. And on Saturday, March 16, 1907, all of the other original members of the Union Labor board of supervisors, except the fortunate Duffey and Sanderson, who was gravely ill, dictated their confessions in Burns' rooms at the Gladstone Apartments. The prosecution was anxious to avoid publicity until these statements were fully on record.

On Monday, March 18, Heney hurried most of the supervisors before a day-long session of the grand jury, where they repeated their confessions in full detail under his questioning. Their stories were alike, with exceptions due to particular circumstances. Gallagher and Wilson had received larger amounts than the others. Rea was substantially innocent. He had received the prize fight and gas rate payments, but nothing more after he realized that these were intended as bribes; and Heney distinquished between Rea and the other members in questioning him before the grand jury. The payments of money in the prize fight, gas rate, Home Telephone, and trolley briberies, and the promises in the Parkside and Bay Cities Water matters, had all been made by Gallagher, who testified that he had received them from Ruef. In only one case did the testimony of the supervisors establish a more direct connection with the source of the bribe, namely in the payment of $5,000 to each of eleven supervisors by Theodore V. Halsey, political agent of the Pacific States Telephone and Telegraph Company.

In the evening of March 18, 1907, after the supervisors had testified before the grand jury, they gave interviews to the newspapers in which they revealed the substance of what they had confessed; and by evening of the next day the sensational details of the briberies, so far as the testimony of the supervisors could establish them, were known to almost everyone in the city.

On March 20 the grand jury returned sixty-five indictments against Ruef, for bribing eighteen supervisors in the "fight trust" incident, seventeen in the gas rate, thirteen for the Home Telephone franchise, and seventeen for the overhead trolley ordinance. On the same day ten indictments were returned against Halsey; and on March 23, after several days of examining other officers and employees of the Pacific States company, the grand jury returned nine indictments against the company's vice-president, Louis Glass, as the executive officer responsible for ordering Halsey to make the bribery payments.

CHAPTER XVI

Ruef negotiates

WHILE the prosecution was scoring these successes, and bringing Ruef's organization to ruin, the harried boss was a prisoner of Elisor Biggy. Detective Burns had visited him several times at the Little St. Francis, to urge him to confess, and Ruef had continued to insist that he had no knowledge of any briberies. On the evening of Saturday, March 16, however, Supervisor Nicholas informed Frank Murphy, one of Ruef's attorneys, that the supervisors had just confessed in Burns' rooms at the Gladstone Apartments, and Murphy carried the news to Ruef.

On Sunday morning, after a sleepless night, Ruef asked for permission to confer with Gallagher and Wilson. Burns telephoned these two former leaders of the board and invited them to come to the Little St. Francis, where Biggy permitted them to talk with his prisoner alone. They confirmed the report that they had confessed. There were some recriminations. Ruef said that if he had been in Gallagher's position he would not have followed such a course. Wilson observed that one could never tell what he would do until he was placed in Gallagher's position. Gallagher defended his actions, and said that in his talks with Spreckels he had gained the impression that Ruef might be able to obtain immunity on terms identical with those granted to the supervisors. According to Gallagher's recollection, Spreckels had said that the prosecution had no feelings of vindictiveness toward Ruef; that political bosses, like public officials, would come and go; and that their punishment was less important than the reform of the public service corporations, which were the real and enduring sources of corruption.

Burns now intensified his efforts to persuade Ruef to confess.

Moreover, on Wednesday, March 20, Ruef found himself faced with sixty-five indictments; and shortly afterward he asked Burns to tell Heney and Langdon that he was willing to confess in return for full immunity. Burns carried this proposal to Heney and urged its acceptance.

Heney denied that he had ever intended to offer complete immunity to Ruef, or to authorize either Spreckels or Burns to make such an offer. According to the affidavit in which Heney later reviewed the disputed history of these negotiations, he told Burns that Ruef, unlike the supervisors, was no mere tool in the briberies, but rather had played a leading part in initiating them. A man of extraordinary intelligence, fine education, dominating personality, and great powers of persuasion, Ruef might have risen to the highest levels of achievement. Instead he had chosen to join hands with vice and with privilege-seeking corporations to rob the people of the city. "To let Ruef go free of all punishment under the circumstances would be a crime against society." Partial immunity was the most that Heney would consider. Ruef, said Heney, was "the greatest rascal" in the whole tangle of corruption.

Burns reminded Heney of the latter's own belief that political bosses in San Francisco were usually the tools of great corporations. Heney replied that Ruef was no ordinary boss. Burns pointed out that it would be very difficult to obtain the convictions of Schmitz, and of men like Ford and Calhoun, without Ruef's testimony—a point in which there was much truth. The supervisors had received money only from Ruef, and from Halsey. Just as Gallagher had been the vital link in the chain of evidence leading to Ruef, so Ruef alone could provide the vital testimony against Schmitz, to whom he had supposedly paid money in the French restaurant matter; and against the Pacific Gas and Electric, Home Telephone, Parkside, and United Railroads officials, from whom he had received money in the bribery cases. If Schmitz were not convicted he would remain in office, controlling the police, the board of public works, and the other administrative commissions which he had appointed. The voters might even reelect him in the fall of 1907, in the belief that the charges against him were false.

Heney finally sent a message to Ruef, through Burns, laying down the conditions on which he would negotiate for an agreement on partial immunity. These conditions were that Ruef must be represented by an attorney in whom Heney had confidence; that Ruef must tell whom he would involve; and that he must give assurance that his testimony would be sufficient to sustain convictions. Ruef proposed Henry Ach as his representative. Heney said that he had no confidence in Ach. Ruef then studied a list of San Francisco attorneys. After several days of delay, he insisted that he could trust no one but Ach. Heney again refused.

From the beginning of these negotiations, Heney and Ruef were deeply suspicious of each other. Ruef told Burns that he feared that Heney would hear his story, use it against him and against others, and then say that it was insufficient, and not worth immunity. Conversely, Heney was afraid that Ruef would try to sell the prosecution a "gold brick," in the form of a confession which would not actually be sufficient to convict his accomplices. One of Heney's reasons for refusing to offer complete immunity was that he wished to keep something in reserve which he could always hold over Ruef's head.

In his dealings with the prosecution, Ruef's strategy appears to have had these main objectives: (1) to secure a promise of complete immunity for himself, in return for a promise to testify fully and truthfully; (2) subsequently to insist that the full truth was that all the payments to him had been as fees to an attorney, without any authorization for him to bribe public officials with part of the money—thus assuring the acquittal of those who had paid him; and (3) when the prosecution should complain that this could not be the whole truth, to accuse the prosecution of attempting to suborn perjury.

Throughout the negotiations, Ruef was a clever lawyer, thoroughly experienced in the twilight zones of legality, and fighting desperately for his freedom. Heney was also an able lawyer, experienced in the prosecution of desperate and clever men, and now more than ever crusading against corruption and vice. In this battle of wits, Heney was aided by the talents of William J. Burns, whose tactics had a special advantage in that they were unofficial and could if necessary be repudiated. Burns was privately employed by Rudolph Spreckels, and was not an official representative of the district attorney's office.

Elisor Biggy had appointed Burns as his deputy. In the capacity of a deputy elisor, Burns had access to Ruef at any time, and he began to visit him regularly, often several times each day or evening, in the hope of persuading him to come to terms. During most of the month of March, Ruef was confined in the Little St. Francis Hotel. These quarters were inadequate for Biggy's staff of guards, and the rent was too high for the city to be expected to continue paying. On March 28, Biggy announced that he had moved his prisoner to a new special jail at 2849 Fillmore Street—a house which had been owned and occupied by none other than Mayor Schmitz, up to the time two years before, when the mayor had purchased a more elaborate residence. The lessee of the house, over the protests of the owner who had bought it from Schmitz, now took in Biggy, Burns, Ruef, and six guards as roomers and boarders. Even in these more economical surroundings, an article in the *Call* asserted, Ruef's captivity was "nearly as expensive as Napoleon's" at St. Helena.

It was Burns who had made these arrangements, and undoubtedly his selection of the former home of Mayor Schmitz, Ruef's codefendant, was more than accidental. It appealed to the colorful detective's flare for the dramatic, and it provided a peculiarly appropriate atmosphere for his efforts to secure Ruef's confession. This element was intensified when Burns discovered, and triumphantly revealed to the newspapers, a velvet-lined "treasure box" built under the floor of Schmitz's former bedroom. Here, said Burns, Schmitz must have hidden his ill-gotten gains; and Ruef was now to sleep in this same room, constantly reminded of the guilt of himself and his accomplice, and of Burns' knowledge of it. Schmitz protested to reporters that the "treasure box" had contained nothing more than his valuable violin; but Burns asserted that it was not large enough to hold a violin of that size.

In his new place of confinement, Ruef was made comfortable physically, and was permitted to order good wines and special food at his own expense. But Burns was making use of psychological pressure to unnerve his prisoner. When Ruef expressed a desire to take his mind off his troubles with light reading matter, several popular novels were carefully selected for him: *Half a Rogue*, by Harold McGrath; *The Malefactor*, by E. Phillips Oppenheim; and *The Fighting Chance*, by Meredith Nicholson. Ruef and his attorneys were unsuccessful in their petitions for relief from the custody of Elisor Biggy, both in the court of Judge Dunne and in the state supreme court. Ach asserted that Ruef's confinement was a "cruel and unusual punishment"; that Ruef's attorneys were not always allowed to speak with him in real privacy; and that his extensive law practice and business affairs were suffering unduly from the elisor's restrictions on the persons permitted to talk with him at all. Ruef, while he did not complain against the treatment accorded by him by Biggy personally, protested that the elisorship would be a dangerous precedent.

"The elisor habit, should it prevail in California," he said, "would mean that every political faction which had a judge on the bench favorable to it might have the Sheriff and the Coroner disqualified and thrust its political enemies into private jails. Private funds, as in my case, and private friends [as] elisors, make any kind of persecution possible under these circumstances."

The story of Burns' efforts to wring a confession from Ruef had a strong appeal to popular imagination, and later became the subject of several magazine articles. An anonymous article appeared in the *Overland Monthly* under the title of "Ruef, a Jew under torture." "William J. Burns does not indulge in physical torture," said this writer. "He has developed a system which is slower and surer." For example, this writer asserted, Burns would feed Ruef heavily, to induce sleep, and tell Ruef the next morning that he had talked in his sleep: consequently, the next night Ruef would suffer from insomnia. Lincoln Steffens wrote an article for the *American Magazine,* based on interviews with Burns, and called "William J. Burns, Intriguer. The Keenest of Detectives and the Story of his Hardest Job." Dana Gatlin, in an article in *McClure's* entitled "Great Cases of Detective Burns," wrote that "Abe Ruef was a foe worthy of his steel, and Burns appreciates him almost tenderly." Gatlin quoted Burns as saying, "I never expect to enjoy anyone more than I did Ruef."

On April 2, after several days in which he had made little progress in forcing Ruef to make a decision, Burns received what he regarded as a welcome offer of aid. Rabbi Jacob Nieto approached Burns in the court room, after the adjournment of a session of impaneling jurors for Ruef's extortion trial, and told the detective that he believed he might be able to persuade Ruef to confess. Dr. Nieto was the minister of the Temple Israel, the largest synagogue in San Francisco, and he had continued to occupy his study and office in the building during its use by the departments of the superior court since the great fire. He had known Ruef for many years, and he now inquired whether Burns would object to his talking with the prisoner. According to Burns, Dr. Nieto told him that "he thought Ruef was being made a scapegoat for those higher up, and that while he was not interested in Ruef personally he thought that in the interests of San Francisco Ruef ought to tell his story." Burns replied that he had no objection, and arranged a meeting between Nieto and Ruef that evening in the house on Fillmore Street.

Nieto discussed the matter with Ruef "from a moral point of view, and urged him to tell the prosecution all he knew," first for the welfare of the city, and second "for his own peace of mind and for the sake of his parents." But Ruef declined, saying "that he had committed no offense under the law," and that his testimony might "implicate other persons and cause them and their families much trouble and anxiety; that he himself was a single man and without family," except for his parents and sisters. Nieto reported this conversation to Burns, and they agreed that the rabbi should continue his efforts.

When Heney heard of Nieto's intervention, he was much less enthusiastic than Burns had expected. Heney was already acquainted with Nieto, who had suggested to him while the grand jury was being impaneled that in questioning prospective jurors he was showing some discrimination against Jews. Heney had denied this heatedly. He now described the episode to Burns, insisted that Nieto's criticisms had been supersensitive and wholly unjustified, and pointed out that "some of the best men" on the grand jury were Jews. "At all times," said Heney, "I looked upon [Nieto] as an ardent admirer of Ruef, who would like to see him escape punishment altogether." Heney warned Burns that the prosecution could not trust Nieto, who would probably "do everything in his power to have Ruef get the best of it in any negotiations which may be had in the matter." Burns replied that Nieto could do no harm, and that his motives would make no difference, if he could help in persuading Ruef to agree to the prosecution's terms. Heney offered no further opposition, "except to warn Burns to be very careful what he said to Nieto."

A day or two later, Dr. Nieto was permitted to take Ruef to the house of his parents, where the rabbi talked earnestly with the family group. This house, in which Ruef himself had also lived until he was taken into custody, was just around the corner from the former home of Mayor Schmitz. Ruef's father and sister had already visited him several times at his place of confinement, but his mother was too ill to do so. Her illness was being aggravated by the troubles of her only son.

On April 8, Burns brought Dr. Nieto to Heney's office, in a former residence now popularly known as the "prosecution house," at 1109 Franklin Street. On this and subsequent visits, Nieto came in by a side gate and by the back door, to avoid recognition by the newspaper reporters who were often in the front hall. According to Heney's recollection, Nieto told him that he was "not interested in the matter as an individual, but only in the welfare of this community," against which Ruef had "grievously sinned."

Heney then assured Nieto that he himself was moved solely by a sense of public duty, that he had no personal animosity toward Ruef, and that he had "always liked him and admired his ability, although I always had a contempt for his character." Heney went on to formulate a statement of his own philosophy as a leader of the prosecution. The greatest benefit which the city and the whole country would derive from the prosecutions, he said, would be "the insight which we will have given them into the causes of corruption in all large cities, and into the methods by which this corruption is maintained." Ruef could be of great service in helping to make it "an object lesson to the world," if he would do so. But in order to impress this object lesson strongly enough to accomplish much good we must punish the principal men who have been involved in it." If the people were to have respect for law, the rich and powerful must be made to obey the law. "It has a greater deterrent effect, in my opinion, to put one rich and influential man in prison than to put a thousand poor ones there. It would do no good to send a few miserable, ignorant supervisors to the penitentiary." Ruef's case was different from that of the supervisors, and Heney would never grant him a promise of immunity on the same terms. To put Ruef in prison would "have a wholesome effect upon other political bosses for the next decade at least." And to "put a few captains of industry there with him" would have an even greater deterrent effect against the bribery of public officials.

Leniency, said Heney, was the most he would promise Ruef, and that only on the strictest conditions. He had already sent an ultimatum to Ruef and Ach through Burns, laying down the condition that Ruef must plead guilty in the French restaurant extortion case in the court of Judge Dunne, in which a jury was then being selected. If Ruef should plead guilty in that case, Heney recalled that he told Nieto in effect, "sentence can be postponed from time to time until we are all through with all the cases in which he is to be a witness, and if I find at any time that he is not keeping his agreement with the prosecution, he can be immediately sentenced in case No. 305 and sent to the penitentiary. I will not trust him without holding that power in my hands."

William J. Burns, in the meantime, was following his own inclinations in his frequent interviews with Ruef. He told Ruef that he would urge Heney and Langdon to grant Ruef a contract for full immunity. Later Ruef asserted, and Burns denied, that at this time Burns claimed to be a representative of the district attorney's office.

The time now approached when Rabbi Nieto was to leave the city on a trip to Europe, to be gone for several months. Ruef asked Nieto to invite another clergyman to be present in his conversations with Heney or Langdon, so that later during Nieto's absence there would be someone to substantiate any promises the prosecution might make. For this purpose, Nieto brought Rabbi Bernard M. Kaplan to Heney's office on April 16. Rabbi Kaplan was a young man, in his early thirties, recently called to San Francisco as minister of the Bush Street Temple. He was already well acquainted with Ruef's family. To Heney, Dr. Kaplan appeared to be "honest and unsophisticated," but also less interested in "the moral issue" than in the possibility of "getting Ruef off without any punishment."

A few days afterward, Nieto and Kaplan came to Heney's office again. Kaplan said that he had talked with Ruef, and that Ruef had assured him that he was not guilty in the French restaurant matter. Heney answered that he had heard the testimony before the grand jury, and was certain of Ruef's guilt. Kaplan replied, according to Heney's recollection: "Well, but Mr.

Heney, I talked with him about it as a minister, and he assures me that he is innocent, and that he took the money as an attorney's fee, and that he refused to take the case until the *Bulletin* abused him and challenged him to do it and that he then took it merely to show the *Bulletin* that he was not afraid to do so." Heney replied that there was no use in arguing the question.

On April 23, Nieto, Kaplan, Ach, Burns, and District Attorney Langdon came to the "prosecution house" for a conference. All entered by the side street and the back door; and in order to preserve the greatest possible secrecy, and to avoid recognition of the participants by the newspaper reporters in the hall, the conference was held in the kitchen. Heney recalled that "Henry Ach, as is usual with him, did most of the talking for his side." Ach stated, according to Heney: "You can't convict Ruef in this French restaurant case, but I realize that you are sure to convict him in some of the bribery cases, and I think it is useless for him to stand out and fight any longer, he had better take the best he can get, and I have told him so. He insists, however, that he ought not to be required to plead guilty in the French restaurant case, or to submit to any punishment." Heney reiterated his "ultimatum" that Ruef must plead guilty to indictment No. 305.

Ach and Heney had both studied the precedents established by higher courts on the question of the power of a district attorney to confer immunity, and it was agreed that technically a district attorney had no such power in California. He could, however, accomplish the same purpose by making recommendations to the court, since the trial judge would usually follow these recommendations if he had confidence in the probity and motives of the district attorney. Ach now proposed that Heney should ask the presiding judge to assign all cases involving Ruef to one department, Judge Dunne's, and that Heney should then ask Judge Dunne to agree to the dismissal of any indictment against Ruef whenever Heney would recommend it. Heney refused to follow this procedure. It was known, however, that only four of the twelve superior judges were hearing criminal cases at that time—judges Cook, Mogan, Dunne, and Lawlor. It was also well known that Heney would refuse to try any case before judges Cook and Mogan, whom he considered to be corrupt tools of Ruef. Thus it was safe to assume that the presiding judge would assign the cases to judges Dunne and Lawlor, and Ach suggested that Heney should "go to those two judges and get them to consent to this agreement."

Heney replied that he would not ask a judge to do anything so collusive; but that he was willing to go with Ach to judges Dunne and Lawlor, and to ask each of them, first, whether he had confidence in Heney, and, second, what his general practice was in cases of similar recommendations by prosecutors in whom he had confidence. Ach, according to Heney's account, hastily declined to accompany Heney on this mission, because he did not wish it to be known that he had taken any part whatever in advising Ruef to turn state's evidence. If it were known, the powerful men whom Ruef would involve would retaliate against Ach, and he would lose some of his best corporate clients.

This conference, which had lasted nearly two hours, proved inconclusive, but it was resumed again three days later, on the evening of April 26, with the addition of Rudolph Spreckels and Charles W. Cobb as observers, in a rear room on the second floor. There, after wrangling until nearly midnight over much the same ground, the participants finally reached what was supposed to be an agreement, complicated and thorny with reservations, and later to be the subject of bitter dispute.

Heney, according to his affidavit, stated that since Ruef was unwilling to say what his evidence would be, in advance of an immunity agreement, the prosecution was unwilling "to swap knives in the dark" by promising immunity before Ruef had given his evidence, in the trials of his accomplices. The prosecution insisted on having the power to reserve judgment on the question of the value of Ruef's testimony, in terms of leniency or immunity, until all of that testimony was finally on the record. This could be done only if Ruef entered a plea of guilty to the French restaurant charge, before Judge Dunne. Heney would then ask Judge Dunne to postpone sentence, from time to time, until the trials of Ruef's accomplices were over. It was possible that Ruef's evidence might be of sufficient value "to entitle even him to complete immunity." This would be true, for example, if his testimony should lead to a conviction of that creator and maintainer of political bosses, William F. Herrin. Heney would make no explicit promise to Ruef or to anyone as to what his final recommendation would be. But in order that Ach, as an attorney, and Nieto and Kaplan, as ministers, might be better able to decide whether to advise Ruef to accept the prosecution's terms, Heney would tell them what his "present intentions" were—provided they would promise not to reveal this information to Ruef, nor to give him the impression that it was part of the actual agreement. In the end, if Ruef's evidence should prove in Heney's opinion to be worth full immunity, then Heney would recommend to the court that Ruef be permitted to withdraw his plea of guilty in case number 305, and that the case be dismissed. If Ruef's evidence should prove worthy only of leniency, or of something even less than that, Heney would make his recommendations accordingly.

Such was Heney's version of his statements to Ach, Nieto, and Kaplan. But it later became apparent that the two rabbis had formed impressions which differed from Heney's in important respects. In particular, Heney's distinction between his "confidential intentions," which they were not to reveal to Ruef, and the explicit offer, which they *were* authorized to convey to Ruef, did not enter clearly into the understanding which the rabbis had formed. Instead, they reported to Ruef that Heney was willing to make a definite promise of full immunity. Kaplan and Nieto believed that the requirement of a plea of guilty was a mere sham, and that the prosecution was insisting on it mainly for the sake of the effect on public opinion. They urged Ruef to accept the offer.

Ruef would not accept it, however, without assurances from the judges themselves that they would concur in the arrangement. On the night of April 29, when Ach, Nieto, Kaplan, Heney, Langdon, Spreckels, and Cobb were again in the room behind Heney's office, it was agreed that Heney should ask judges Lawlor and Dunne, in the presence of rabbis Nieto and Kaplan, what the practice of the judges was in cases involving such recommendations as Heney might make in his capacity as representative of the district attorney. Nieto pointed out that this would have to be done that night, since he was leaving for Europe the next morning. Burns then set out in his automobile to find the judges.

Judge Lawlor, Burns discovered, was at the Van Ness Theatre. There, between acts, Burns told him that Heney, Nieto, and Kaplan wished to see him on an important matter, and explained

why it could not wait until a less unusual time. With some reluctance, Judge Lawlor consented to grant the interview, provided it be held at his chambers, and after the play at the theater
was over. Burns returned to Heney's office to drive Heney, Nieto,
and Kaplan to the Temple Israel. There he left them to wait for
Judge Lawlor, and set out to look for Judge Dunne.

When Judge Lawlor arrived at his chambers in the Temple,
and after an exchange of amenities, there was a brief discussion
which Heney began by saying, in effect: "Judge, we came up
here tonight to ask you what the practice of your court is in
criminal cases in relation to recommendation which may be
made by the District Attorney." At this point, Judge Lawlor
interrupted to say that he did not wish to know the particulars
and would speak only of his practice in general. It was his duty,
he said, to give the most careful consideration to any recommendations made by the district attorney as the representative of
the people, when made in open court and accompanied by a
full statement of the facts. If he considered such a recommendation to be in the interest of justice, he would follow it. Judge
Lawlor then excused himself and left the building.

In the meantime, Burns had been waiting at the residence of
Judge Dunne, who was not at home. When the judge came in,
it was nearly midnight, and at first he flatly refused to go to the
Temple at such an hour. Finally, however, he agreed to go there
on foot, refusing to go in Burns' automobile. He arrived a few
minutes after midnight, and met Heney, Nieto, and Kaplan,
who had been waiting just inside the Webster Street door. The
later accounts of all four of the participants agreed that the
conversation lasted scarcely more than one minute. Judge
Dunne expressed confidence in Heney as assistant district attorney, and said that he would be guided by his recommendations made in open court, if they were in the interest of justice.
Rabbi Kaplan asked whether a plea of guilty, once entered,
could afterward be changed on such a recommendation. The
judge, according to his own version, replied that while the final
decision would rest with him, he would give "great weight" to
such a request from Heney or Langdon. According to the accounts of Heney and the judge himself, there was no specific
mention of Ruef. According to Nieto and Kaplan, however,
Kaplan's question mentioned Ruef and the French restaurant

case specifically, and the Judge's answer was, "Yes, certainly."

After the departure of Judge Dunne, Nieto and Kaplan asked Heney to advise them whether they could interpret the statements of the two judges as giving the assurances they required. Heney told them to have no further doubt that he could carry out his own part of the proposed agreement—if Ruef carried out his part of it.

From the Temple Israel, Burns drove Nieto and Kaplan to the house on Fillmore Street, where, between one and two o'clock in the morning, they urged Ruef in the strongest terms to accept the prosecution's offer. According to Kaplan, he and his colleague "pledged to [Ruef] our sacred honor as men and as ministers . . . that the promises of the prosecution would be sacredly and absolutely kept." Still Ruef balked at the condition that he plead guilty to the extortion charge.

On the night of May 1, after Heney had retired, Burns telephoned to say that he believed Ruef was almost ready to give in if Heney would grant him an interview. Heney consented, and Burns drove Ruef and Elisor Biggy to Heney's residence. When he arrived, however, Ruef launched into a series of arguments against pleading guilty. He suggested that if he were to admit that he was guilty of extortion, it would lessen the value of his testimony against his accomplices in bribery. Heney was not impressed. According to Heney, Ruef went on to say that public opinion would approve his being permitted to escape without punishment, and that "Ninety per cent of the people of this city would sign a petition for my pardon tomorrow," to which Heney replied: "You fooled the public a long time here, Abe, but you can not fool them all the time, and you are now fooling yourself instead of them. Ninety per cent of the people of this state want to see you in the penitentiary for life, and that is what I am going to do with you unless you make up your mind very quickly to help undo some of the wrongs which you have committed."

Unmoved by any of Ruef's arguments, Heney finally issued an ultimatum with a definite time limit. Ruef was given until eleven o'clock on May 3 to make up his mind. Otherwise, Heney threatened to offer immunity to Patrick Calhoun, and on Calhoun's testimony, combined with that of the supervisors, to make it certain that Ruef, if no one else, would go to prison for the trolley franchise bribery.

On the morning of May 3, Ruef told Burns that he had decided to accept the prosecution's offer and was ready to begin his confession. Burns was overjoyed. He congratulated Ruef and suggested that Ruef make a preliminary statement to be shown to Heney as evidence of his good faith.

This first confession of Ruef to Burns was concerned mainly with Ruef's employment as attorney for the United Railroads; with the payment of the $200,000 to Ruef by Tirey L. Ford, after the trolley franchise had been granted; and with Ruef's payments to the supervisors and the mayor. Burns wrote down Ruef's statements, and hurried to Heney's office, where he read his notes to Heney, Langdon, Spreckels, and Cobb. Heney pointed out that Ruef had revealed nothing of importance which the prosecution did not already know. In particular, Ruef did *not* say that Ford had paid the money to him with an understanding and expectation that he should pay any of it to the public officials involved. Heney asserted that Ruef must be keeping something back, and that if this were his intention the prosecution should break off negotiations with him. Burns replied that Ruef had at least made a definite confession of the origin of the money, and that this was only his preliminary statement. Burns reminded Heney that in their past relations with criminals who confessed, they had seldom been able to get the whole truth at the outset. Heney finally consented to dictate a draft of a written immunity contract.

On May 7, Ruef made a series of further statements to Burns, concerning his knowledge of the "fight trust," gas rate, Parkside, Home Telephone, and United Railroads matters; of the sharing by Schmitz and himself of the fee from the French restaurant keepers, and the profits from the "municipal crib" at 620 Jackson Street; of his relations with the Bay Cities Water Company; and of his arrangement with Herrin to receive $14,000 as campaign expenses in the 1906 primaries. On May 8, Heney, Langdon, and Ruef signed the "immunity contract" which Heney had drafted. It provided that if Ruef should make "full and fair disclosure" of "the truth, the whole truth, and nothing but the truth," the prosecution would "grant and obtain for said A.

Ruef full and complete immunity"; but the final clause provided that this agreement was not to apply to indictment No. 305 in the French restaurant matter, a weapon which Heney insisted upon holding in reserve.

During all of these negotiations, the selection of a jury to try Ruef for extortion on this same indictment had been proceeding intermittently. The defense had secured various delays, including one occasioned by a conveniently protracted illness of Henry Ach. But on May 13, the twelfth juror was finally accepted, and the jury was sworn. Heney had warned Ruef that if he failed to enter a plea of guilty before testimony began in the trial, the immunity contract would be canceled, and the prosecution of Ruef for extortion and then for bribery would proceed.

When court opened on May 15, Heney was ready to make the opening statement for the prosecution, and to call the first witness. But Henry Ach rose to say that Ruef had asked for a private conference with his counsel. Judge Dunne granted a recess of half an hour, and permitted the use of his chambers for a conference between Ruef and his attorneys, Henry Ach, Samuel Shortridge, Frank J. Murphy, and Charles Fairall. A moment after this group entered the chambers, Ach hurried back into the courtroom for a glass of water, and sent a messenger for a flask of brandy. The report spread through the courtroom that Ruef had fainted.

Up to this time the spectators had had little reason to suppose that Ruef was contemplating any very extraordinary decision, although it had been obvious for several days that he was under a great strain. Several newspaper reports of his appearances in court had remarked that he appeared pale and careworn, with streaks of gray beginning to appear in his hair; and he had unsuccessfully sought a further delay in the trial on the ground that his health was in danger.

When Ruef and his attorneys emerged from Judge Dunne's chambers, Henry Ach led the way, and walked to his seat with an air of great anger and disappointment. When the court was called to order, Ach asked permission to withdraw as Ruef's counsel, because of a disagreement with his client on the conduct of the case. Shortridge also withdrew from the case and left the courtroom. Murphy and Fairall remained.

Ruef now asked permission to make a statement. It would

be made, he said, against the protests of his attorneys, whom he thanked for their services, fidelity, and friendship. But he assured the court that neither his own health nor that of the members of his family could stand the strain of a long trial.

Alternately reading and looking up from a manuscript on several sheets of yellow paper, pausing often for sips of water, and with tears running down his cheeks, Ruef continued his dramatic statement. He had occupied, he said, "a somewhat prominent position in this city of my birth, in which I have lived all my life." He had borne an honored name. There had been no stain in his private and in his professional life. And in his "public affiliations," it was only after the election of the present board of supervisors, in 1905, that "the assaults of the press" and "a desire to hold together a political organization which had been built up with much effort" had influenced him "in a measure" to lower his ideals.

It would be folly to offer excuses for the past. But he had decided that "whatever energy or abilities I possess for the future shall be . . . re-enlisted on the side of good citizenship and integrity." He was resolved to assist in "making more difficult, if not impossible, the system which dominates our public men and corrupts our politics"; and to have "some small part" in reëstablishing "just reciprocal relations between the constantly struggling constituent elements of our governmental and industrial life.

"As an earnest I have determined to make a beginning," Ruef concluded, "I am not guilty of the offense charged in this indictment. I ask now, however, that this jury be dismissed from further consideration of this case. I desire to withdraw my plea of not guilty heretofore entered and to enter the contrary plea, and at the proper time submit to the Court further suggestions for its consideration."

With the consent of the prosecution, Judge Dunne permitted Ruef to change his plea to "guilty." The jury was dismissed, and sentence was postponed.

CHAPTER XVII

The conviction of Mayor Schmitz

THE public had had no inkling of the negotiations leading to Ruef's plea of guilty and to his asserted "re-enlistment" on the side of reform, and the effect was tremendous. During the afternoon, Ruef gave the Associated Press a long statement which it sent out as part of a 3,000 word dispatch, along with a detailed description of the scene in the courtroom. The *Call* observed with a kind of civic pride that this story "interested the largest number of outside readers that have ever been interested in a San Francisco occurrence, with the exception of the earthquake and fire"; and that the story not only appeared in New York and London, but was translated into several foreign languages, and published in such countries as China and Japan, where "kimonoed figures read bulletins on the ginze about Abe Ruef-San and his confession of guilt."

There was, of course, a curious contradiction in Ruef's claim to being innocent of the particular extortion charge to which he had entered his plea of guilty. And there was a strong mixture of self-justification with his self-abasement in many parts of his interview with the Associated Press:

. . . I have made no confession. I know much. Some things I shall tell; some things I shall not tell. Wherever an innocent man has been forced into corruption against his will, that man I shall protect. Wherever a man, be he high or low, has entered into corruption willingly, with his eyes open, that man I shall expose.

I will not say at the present moment that Mayor Schmitz is guilty of the charges that have been brought against him, or that he is innocent. I will say this: I wanted to break away from Schmitz before his re-election a year ago last November. I told him: "I am sick of the whole thing and I want to get out. I can't stand for all these labor union bums you have gathered around you and will appoint. They would eat the paint off a house." In answer, the mayor begged me to stay with him and put up the argument that those fellows must be allowed their share or we could never hold the machine together. There was all too much truth in that.

I stayed with Schmitz and I stayed with the machine that I at great labor and pains had built up and assembled. I found then that I had taken a step away from the high and clean ideals with which, I earnestly assure you, I originally entered the political field. I found, in short, that to hold this machine together I had to permit and connive at corruption. In the state of affairs existing it was necessary. But I myself never asked for a dollar from any man, never took a dishonest dollar from the public. The things I did were things that hurt no one.

Before the "boodle" board of supervisors was elected I warned them against crookedness in office. Immediately after their election I got them together and I said to them: "Now, you —— —— ——, if any one of you takes a dollar, I'll prosecute him myself." And I meant it. I was in earnest. But I couldn't carry out my threat and keep the machine from going to pieces. Schmitz was right about that. . . .

Ruef insisted the next day that in his references to labor union politicians he had been misquoted. He was loyal to the Union Labor party, he told a *Bulletin* reporter, and would "never disparage its principles." But the expression, "They would eat the paint off a house," soon entered into the folklore of the city, along with a saying of less certain origin that on the night of the election of the Union Labor supervisors "every burglar alarm in town rang of its own initiative."

During the next few days, the newspapers observed that Ruef seemed to have had a great burden lifted from his shoulders. He was encouraged by hundreds of letters of sympathy, not only from friends, but from strangers all over the nation. One of his old public school teachers wrote, "I have as much interest in you now as I had in that little boy who led my second grade years ago." Relieved and encouraged, Ruef seemed to achieve an almost miraculous recovery of his health. There were some, on the other hand, who regarded this miracle with skepticism, and considered Ruef's actions to be highly disingenuous and carefully planned for their effect on reporters and the public. William J. Burns had noted that on the morning when Ruef was to make his famous statement in court, he had sent for the barber and had his hair cut. Supervisor Coleman protested to a *Chronicle* reporter that "Ruef is of age, and I don't think we led him astray. It was the other way about." Heney took particular notice of Ruef's statement to the Associated Press that "no man possesses physical nerve more than I do. . . . I do not know what my sentence will be. If it be five years across the bay, I can meet that when it comes. I believe that with my personality, and leaving out of consideration the feelings of those who love me and have stood by me, I could spend five years at San Quentin almost as comfortable as in a hotel at Napa Springs. But if the step I took this morning had meant five years or fourteen years or fourteen-hundred years, the fear of that would not have deterred me."

Heney wrote later that Ruef possessed "not only . . . 'physical nerve' but immaculate gall. Indeed I do not know anyone who is his equal in these respects, unless it be his leading counsel, Henry Ach."

The news of Ruef's plea of guilty began a period of avid public curiosity to know how far his promised revelations would extend. A reporter had asked him whether he would involve the railroad capitalist Edward H. Harriman, and his western attorney and political boss, William F. Herrin. Ruef's reply was, "I have never had any dealings with Mr. Harriman, and as far as Mr. Herrin is concerned I have had financial dealings with him, but they were not of a nature to warrant an indictment." Some of Ruef's other statements to reporters were still more enigmatic.

On May 16 Ruef was called to testify before the Oliver grand jury, and the newspapers began an intense rivalry in their efforts to satisfy their readers' desire for information on what he would say. The public and the press were in no mood to respect the traditional secrecy of proceedings in a grand jury room. A few weeks earlier the *Call* had somehow obtained possession of a copy of the stenographic transcript of the confessions of the supervisors in their testimony before the grand jury on March 18, and also of the testimony of several officials of the Pacific States Telephone and Telegraph Company in two subsequent sessions. The *Call* had published this transcript verbatim in its issue of April 26, in six full, seven-column pages of fine print. The publication of this tremendously important and striking "human document," the *Call* said proudly, "was merely a question of newspaper energy and enterprise in getting and printing it—and the *Call* had the energy and the enterprise. Its contemporaries had not."

When Ruef went before the grand jury on May 16, however, it was the *Bulletin* which scooped its rivals. That afternoon its front page bore the headline: RUEF INDICTS, followed by the names of Schmitz, Calhoun, Herrin, Tevis, Drum, Mullally, Ford, and Abbott. Purporting to describe what Ruef "is . . . testifying," the *Bulletin* supplied a wealth of detail, quite without explanation of how it could know what Ruef was testifying. There were such sub-headlines as "Herrin Charged with Grave Felony," followed by a description of the $14,000 bargain between Herrin and Ruef in the 1906 campaign; and "Brothel Funds went to Schmitz," with a description of the "municipal crib." Greatest emphasis was given to the details of the $10,500,000 project of William S. Tevis and his Bay Cities Water Company.

The fact was that all of this information came from confessions which Ruef had made to William J. Burns several days before, particularly on May 7. Burns had turned his notes over to the *Bulletin* with the idea of rewarding Fremont Older for his important and still secret part in the prosecution. But the source of the *Bulletin's* information was not generally known until several months afterward; and other leading newspapers, unwilling to let the *Bulletin* outshine them, began to use all of their ingenuity in devising accounts of what Ruef "was testifying." During the next few days the *Call*, the *Chronicle*, and the *Examiner* published what were represented to be accurate circumstantial reports. Actually, these were mainly reshufflings of the confessions of the supervisors, Ruef's public statements, and the *Bulletin's* revelations. Some purely imaginary details were added, which later proved to be entirely wrong. The *Call* published long verbatim passages of Ruef's alleged testimony on the United Railroads matter, when in fact there had been no stenographer present at that particular session.

Ruef did testify before the grand jury, entirely on the subject of the United Railroads trolley ordinance, on May 16. The next morning, he testified concerning the gas rate matter; and a few hours later the grand jury proceeded to the affair of the Parkside franchise, in which it heard the testimony of several of the principals, including Ruef. A few days later, the grand jury took action. It returned fourteen indictments for bribing fourteen supervisors in connection with the trolley ordinance, directed jointly against Ruef, Schmitz, Patrick Calhoun, Thornwell Mullally, Tirey L. Ford, and William M. Abbott. Fourteen similar indictments, in the gas rate matter, were returned against Ruef, Schmitz, and three officials of the Pacific Gas and Electric Company, Frank G. Drum, Eugene de Sabla, and John Martin. And fourteen more indictments, in connection with the Parkside franchise, were returned jointly against Ruef, G. H. Umbsen, J. E. Green, and W. I. Brobeck.

Now that Ruef's testimony had led to these sensational developments, a matter of at least equal importance was the question of what he would testify against Mayor Schmitz, who was about to be tried on the same French restaurant extortion indictment on which Ruef had avoided trial only by pleading guilty. When they had been jointly indicted on the French restaurant charges six months before, Ruef and Schmitz had asked to be tried separately; and since then each had made use of every delay which might postpone his own trial. The personal friendship between them had been steadily deteriorating for more than a year. Ruef had resented the mayor's increasing ideas of his own importance; his efforts to secure the Republican nomination for governor; and his trips to Europe and Washington, D.C. Since Ruef's arrest and confinement in March, followed shortly by the confession of the supervisors, the relations between Ruef and Schmitz had been particularly strained. Ruef was now a prisoner, and his power as a boss was broken. Schmitz was still mayor of the city and free on bail. Messages passed between them through George Keane, now almost the only man whom they both trusted. But during this period, Ruef and Schmitz conferred directly with each other only once, in April. The scene

ATONEMENT

"ATONEMENT"

A cartoon from the San Francisco *Examiner*, May 16, 1907.

of this private conference, ironically enough, was Schmitz's own former bedroom, now serving as Ruef's place of detention. Burns and Heney believed that Schmitz came there to try to persuade Ruef not to turn state's evidence, after learning through Keane that Ruef was negotiating for immunity.

A few days after Ruef pleaded guilty, Judge Dunne set aside the last obstacle to the beginning of the trial of Schmitz. The mayor's attorneys had filed a motion for change of venue, that is, a transfer of the case to some other court, on the ground that Judge Dunne was biased against the defendant. Schmitz had supported the motion with an affidavit stating that Judge Dunne had been for years a close and personal friend of Fremont Older, a bitter enemy of Schmitz; that the judge (a Democrat), had long been a political opponent of the mayor; and that "the said Frank H. Dunne is acting and will continue to act in perfect harmony with the dictates of the . . . newspapers, and with one Rudolph Spreckels and others interested through their private malice and personal motives in the prosecution and persecution of this affiant."

On May 21, 1907, Judge Dunne denied the motion, and the selection of the jury began. On June 5, Heney made the opening statement to the jury and called the first witness for the people, former Police Commissioner Thomas Reagan, whose vote had held up the renewals of the liquor licenses of the French restaurants.

During the several days occupied by the selection of the jury for the trial of the mayor, increasing numbers of would-be spectators had sought to crowd into Judge Dunne's courtroom, in one of the smaller rooms of the Temple Israel. Those who were denied entrance formed noisy crowds in the halls, and interfered with the business of the other courts. To alleviate this congestion, Judge Dunne's department was transferred to another synagogue, the Bush Street Temple, a few blocks away, and it was there that the scenes in the main part of the trial of the people against Eugene E. Schmitz were enacted. The Bush Street Temple was somewhat less imposing than the larger brownstone Temple Israel. One observer described the smaller and older building as constructed of wood, with "Moorish arches and . . . curious Tartar-like minarets." "This strange Old World association," the same writer remarked, "makes a weird contrast with the sordid, degraded testimony being given in the audience-room beneath, where the Judge sits under a gold-lettered Hebrew inscription suggesting virtuous conduct."

The evidence in the trial of Mayor Schmitz was expected to turn upon three main questions: (1) whether as mayor he had caused the police commission to hold up the renewals of the licenses and then to grant them again after the owners had agreed to employ Ruef; (2) whether he had received any of the money from Ruef; and (3) whether he had entered into a conspiracy with Ruef to commit the crime of extortion as defined by the law.

Ex-Commissioner Reagan testified very positively on the first of these questions. "In compliance with [the mayor's] request," he said, "I assisted in holding up the French restaurants." Reagan also told of the mayor's later removal of Commissioner Hutton in order to secure a majority vote for renewal of the licenses after Ruef had been employed; and on this point ex-Commissioner Poheim's testimony substantiated Reagan's. Several of the French restaurant keepers testified that they had gone to Ruef, and had paid money to him, because he was political boss and not because he was an attorney. But having carried its evidence of conspiracy this far, the prosecution rested its case, without calling Ruef as a witness and without attempting to prove that Schmitz had received any of the money from him.

When this occurred, on June 10, there was general astonishment among the spectators. Why had Ruef not been put on the stand? Why had the prosecution not called the very witness whose testimony had been expected to clinch its case? If Ruef himself had pleaded guilty, why should he not testify against his codefendant?

The explanation lay in a new and bitter dispute between Heney and Ruef, which was still unknown to the public. In this dispute, Heney had made up his mind that Ruef would not be a trustworthy witness, but instead would try to save Schmitz from conviction. About May 19, shortly before the opening of Schmitz's trial, Heney had asked Ruef to tell him the facts in the French restaurant extortion cases. This conversation took place in Heney's office, with District Attorney Langdon also present. According to Heney's account, Ruef admitted that he had given half of the French restaurant money to Schmitz; but

Ruef also made several statements which tended to justify his own part in the matter. One was that he had no intention of taking the cases of the French restaurant keepers until the *Bulletin* had published an article denouncing him, and daring him to take them. Another was that he had then accepted an agreement with a regularly constituted French Restaurant Keepers Association, to represent them in all their legal business for two years.

From the testimony of the French restaurant keepers before the grand jury, several months before, Heney knew "that the French Restaurant Keepers Association was a mythical creation of Ruef's own brain"—that the proprietors had not known that they were members of any such association until Ruef told them they were. Moreover, after Ruef had left his office, Heney sent out for a file of the *Bulletin,* and discovered that its first article denouncing Ruef in the French restaurant matter had appeared in the last edition for January 7, 1905, the day *after* the date of Ruef's written contract with Priet.

Having satisfied himself that two of Ruef's statements in his own justification were false, Heney had refused to believe his other statements, particularly that there had been no prior understanding or corrupt conspiracy between Schmitz and himself. Heney had Ruef brought to his office again, and confronted him with the *Bulletin* file. As Heney recalled the conversation which followed, he told Ruef, "You will have to admit yourself that I have demonstrated that you have been lying to us about your motives in accepting this pretended employment from the French restaurant keepers, which was in fact as clear a hold-up as any highwayman ever committed."

Ruef then "simply laughed in my face and, shrugging his shoulders, said, 'Well, what of it?' "

Heney replied: "This of it. You are an unmitigated liar, and I would not believe you under oath in any material matter where you were not corroborated by reliable evidence." He accused Ruef of lying, and of withholding facts, in his statements to Burns and to the grand jury on the trolley ordinance, the gas rate, the Parkside case, and other matters.

"I don't believe you ever acted in good faith with anybody in your life," Heney told Ruef, "but you have overreached yourself this time. You think you have handed us a gold brick, but

you will find that you have that gold brick left on your hands."
Heney then ordered Ruef out of his office, and told him never
to come back. "The immunity agreement is off," he concluded,
"and if I have my way you will be prosecuted on at least one of
each set of cases in which you have been indicted." A few days
later, when Burns again brought Ruef to Heney's office, Heney
refused to see him.

It was this break with Ruef which led Heney, with the consent
of District Attorney Langdon, to rest the people's case against
Schmitz on June 10 without calling Ruef as a witness. Several
of Heney's associates in the prosecution were very doubtful
that this was the best policy. Hiram Johnson, Charles Cobb, and
Joseph J. Dwyer urged that Ruef's testimony that he had paid
the money to the mayor would greatly strengthen the case.
Heney admitted this, but he insisted that Ruef's testimony on
other points would do the case more harm than good.

Heney was forced to modify this opinion, however, when on
June 11 the mayor proceeded to take the stand as a witness in
his own defense. Schmitz denied the charges of ex-commissioners
Reagan and Poheim. In cross-examination, Heney asked the
mayor whether Ruef had paid him part of the five thousand
dollars he had received from the French restaurants. Over the
strenuous objections and against the repeated advice of his
own counsel, Schmitz answered the question. He replied, "I
didn't know that Mr. Ruef got any five thousand dollars, nor
did I receive any part of it."

After the adjournment of the session of the court in which the
mayor had made these flat denials, Burns and Johnson urged
Heney to put Ruef on the stand as a witness in rebuttal. Heney's
accounts state that he finally agreed, under certain conditions.
First, he wrote out a list of questions, and instructed Burns to
take them to Ruef and bring back Ruef's written answers. The
questions were concerned with how much money Ruef had received, and when; and how much money he had paid Schmitz,
and when. Heney would hold no further conversation with
Ruef before he was put on the stand; and he would give Ruef no
assurance that his immunity agreement would be renewed.
Burns returned with Ruef's written answers to the questions.

The next day, after the defense had rested, Heney called Ruef
to the stand as a prosecution witness in rebuttal. "Did you," he

asked, "in January or February, 1905, in this City and County, at the house of Eugene E. Schmitz, the defendant, at number 2849 Fillmore Street, give to Eugene E. Schmitz any money, and if so how much, and in what kind of money?"

An objection was overruled, and Ruef answered, "I did, $2,500 in currency."

Heney asked, "Did you then and there tell him that it was his share of the money you had received from the five French restaurant keepers?" This was objected to as a leading question, and Heney changed it to "What did you then and there say to him when giving him the money?"

Ruef answered, "I didn't say to him that it was his share of the money which I had received from the French restaurants. I did say to him that I had received from the French restaurants the sum of $5000, and that if he would accept half of it I should be glad to give it to him. Thereupon I gave it to him."

Ruef also testified that he had paid the mayor $1500 in currency about a year later, out of the second installment of his fee.

When Schmitz's leading counsel, Joseph C. Campbell, began his cross-examination of Ruef, it was clear that the defense had been prepared for the possibility that Ruef might testify as he did. Campbell was well supplied with ammunition for an attempt to discredit Ruef's testimony. He began with a series of questions designed to show that Ruef was testifying under coercion by Burns and Heney. He drew from Ruef the statements that Burns had visited him "probably . . . 150 times in the last 60 days," and that Ruef had also had several conversations with Heney and Langdon. Then Campbell proceeded:

Q. It is a fact, is it not, Mr. Ruef, that at the present time you expect these gentlemen connected with the prosecution in this case to use what influence they have in your favor to secure for you leniency upon certain criminal charges now pending against you?

A. Upon my testifying fully and fairly to the truth in these matters, yes, sir.

Q. Please answer the question.

A. That is an answer. . . .

Q. Who is to be the judge, Mr. Ruef, as to whether or not your testimony is true, you or the prosecution?

A. Well, I shall insist that I am.

Q. What is their situation about it?

A. They can tell you better than I can.

Q. You don't know yourself?

A. No, I presume they—knowing me as they do, that they take my word. . . . The testimony which I am giving here now is true. I expect the prosecution will believe it to be true, and expect that they will carry out what they have said, namely that they will do what they can to assist in securing leniency.

Campbell also asked a series of questions referring to statements which Ruef had made in the past, and designed to show that Ruef had lied in making these statements. He asked why Ruef had pleaded guilty, and why he had said, at the same time, that he was not guilty. Heney objected to these questions as not within the scope of proper cross-examination, and Judge Dunne sustained the objections. Campbell continued:

Q. Mr. Ruef, were you present at the house of the defendant in the month of December, 1906, in the presence of Mr. Drew, Mr. Metson, the Mayor and myself one afternoon when it was raining?

A. December, 1906.

Q. Just at that time, if you can fix it that way, at the time our firm were employed in the case of the defendant one Sunday afternoon?

A. I recall meeting you there.

Q. In the parlor of the Mayor's house on that afternoon?

A. Yes, sir.

Q. In the month of December, 1906, in the City and County of San Francisco, in the presence of the parties named, . . . did you not say that you had never given the Mayor one dollar of the money received from the French restaurants?

A. I do not recall having said that.

Q. Will you say you did not?

A. I can only say that I do not recall having said that at that conversation. I have said that at other times.

Having thus suggested to the jury that Ruef would say anything at any time that might be in his own interest, Campbell concluded with a question designed to show what Ruef's present interest was: "Now, I will ask you . . . if you are not now giving your testimony under the expectation and hope of immunity, complete immunity?"

Heney objected: "What his hopes or expectations may be is immaterial, incompetent and irrelevant." The objection was sustained.

In re-direct examination, Heney asked Ruef:

Q. At the time you stated that you had not given the Mayor any part of the money from the French restaurants, you were not under oath?

A. No.

Q. Were you telling the truth?

A. I am telling the truth now.

Q. So you were not telling it then?

A. Well, that is the natural deduction, that I was equivocating about the proposition.

"It will be noticed," Heney wrote later in recalling this episode, "that Ruef draws a line of distinction between not telling the truth and equivocating. It would be interesting to know what definition he would give as constituting plain ordinary lying."

Early in the evening of June 13, the jury retired to consider their verdict. They took only one ballot, on which they found the defendant, Eugene E. Schmitz, guilty of extortion. Convicted of a felony, Schmitz was ordered into the custody of the sheriff to await sentence. His attorneys asked that he be admitted to bail, on the ground that he was still mayor of the city, and that many matters of great importance required his attention. Judge Dunne denied the request, and Schmitz was confined in the county jail.

What followed was a strange interlude in the history of the mayoralty of San Francisco. The law provided that if a mayor was convicted of a felony, he automatically vacated his office; and there was little doubt that the vacancy occurred as soon as the jury rendered its verdict. Under the charter, the election of a new mayor to fill an unexpired term devolved upon the board of supervisors. But sixteen of the supervisors, as a result of their confessions, were guided at this time mainly by their hopes that the prosecution would honor their conditional immunity contracts. They were, as Lincoln Steffens put it, "good dogs." In the opinion of Steffens, the country's best-known authority on municipal corruption, they were "the best board of Supervisors in

America," and he recommended that other cities adopt the same method of putting their law-makers on good behavior. Obviously this board was not likely to take a step as important as the election of a mayor without specific instructions from the prosecution. In other words, the selection of a mayor devolved upon the district attorney's office. But this election was a very delicate matter, and the prosecution was not ready with a candidate.

The status of the mayor's office had already become a subject of bitter controversy, especially between business and labor. While Schmitz was still mayor, a "Committee of Seven," composed of representatives of the Chamber of Commerce and other leading commercial bodies, had offered to take over the reins of government. Organized labor had strongly resented this proposal; and the district attorney's office had rejected it because of a fear that, in the words of Rudolph Spreckels, it would serve the interests of "Calhoun, Herrin and the coterie who are inimical to the Prosecution."

When Schmitz was convicted, various factions were anxious to influence the naming of his successor. In order to allow time for a thoughtful solution of the problem, the prosecution resorted to a stopgap. Although Schmitz was in the county jail, awaiting sentence, the office of mayor was not immediately declared vacant. On the theory that the mayor was "temporarily unable to perform his duties," and under the charter provision for that contingency, the district attorney advised the supervisors to elect one of their own members as acting mayor. On June 17, they elected Supervisor Gallagher. Schmitz, clinging to the theory that he was still mayor himself, sent an order to Chief Dinan for a policeman to be stationed at the door of the mayor's office, and to keep Gallagher out of it. But the next morning agents of the district attorney forcibly removed the policeman, and Gallagher entered to undertake his duties as acting mayor.

On July 8, Judge Dunne sentenced Schmitz to five years in the state penitentiary at San Quentin. Before pronouncing sentence, the judge addressed some remarks to the prisoner. He began by describing the verdict of the jury as "a message to all the people that in the city of San Francisco law and order are supreme, that no man, no matter how exalted his station or how strong and powerful the social and financial influences which surround him, is above the law." The judge went on to express regret that five years was the maximum sentence which the law provided. "However," he said, "by your conviction you will lose the respect and esteem of all good men."

Schmitz did not listen calmly. He interrupted several times, protesting angrily against the humiliation of "this lecture." He shouted that the higher courts would overrule his conviction, and that the people would reëlect him as their mayor. After the court had adjourned he told a reporter: "It has been impossible to secure a fair trial from Judge Dunne. The animus nurtured in his heart for years came out this morning." He was returned to the county jail, where he was to be confined for several months, awaiting the outcome of the slow and tedious process of appeal.

With the sentencing of Schmitz, it was no longer possible to postpone the declaration of a vacancy in the mayor's office and the election of a new mayor, rather than an "acting mayor." But although more than three weeks had elapsed between the verdict and the sentence, the prosecution had still not been able to solve the problem of whom it should instruct the supervisors to elect as Schmitz's successor. The result was another remarkable expedient. The prosecution decided that another member of the board of supervisors should be elected mayor with the understanding that he would resign when a more suitable successor could be found among the eligible citizens.

The dubious honor of this choice fell upon the unfortunate Boxton. On July 9, the board resolved that the mayoralty was vacant, Boxton resigned as supervisor, and the board elected him to the higher office. The unhappy dentist, a criminal who had turned state's evidence to escape punishment, became "The Honorable Charles Boxton, Mayor of the City and County of San Francisco." The *Examiner* commented acidly: "Having put our bribe-taking Mayor in jail, and having put in his place a taker of smaller bribes, we have now substituted for Gallagher, Boxton, who differs from Gallagher principally in having sold his vote for still less of the bribing corporations' money."

For Boxton himself, the position was one of excruciating embarrassment. "When I think," he said on taking the oath of office, "of the things that have come into my life in the past ten years, I realize how few of them were of my own planning. When we came back from Manila, I had no idea of politics, but they insisted on making heroes of us, and I had to run for Supervisor.

Now I wish I had not done it." And a little later he told reporters: "This has come to me as a great surprise. I very much regret the circumstances which have led up to this appointment. I hope that the people will bear with me for the few weeks that I am in office. As to my official policy, I cannot discuss that at present. . . . The only thing I can say is that I believe during the short time I will hold the office the people will have no cause to—to again find fault with me."

Once again, Schmitz asserted his claim that he was still mayor. This time, a crowd of his followers stationed themselves outside the door of the mayor's office to prevent Boxton from entering. Boxton announced that he would undertake his duties in another place; and his first official act was an order discharging the secretaries who did not appear at the new "mayor's office." In the subsequent confusion, the city auditor was in doubt as to whose signature he should recognize as that of the mayor, and in at least one case the auditor refused to approve a claim on the treasury until it had been signed by *three* "mayors," Schmitz, Gallagher, and Boxton.

On the day of Boxton's election, the district attorney announced a plan for a convention, to choose a candidate whom he would then instruct the supervisors to elect. Langdon proposed a convention of thirty members, fifteen from organized labor and fifteen from commercial bodies. The Labor Council would have eight delegates, and the Building Trades Council seven; the fifteen business delegates would be apportioned three each among the Chamber of Commerce, the Merchants' Association, the Board of Trade, the Real Estate Board, and the Merchants' Exchange. But this project broke down in a tangle of jealousies and suspicions. Langdon, Heney, and Spreckels decided that they would have to choose a candidate themselves.

The man they sought must be free of associations with the large interests which the prosecution was attacking; his standing must be such as to convince the public that he was no mere tool of the prosecution; and he must be willing to accept the office under the highly unusual circumstances which prevailed. This was not an easy combination to find. The position was offered to Dr. John Gallwey, who refused it, partly on the ground that he could be of more service to humanity in the practice of medicine. And Judge Ralph Harrison, a former member of the state supreme court, declined to undertake such an onerous assignment at his time of life.

The man who accepted was Dr. Edward Robeson Taylor, one of the most distinguished professional men in the city. Taylor was both a physician and an attorney, and was widely known and respected in both fields. For many years he had been president of the Cooper Medical College; and at this time, at the age of sixty-eight, he was dean of the Hastings College of Law.

On July 16, after Boxton had served as mayor for one week, he resigned, and the supervisors elected Taylor in his place. Then, at last, the prosecution could order the resignations of the supervisors who had confessed to bribery. There had been some public criticism of the prosecution for keeping these members of the "boodle board" in office during the period of more than four months since their confessions. But when supervisors resigned, the mayor had the power to appoint their successors. While Schmitz was mayor, this would simply have presented him with control of the legislative branch of the government. Under Gallagher, or Boxton, the prosecution itself would have had to select nearly a whole new board. This task could now be turned over to Mayor Taylor; and as soon as the new mayor had found the necessary number of well-respected citizens who were willing to serve, the disgraced officials resigned and their successors were appointed. There were no labor representatives on the new list, but Taylor explained that this was because such labor leaders as Walter Macarthur, Michael Casey, and Will French had declined. Schmitz, from the county jail, "appointed" fifteen men from various labor unions. This was a forlorn hope, and the state supreme court soon confirmed the validity of Taylor's election and hence of his appointments.

Most of the newspapers received the new regime with approval. But the *Examiner* was dissatisfied. Hearst had asked Langdon to give the mayoralty to Joseph J. Dwyer. Rudolph Spreckels had opposed this suggestion. The *Examiner* then published editorials ridiculing the elections of Boxton and Taylor, and charging the prosecution with "doing politics." When the first of these editorials appeared, the *Bulletin* called it "the *Examiner's* first overt act" of "abandoning reform." Said the *Bulletin:* "Hearst and Harriman having entered into an alliance in New York, the *Examiner* has broken away from the prosecution."

Up to this time, the prosecution had received relatively little criticism, and fairly general praise, from the newspapers. Its achievements were beyond dispute. With firmness and ingenuity it had broken a corrupt political machine. It had forced the boss to plead guilty to extortion. It had convicted the mayor of extortion and removed him from office. It had forced the supervisors to confess to bribery, and had removed them from office as soon as it was practical to do so. Thus far its main successes had been achieved against corrupt politicians, corrupt "Union Labor" politicians. It was now ready to enter a new phase, a relentless attack upon the bribers instead of the bribed, and upon men of great wealth, prestige, and social influence.

CHAPTER XVIII

The telephone cases

THE prosecution's cases against Louis Glass, vice-president and general manager of the Pacific States Telephone and Telegraph Company, and Theodore V. Halsey, the company's political agent, were unlike the other bribery charges in that the vital evidence was in no way dependent upon the testimony of Ruef. Of the corporations involved in the various charges, only the Pacific States company had paid money directly to public officials, that is, to the supervisors. The others had paid money to Ruef, an attorney and political boss, and Ruef had paid some of it to the supervisors.

In their confessions before the grand jury, several members of the board had told of receiving $5,000 bribes from Halsey in a room in the Mills Building. The grand jury had returned indictments against Halsey for bribing ten supervisors, on their testimony alone. After examining a number of officials of the company, the grand jury had concluded that Glass was the executive official who had approved the payment of the money to Halsey out of the corporation's funds. From the evidence, it appeared that Glass had conspired with Halsey, who was his brother-in-law, as well as his subordinate in the company, in committing the crimes charged. The bribery indictments against Glass had followed.

Glass was a very able executive and capitalist. He had risen from the position of telegraph operator, and had become first vice-president and general manager of the Pacific States company in 1898. He was also the leading organizer of the telephone service in the Philippine Islands. In 1905 he had organized the Philippine Telephone and Telegraph Company, of which he was president and one of the leading stockholders. He was planning to leave the Pacific States company in order to give his full time to the Philippine enterprise; but in the fall of 1905 the Pacific States company's president, John I. Sabin, had died. Sabin had been a brother-in-law both of Glass and of Halsey. His death came at a critical time, when the rival Home Telephone Company was making a strong bid for a franchise to set up a competing telephone system in San Francisco. Glass had agreed to continue with the Pacific States company as acting president until the Bell system could find a suitable man to take Sabin's place.

It was while Glass was still acting president that Halsey had made the bribery payments in the Mills Building, on February 23 and 24, 1906. The payments had failed to achieve their purpose. Most of the supervisors had failed to stay bought, and instead had followed Ruef's orders to vote for the competitive franchise.

In January, 1907, there was a reorganization in which the Pacific States company was consolidated into the new Pacific Telephone and Telegraph Company. Glass had continued as first vice-president, though expecting to transfer his activities entirely to the Philippine company as soon as possible. In the meantime he had sent Halsey to Manila, essentially as his personal representative, with an understanding that Halsey would also be promoted to an executive office in the Philippine Island system. Halsey was in Manila when he was indicted for bribery in San Francisco; but he waived extradition and returned to face trial.

Following the indictments of Halsey and Glass, in March 1907, the newspapers generally assumed that they were guilty, especially after the *Call* published a full transcript of the grand jury testimony in its issue of April 26. Early in May the telephone operators went on strike. "The girls," said the *Call*, "argue that the company paid out more than $80,000 for corrupt purposes last year," and that if it could afford to spend that much on bribes to politicians, it could afford to raise the wages of its own underpaid employees. The company was not inclined to agree with this reasoning, particularly in view of the triple disasters it had suffered—the destruction of most of its San Francisco installations by the earthquake and fire, the beginning of a competing system by the Home Telephone Company, and the indictments. Although the strike lasted three months, the company steadfastly refused to give in or to arbitrate. Instead it hired and trained a new staff of operators, and when the nearly five hundred striking girls at last offered to return to work, the company reëmployed less than half of them.

In their court battles, the harrassed telephone executives were equally stubborn and resourceful. Hopeless as the case might appear, they were resolved to spare no effort for the best possible defense. As chief counsel for Glass, they selected Delphin M. Delmas, a San Francisco attorney who was at that moment undoubtedly the most celebrated criminal lawyer in the United States.

In appearance, Delmas strikingly resembled Napoleon Bonaparte, and he was often referred to as "the Napoleon of the bar." When Glass was indicted in San Francisco, Delmas was in New York as chief counsel in the defense of Harry Kendall Thaw, who had murdered the architect Stanford White. The defense of Thaw by Delmas had been hardly less sensational than the circumstances of the murder itself, which was committed before a large crowd at Madison Square Garden. The Thaw jury had failed to agree upon a verdict. But San Franciscans drew pride from the belief that Delmas had won a brilliant victory over the famous New York district attorney, William Travers Jerome. Fresh from this dubious triumph, Delmas returned to San Francisco to take charge of the defense of Louis Glass.

The indictment on which Glass was first brought to trial happened to be the one which charged him with the bribery of Supervisor Boxton. And the day on which Boxton was called to the stand as the first witness of the trial, to repeat his confession of bribe-taking, was the same day, July 10, on which he was required to perform his first duties as mayor. During the greater part of the week when he was chief executive, Boxton was kept hurrying back and forth between the witness stand and the mayor's chair. Under direct examination by Heney, he testified in painful detail to receiving the $5,000 bribe. Delmas, in cross examination, introduced the text of the affidavit which Boxton had signed along with the other supervisors in October of the previous year, claiming that he had never committed any crime. Thus Boxton was forced to admit that he had once lied under oath. For hours, Delmas subjected his honor the mayor to merciless humiliation, the more effective in that on the surface it was scrupulously polite.

Delmas did his best to discredit Boxton's testimony that he had received a bribe from Halsey. But Glass, not Halsey, was the defendant in this particular trial, and the main plan of Delmas was to prevent the prosecution from establishing a conspiratorial connection between Halsey and Glass. In the grand jury hearings, this connection had appeared chiefly through the testimony of Emil J. Zimmer, who had been the company's auditor and confidential secretary at the time of the bribery payments. Zimmer had testified that during that period he had paid several large amounts to Halsey, in currency, without receiving vouchers, without knowing the purpose, and simply on instructions from Glass as acting president. During the same period Zimmer had also approved a number of vouchers submitted by Halsey for "special expenses . . . as per detail on file," but the details were apparently filed only in Glass' memory. On the company's books, all such payments to Halsey came out of the "reserve for contingent liabilities," and were eventually attributed to "legal expense." Subsequently, in September, 1906, Zimmer had been promoted from auditor to second vice-president.

When Heney called Zimmer as a witness in the trial of Glass, he expected him to repeat the testimony which he had given before the grand jury. But to Heney's surprise and irritation, Zimmer now refused to testify at all. Addressing Judge Lawlor, Zimmer said: "Your Honor, meaning no disrespect to the court, I have decided not to be sworn as a witness in this case." The grand jury, he continued, had "indicted a number of gentlemen on evidence which I have read, and it seems to be insufficient, and for that reason I have taken this stand to protect my own interests."

Heney rose with visible anger to protest that the witness had concealed this intention until the last moment, and had purposely waited to reveal it until after the beginning of the trial had placed the defendant once in jeopardy. Delmas protested suavely against such a conclusion by the assistant district attorney. Judge Lawlor ordered Zimmer to take the oath. Zimmer did so, but he still refused to answer questions. The judge then instructed him as to his rights and duties as a witness. Zimmer stated emphatically that he did not place his declination on the ground that his testimony might incriminate him. In fact, according to Heney himself, the prosecution had assured Zimmer that in carrying out the orders of his superior he had not been criminally involved.

For his refusal to testify, Judge Lawlor sentenced Zimmer to five days in the county jail for contempt of court. Zimmer served the sentence, and was again called as a witness. He still refused to testify, and was sentenced to serve another day. He then refused for the third time, went back to jail, and paid a fine of $500.

Delmas denied that he had ever seen Zimmer until the day when he first refused to give evidence. But Heney felt sure that it was Delmas who had planned the maneuver of Zimmer's refusal, and for a time Heney's anger was so apparent that Delmas sought to capitalize on it. He baited Heney unmercifully. "I have always assumed," said Delmas, "that the office of a prosecutor, who holds in his hand the official sword of justice, was to be administered in a spirit of justice, and that . . . the hand which . . . directed the blow did so in sorrow and not in anger." He had supposed, he said, that the prosecutor did not come to the bar with "his face flushed with blood and the veins of his temples swollen with malice and revenge, and with a voice vibrating with passion." This, said Delmas, was "a spectacle that no one could behold without sorrow or regret." He called Heney a "human bloodhound," who was "ready to sell his services for blood money wherever they are required." And he referred to "a certain fiendish and insatiable desire to inflict pain upon others, which seems to characterize the learned gentleman from Arizona, who can speak of this city as 'my' city."

Heney protested. "I am indignant, it is true," he said, "at the way my city has been crucified. If I say that our laws have been trampled in the dust, I say it in indignation and not anger."

After a number of such passages, Judge Lawlor requested counsel on both sides to confine themselves more closely to the evidence.

Heney closed his case against Glass on July 25, without the direct testimony which he had expected Zimmer to provide, and relying instead upon the circumstantial evidence connecting Glass with the bribery. The defense called no witnesses, and introduced no evidence of its own. Instead, in a remarkable closing argument to the jury, Delmas contended that the prosecution's evidence had not established the defendant's connection with the crime beyond a reasonable doubt. He did not admit that any crime had been committed, or that the testimony of the discredited Boxton was sufficient to establish that Halsey had paid a bribe. But he assumed for the sake of argument that if Halsey had made such a payment, some higher officer of the company must have authorized it. The prosecution had rested its case on evidence which tended to show that Glass as acting president was the *only* executive who could have been Halsey's confederate in bribery. Delmas now contended that there were other excutives who *could* have given authorization for the payments at the particular time that they were alleged to have been made. In particular, Delmas suggested that Henry T. Scott, who had been elected president of the company shortly before the dates of the alleged briberies, could have provided the money.

In this *tour de force,* Delmas ignored one aspect of Scott's own testimony in the trial. Scott himself had testified that he did not take over the actual duties of the presidency from Glass until after the fire, in April, and that until that time he had not authorized the payment of any money whatever. Glossing over this flaw in his main edifice, the Scott theory, Delmas went on to construct other theoretical possibilities. In the absence of Zimmer's testimony, Delmas argued, the jury must assume that Zimmer himself, in an excess of zeal, might have cashed the checks *without* authorization from Glass. And still another possible suspect, said Delmas, was none other than Frederick P. Fish, president of the American Telephone and Telegraph Company, which controlled the entire Bell system. Fish and his assistant, Pickering, had been in the West in February 1906. Either of them could easily have brought in the money from New York.

It was soon to become apparent that the complexity of the evidence, not to mention the arguments of counsel, had left the jury completely at sea. They retired to consider their verdict late in the afternoon of Friday, June 26, 1907. In their quarters at the Fairmont Hotel, they debated and balloted until midnight. On Saturday they returned to the courtroom in the Temple Israel, but only to ask that the full testimony of five officials of the company be read to them from the transcript. This took four hours. They did not return to the courtroom again until

Sunday afternoon. Then, having been out forty-seven hours, they announced that they were hopelessly divided.

They were dismissed, and the five jurors who had stood for acquittal explained to newspaper reporters that, in their opinion, the evidence had not identified Glass, beyond a reasonable doubt, as the only executive who could have been the guilty one.

Under the circumstances, a hung jury was no mean accomplishment for the defense. But it was not enough. Within a few days, a new jury was impaneled and Glass was brought to his second trial, this time for the bribery of Supervisor Lonergan. In some respects the second trial was to be a repetition of the first, but with the important difference that the defense had now fully revealed its strategy, and had lost the advantage of surprise. The prosecution, in the meantime, had had the opportunity to seal the holes in its case.

When Heney made his opening statement in the second trial, one of the most interested spectators was Charles Fonda, foreman of the first Glass jury and one of the five who had held out for acquittal. Fonda brought his wife, and asked Heney to get her a seat. He explained to a *Bulletin* reporter that he had received very strong criticism from his wife and his friends since the first trial, and that he wanted his wife to hear the evidence in detail, in the interests of peace in the Fonda household. "After all," he said, "it was simply a case of a 'Scotch verdict,' " by which he meant, presumably, a verdict of "not proven; but don't do it again."

In the second trial, Zimmer again refused to testify, this time on the ground that he might incriminate himself. His earlier refusals had led to his indictment for contempt of court, and he had been convicted in a trial before a justice of the peace, who sentenced him, shortly afterward, to three months in the county jail. He appealed to the higher courts. In any event, the prosecution was now fully prepared for Zimmer's refusal to give testimony against Glass, and had built a case which did not rely upon it. This time, the prosecution proved from the company's records and the testimony of its treasurer, Frederick W. Eaton, that only Glass could have authorized checks cashed on February 23 and 24, 1906, and that in particular President Henry T. Scott could not have done so.

Again the defense introduced no evidence, and again Delmas relied on his closing argument. But that argument had now lost its force, and Delmas' famous way with juries was perceptibly less effective. Instead it was Heney who won the battle of the closing arguments. Over the strenuous objections of counsel for the defense, Judge Lawlor permitted Heney to bring in a large chart representing the alleged events of February 23, 24, and 26, 1906. This chart listed six of the company's checks, cashed at various banks, and totaling $50,000. It also listed the names of eleven supervisors, and the specific amounts they had received, also totaling $50,000.

The second Glass jury was out only twenty-five minutes, and its first ballot was unanimous for conviction. Five days later, on September 4, 1907, Judge Lawlor sentenced Glass to five years in San Quentin penitentiary. Glass was confined in the county jail, where he was to remain for several months, awaiting the outcome of his appeal.

During this period, Glass and Zimmer were temporarily relieved of their active duties as vice-presidents of the Pacific Telephone and Telegraph Company. But the company stood by them. They were not removed from office; and in fact they were to continue to be listed as the first and second vice-president, respectively, until 1912.

While the second trial of Glass was in progress, Theodore V. Halsey had also been brought to trial for the bribery of Supervisor Lonergan. Before the selection of the jury could be completed, Halsey was stricken with appendicitis. He underwent an operation, and, his health continuing to be poor, his trial was indefinitely postponed.

In one aspect of the telephone cases, there was a certain poetic injustice. The alleged bribes paid on behalf of the Pacific States Company had been entirely unsuccessful, while those paid on behalf of the Home Telephone Company had fully achieved their object, the competitive franchise. Yet it was the Pacific States officials who were being prosecuted, while the Home Company officials were not. The main reason for this was simply that Abram K. Detwiler had disappeared from his home in Toledo, Ohio, at the time of his indictment, and could not be found. Heney explained in a statement to the newspapers that Detwiler had apparently paid the money to Ruef out of his own pocket, rather than from funds of the Home Telephone Company, and that there was no way to trace the money except through Detwiler himself.

CHAPTER XIX

The trials of Tirey L. Ford

O F T H E various bribery payments revealed by the confessions
of the supervisors in March, 1907, the largest had come indirectly
from the United Railroads. Seventeen supervisors had confessed
to receiving a total of $85,000 from Ruef for their votes in favor
of the ordinance permitting the United Railroads to convert all
of its remaining cable car lines to overhead trolleys. The indictments of President Patrick Calhoun, Chief Counsel Tirey L.
Ford, and other officials of the company had been delayed until
May, while the prosecution was seeking to persuade Ruef to
furnish more direct evidence against them.

When the confessions of the supervisors were first announced,
on March 18, Calhoun was in New York. He immediately issued
a statement denying that his company had ever "paid or authorized any one to pay . . . a single dollar to the Mayor,
Supervisors or any public official of the city of San Francisco
or the State of California." Calhoun also told the New York press
that he had "a warm personal regard for Mayor Schmitz," and
that when Schmitz was in New York he had invited him to his
home. "Anyone who knows me," said the proud Calhoun,
"knows that if I had bribed him I would not have invited him
to my house."

A few hours later Calhoun's assistant, Thornwell Mullally,
in charge of the corporation's affairs in San Francisco, issued a
statement which also denied that money had been paid "to any
official." The *Bulletin* remarked the next day that "that word
'official' is bound to become historic"; and events were to bear
out this prediction. During all the controversies which raged
around this matter for years afterward, the United Railroads

executives neither denied nor affirmed that they had paid $200,-
000 to Abraham Ruef, attorney at law.

Calhoun returned to San Francisco in April, and was called
before the grand jury on May 3. He exercised his constitutional
rights of refusing to answer questions. In a public statement he
insisted that this action should "not be misconstrued." It was
not for him, he said, nor for any officer of his company to disprove
"these grave charges. It is for those making them to prove them.
. . . We know that they cannot produce any truthful evidence
connecting . . . any officer of the United Railroads with this
alleged crime." A few days later, Tirey L. Ford was called, and
also declined to testify. In a long statement to the newspapers, he
did his best to avoid the implication that his testimony would
have incriminated him.

On May 16, Ruef gave his testimony before the grand jury
on the trolley matter. The next day, Calhoun gave out a statement addressed "To the American People," charging the prosecution with having "prostituted the great office of the District
Attorney to further the plans of private malice" on the part of
Rudolph Spreckels, Claus Spreckels, and James D. Phelan, who
had organized the Municipal Street Railways of San Francisco
and subscribed to the bulk of its stock. The purpose of these men
in establishing Heney as their private prosecutor, said Calhoun's
statement, had been above all to defame and injure the United
Railroads, for the sake of their own private profit. To serve this
end, Heney and Langdon had "been willing to purchase testimony with immunity contracts, purporting to grant immunity to
self-confessed criminals." The officials of the United Railroads,
said Calhoun, "are ready to meet their enemies in the open,
and before they are through, they expect to show the whole
country the infamy of the methods of the prosecution."

While the threat of indictment was hanging over the heads of
the United Railroads officials, the whole situation was still further complicated by the beginning of the longest, most stubbornly contested, and most violent street car strike that had ever
occurred in an American city. Calhoun resolved not only to
break the strike, but to break the union, and he was to be successful in doing both. The strike began on May 5, 1907. It
paralyzed service completely for many days, and the gradual resumption of traffic with strikebreakers led to a series of riots in

which there were dozens of casualties. Calhoun refused to negotiate with the union. And the strike did not end officially until December, when the union, broken and scattered, finally gave up its charter and went out of existence.

Almost from its beginning the strike was highly unpopular with the general public, and before it was over the question of who was to blame for it became shrouded in controversy. Calhoun sought to connect the prosecution with it, and charged that the strike was another conspiracy of the Spreckels', ex-Mayor Phelan, and their associates to ruin his company in order to secure possession of it for themselves. Fremont Older leveled the counter-charge that Calhoun had precipitated the strike, in order to pose as a man who could free the city from the grip of unionism. It is quite probable, however, that both of these charges were untrue, and that in reality the strike was simply the climax of the union's industrial disputes with the company which had been intensified by the nerve-wracking conditions prevailing since the earthquake and fire.

Calhoun succeeded in making himself a hero in the eyes of many San Francisco employers by his policy of fighting a union to the bitter end. He had caught the union in a very unfavorable position. Outside the ranks of organized labor, sentiment was preponderantly against the strikers, even on the part of many who would have supported them in better times. Among the newspapers they found active sympathy only in Scripps' *Daily News*, which had most of its circulation among workingmen. The *Bulletin* and the *Call*, while full of denunciations of Calhoun, were lukewarm toward the strikers. The *Examiner*, in the past usually prolabor, gave them virtually no support. The *Chronicle* was frankly unsympathetic with the strike, and went so far as to praise the character and demeanor of the "new men," most of whom Calhoun had imported from the East under a contract with the strikebreaking organization of James Farley. Union men, of course, took a very different attitude toward the "scabs," or "finks," and the latter were forced to live in the carbarns, which were converted into fortresses and kept in a state of siege. For months no "Farleyman" dared venture out of a carbarn at night. Throughout the summer and fall of 1907, the newspapers carried almost daily accounts of street car smashups, some of them caused, it was charged, by strikers greasing the tracks on hills.

It was while these tragic events were occurring that the prosecution placed Tirey L. Ford, the distinguished general counsel of the United Railroads, on trial for bribery. Thus the history of the strike, with all of the suffering and danger which it brought to the whole population of the city, paralleled the beginning of the prosecution's long and stubborn efforts to send the leading officials of the United Railroads to prison. Inevitably the emotional controversies aroused by the strike became entangled with the controversies aroused by the "graft prosecution," and each intensified the bitterness of the other.

Ford was a handsome and able man of charming personality, and he had been for years one of the most popular and respected figures in California. The success story of his career had captured the admiration of high society and the common man alike. Beginning as a ranch hand in the Sacramento Valley, he had studied law in the office of a small town lawyer. After serving as a county prosecutor, and a state senator, he had risen to the office of state attorney general, and then to what many had regarded as the still more honorific position of head of the law department of the United Railroads of San Francisco. When Ford was about to be indicted, in May, 1907, even the *Bulletin* described him as "a man whose error was caused by a mistaken loyalty to a corrupt corporation and in whose fall many will sorrow and none will rejoice." Ford's position was made peculiarly embarrassing by the fact that in 1905 he had accepted appointment as a member of the state board of prison directors. He continued to serve in this capacity during the whole period when he was in danger of going to prison himself.

The prosecution's hopes of convicting Ford and Calhoun of the crime of bribery depended on the furnishing of evidence that the United Railroads executives had entered into a conspiracy with Ruef, who was not a public official, to bribe the supervisors, who were. Evidence of such a conspiracy might be either direct, or circumstantial, or, preferably, a combination of both. An important part of the direct evidence would have to come, if at all, from Ruef. Only Ruef and Ford knew precisely what had transpired between the two of them, and there was no way of persuading Ford to tell. The confessions of the supervisors, of course, provided important circumstantial evidence. It was hardly reasonable to suppose that Ruef would have paid them $85,000 for their votes in favor of the trolley ordinance if he had not received all of that and more from the United Railroads. But the prosecution would have to do more than prove that the money had come from the United Railroads. It would have to prove that in promising Ruef a huge "attorney's fee," and later in paying it to him, Ford had not only understood that Ruef would bribe the supervisors with part of it, but had also authorized Ruef to do so.

On May 3, in his first confession to Burns, Ruef had admitted making bribery payments to the supervisors and the mayor out of a $200,000 attorney's fee which he received from Ford. But in this confession, and in all of his statements on the subject during the remainder of his life, Ruef insisted that in his dealings with Ford neither of them had ever made the slightest reference to the possibility that any of the money might have any other purpose than to compensate Ruef for his legal services to the United Railroads, in preparing the text of the proposed ordinance and in advocating it before the board of supervisors. As for the relations between Calhoun and himself, Ruef insisted that not even the subject of his employment as an attorney had ever been mentioned between them.

There is much to be said for the theory that these statements were true. Ford, Calhoun, and Ruef were all attorneys of outstanding ability. Ford was a former attorney general of the state. Calhoun was one of the leading corporation lawyers of the country. And Ruef himself was well known as one of the cleverest practitioners at the California bar. Certainly all three were too well versed in law to have said anything of a conspiratorial nature if they could avoid saying it. It is highly probable that whatever conspiracy there may have been among Calhoun, Ford, and Ruef had remained implicit in the circumstances, and was never put explicitly into words.

Francis J. Heney, however, refused to believe Ruef's assertions on these important points. Heney's state of mind at this time was one of intense and stubborn determination to send Ford and Calhoun to the penitentiary. He had convinced himself that in promising Ruef his huge "attorney's fee," and in paying it to him after the passage of the ordinance, the United Railroads officials must have had some perfectly clear and definite understanding with him that he would have to commit bribery by dividing the money with the supervisors and the mayor. Heney had caught Ruef in false statements about several lesser matters, and he tended to reason from these to the conclusion that Ruef was also lying on this most vital point.

Ruef insisted repeatedly to Heney, Burns, Langdon, and rabbis Kaplan and Nieto that there was no way of knowing what Ford and Calhoun may have known or suspected about the question of whether Ruef would have to share his fee with public officials. Ruef argued further that Ford and Calhoun would not have wanted to know, and would have had every reason to be extremely careful never to mention the subject. Rabbis Kaplan and Nieto became convinced of this. But Heney firmly refused to believe it. Burns informed Ruef that the prosecution would not accept it as "the whole truth" and "a full and fair disclosure," and that as long as Ruef should continue to insist that it was the whole truth, the prosecution would consider his partial immunity agreement as void. Unfortunately, the nature of the "truth" involved was complex enough to have hardened the skepticism of Pontius Pilate.

During the summer of 1907, while the trial of Tirey L. Ford was in preparation, Ruef continued to hope that his immunity agreement might still be made effective. Detective Burns continued to urge Ruef to agree to give testimony against Ford which would satisfy Heney. Rabbi Kaplan urged Heney to accept Ruef's version of the matter. And Rabbi Nieto, after his return from Europe in August, added his efforts to Kaplan's.

Ruef charged in an affidavit filed several months later that Burns had repeatedly asked him to tell more than the truth— to say, for example, that Ford had paid him the money "to put the matter through the Board of Supervisors." Ruef quoted Burns as saying that there was "not much strain in that language, and that I could safely say that, and that it would please Mr. Heney and the prosecution." According to Ruef, he refused to make such a statement, and Burns then asked him to testify "that I thought that Ford understood that money would be given to the Board of Supervisors to pass the trolley franchise," whereupon Ruef replied that even if he were willing to say this, no court would admit as evidence the conclusions of any witness about what anyone else might have thought or understood. Burns, on the other hand, later asserted under oath that Ruef had told him several times: "I am willing to go as far as I can for you, and while I don't remember it that way I will say it." According to Burns, Ruef said this in the presence of Rabbi Kaplan, in the hope of giving the impression that Burns was trying to put words into Ruef's mouth. Burns asserted that he had always strongly disavowed any such intention.

As yet the public had little knowledge of the deadlock between Ruef and Heney. On the first of September, for example, the *Chronicle* speculated that Ruef's testimony as state's evidence would be "the great sensation" of the approaching trial of Ford. But actually Heney had no intention of calling on Ruef to give his testimony as part of the prosecution's case, unless Ruef should be willing to change his story. Ruef was not willing.

For the defense of Ford, Calhoun was ready to do everything possible, and to spare no expense. The *Examiner* remarked sarcastically that "Calhoun probably would have found it cheaper to put in an underground conduit system." The private detective force of the United Railroads, already augmented as a result of the strike, was increased to the proportions of a small army, partly in order to counter the efforts of the prosecution's detective force under William J. Burns in such matters as the questioning of prospective jurors. As counsel, the defense had the services of a battery of able lawyers. These included A. A. Moore and his son and partner, Stanley Moore, attorneys for the United Railroads and the Southern Pacific; Alexander King, Calhoun's law partner in New York, who secured admission to the California bar in order to participate in the defense of Ford; and Lewis F. Byington, Ford's brother-in-law and a former district attorney of San Francisco.

The chief counsel for Ford, and the most colorful figure among his defenders, was Earl Rogers of Los Angeles. Rogers had a fabulous though mainly a local reputation as a criminal lawyer. In Southern California he had established an extraordinary record for securing acquittals in murder cases, usually by spectacular devices of a kind seldom encountered outside the pages of fiction. At this period of Rogers' career his drinking, while heavy, had not yet begun to injure his health or to dull his wits. He excelled in cross-examination, and in baiting a prosecuting attorney into a state of maudlin and impotent rage. His biographers assert that these qualities were the ones which recommended him to the indicted officials of the United Railroads, and that the person who probably suggested the employment of Rogers was Luther Brown, a Southern California lawyer and politician who had become the head of the United Railroads' secret service. Luther Brown had been, among other things, a jury investigator for Rogers in Los Angeles.

The prosecution registered bitter complaints against the character of some of the persons the defense employed. Heney asserted in court that the United Railroads detective force included such notorious "desperate characters" as "Dave" Nagle, "Bogie" O'Donnell, and Harry Lorentzen, known as the "Banjo-eyed Kid." Heney also claimed to have seen these individuals in the courtroom itself. The *Call*, owned by Rudolph Spreckels' brother John, and strongly sympathetic with the prosecution, denounced "the retinue of the trolley magnates," and asserted that behind such "lawyers of last resort" as Earl Rogers and Porter Ashe, there trooped "a motley train of gun fighters, professional pluguglies, decoys, disreputable 'detectives,' thugs, women of the half world, and the wolfish pack of gutter journalism." The defense, on the other hand, made almost equally uncomplimentary references to some of the agents of the prosecution.

The selection of the jury for the first trial of Ford began on September 12, 1907; and Earl Rogers immediately took the center of the stage. To the delight of the newspaper reporters, though somewhat to the irritation of the other attorneys on both sides, Rogers appeared in a cutaway morning coat, striped trousers, patent leather shoes, and spats, "his shirt and necktie a symphony of hues that blended more or less harmoniously with his checked waistcoat." In his questioning of veniremen, Rogers promptly began to demonstrate the tactics which had helped to win many of his cases. The questions which he addressed to the prospective jurors made it obvious that his secret agents had canvassed the lists of talesmen to be called, and had secured remarkably detailed information about the backgrounds and prejudices of most of them. Rogers asked one talesman whether he had not said in a saloon conversation that Patrick Calhoun was "one of those dam' Southerners," and "a slave-driver, like his grandfather John C. Calhoun." He asked another whether he was acquainted with "William J. Burns, said to be a detective." Moreover, and to the intense irritation of Heney, Rogers began to ask loaded questions which would tend to put prejudices into the minds of the jurors who were already accepted and sworn, and listening to the further proceedings. For example, Rogers asked a venireman what his attitude would be "if it were proven" that Spreckels, Langdon, and Heney had conspired to seize control of the government of San Francisco "in order that the Spring Valley Water Company might sell its plant to the city."

After more than a week of such proceedings, the twelfth juror was finally admitted. On September 23, Heney made the opening statement for the people in the first trial of Ford, in which the charge was that of offering and paying a bribe to Supervisor Thomas F. Lonergan for his vote on the trolley ordinance. Heney explained to the jury that the prosecution did not expect to prove that Ford had made the offer to Lonergan personally, but rather that Ford had authorized Ruef to make the offer, that Ruef had authorized Supervisor Gallagher to make it, and that Gallagher had caused Supervisor Wilson to make the actual offer to Lonergan.

Lonergan, a baker and former driver of a bakery delivery wagon, took the stand the next day. Under Heney's questioning the embarrassed ex-supervisor testified that Wilson had indeed offered him money for his vote, and that Gallagher had later paid him money for it.

Earl Rogers then cross-examined Lonergan, and he had not proceeded far before introducing a document which created a sensation among the spectators in the courtroom. This was a statement signed by Lonergan only a few days before, flatly contradicting the testimony he had just given, and thus seeming to demolish the credibility of the prosecution's most important witness. The document was in the form of an interview which Lonergan had given to one Walter E. Dorland, who claimed to be a representative of "an Eastern magazine." In it, among other statements defending the policies of himself and the other Union Labor supervisors while in office, Lonergan had said that he had voted for the overhead trolley privilege "for the good of the community," and that no one had promised him any money for his vote.

Confronted with this, Lonergan could only protest weakly that he had not been under oath when Dorland had persuaded him to sign the "magazine" statement. Rogers now seemed to have brought off a sensational coup. When the morning session was over, a *Daily News* reporter hurried to the telephone to say that the prosecution had been "thunderstruck." The *Evening Post* reporter said that "how the brilliant young attorney from Los Angeles . . . got the statement from Lonergan can only be surmised"; but that during the noon recess, when newspaper men asked him what magazine Dorland represented, Rogers had grinned and replied, "Rogers' Magazine."

The fact was that Dorland was not a magazine writer at all, but a secret agent of Rogers and the United Railroads. And when Heney took Lonergan under redirect examination that afternoon it became clear that the prosecution, far from being taken by surpise, had known much more about the matter than Rogers had suspected, and was prepared to make some startling revelations on its own part.

Dorland had first approached Lonergan early in September, and had described himself as a magazine writer preparing an article which would give the former Union Labor supervisors "a square deal," and put them in a better light before the reading public in the eastern part of the country. He had expressed strong sympathy for Lonergan, treated him cordially, and entertained Lonergan and his wife and children with automobile rides. Lonergan had signed the "interview" statement on September 5. A few days later Heney had called him in to ask whether anyone had spoken with him. Lonergan described his relations with Dorland. Heney told Lonergan that Dorland was a United Railroads detective, and that if Dorland made any further approaches to him he should inform Burns at once.

On the evening of September 23, the night before Lonergan took the stand in the Ford trial, Dorland had called Lonergan to invite him for another automobile ride, this time without Mrs. Lonergan. Lonergan told Dorland to call again a little later. He called Burns, and asked his advice. Burns told him to say that he would go, but to take his wife out to the automobile with him. Lonergan followed this course, whereupon Dorland took Lonergan aside, told him that he was embarrassed to see Mrs. Lonergan, and explained that his plan had been for the two men to "make a night of it" with the "two nice young ladies" who were in the automobile. Lonergan declined, and Dorland and the "two nice young ladies" drove away.

On the evening of the 24th, after these developments had been revealed in court, Burns gave a statement to the newspapers. According to Burns' account, he and his men had trailed Dorland and his female companions in another car. After leaving the Lonergans, the party had been joined by J. C. Brown, another United Railroads detective. Dorland and Brown had spent the remainder of the night with the two women, Burns added, under circumstances which established the disreputable character of the latter. Burns asserted that the plan had involved a frame-up designed to compromise the prosecution's key witness, and that one of the women was to have charged Lonergan with attempting a criminal attack upon her.

In an interview with a reporter for the *Examiner,* Dorland insisted that he was not a detective, but a bona fide "historical writer." Asked to name some of his writings, he admitted that he could not, but asserted that he had been collecting material for "a history of California."

The Lonergan-Dorland affair led indirectly to another and even more melodramatic example of the flamboyant tactics to which the defense was resorting. This episode came to be known as the "kidnaping" of Fremont Older.

Because of a blunder on the part of one of Older's reporters, the *Bulletin's* account of Burns' charges confused J. C. Brown, the United Railroads detective, with Luther Brown, the head of the United Railroads detective bureau. Thus through mistaken identity the *Bulletin* described Luther Brown as carousing with the loose women with whom he had been trying to "frame" a witness. The next day, Earl Rogers denounced Older and the *Bulletin* for criminal libel against his friend Luther Brown, who could prove that he had been at home with his family on the night in question.

Rogers and Luther Brown then made secret arrangements to have Older prosecuted for criminal libel in Los Angeles. A Los Angeles justice of the peace, who owed his position to Luther

Brown, issued a warrant for Older's arrest, and two Los Angeles constables made a secret trip to San Francisco to serve the warrant. In order to make it valid, the constables needed the approval of a San Francisco court, and on arriving in the city they proceeded to the chambers of Superior Judge Carroll Cook. Judge Cook himself had been the recipient of much criticism from the *Bulletin* for several years; and he signed the warrant, at four o'clock in the afternoon of September 27.

About an hour later, according to his own account, Fremont Older received a telephone call at Heney's office in the "prosecution house" on Franklin Street. A "Mr. Stapleton" offered to give him some important information if he would come to the Savoy Hotel, nearby on Van Ness Avenue. Older could seldom resist such an offer, and he went. As he walked along Van Ness, an automobile with four men in it drew up beside him. One of the occupants emerged, showed Older a constable's star and the Los Angeles warrant, and ordered him to get into the machine. Older asked that he be permitted to see his lawyer and to arrange bail, and the constable told him that they would go to Judge Cook's chambers where an order for bail could be secured. But as the car drove rapidly toward the southwestern suburbs, Older realized that this promise was not being kept. He noticed that there was another car ahead, and that Luther Brown and Porter Ashe were in it. Older tried to rise in order to attract the attention of someone he knew, or of a policeman. The man beside him pulled him down, and pressed a gun against his side.

Older was now thoroughly shocked and frightened, and as the car drove along "at fully forty miles an hour" he decided that his captors meant to take him to some deserted spot and kill him "while attempting to escape." But instead they drove him to Redwood City, boarded the night train for Los Angeles, and confined Older in a stateroom on the train. Apparently one of the passengers overheard a conversation between Brown and Ashe in the diner, became alarmed for Older's safety, and telephoned the San Francisco *Call* from a station stop. Rudolph Spreckels and Francis J. Heney telephoned Santa Barbara, where Superior Judge Crow issued a writ of habeas corpus shortly after midnight. Early the next morning, when the train drew into Santa Barbara, Older was surprised to see a large crowd gathered at the station. Soon a Santa Barbara officer knocked on the stateroom door, served the writ, and took Older and his erstwhile captors before Judge Crow, who released Older on bail.

The attempt to prosecute Older in Los Angeles was given up, and instead Luther Brown and Porter Ashe were indicted for kidnaping in San Francisco. More than a year later Brown was brought to trial on this charge, and acquitted.

The bizarre developments growing out of Lonergan's appearance as a witness were not the only difficulties which the prosecution encountered in attempting to prove its case against Ford. Fifteen other ex-supervisors followed Lonergan on the stand. James L. Gallagher, and most of the others, repeated fairly closely the details on the trolley matter which they had confessed before the grand jury; but two ex-supervisors changed their stories on highly important points. Andrew M. Wilson now proved unable to remember having carried the offer of a bribe from Gallagher to Lonergan. And Michael W. Coffey asserted that he had voted for the overhead trolley ordinance on its merits, and that he could not remember receiving an advance offer of money for his vote. District Attorney Langdon stated publicly that Wilson and Coffey must have been "reached" by agents of the United Railroads. The prosecution canceled their immunity contracts, and both were promptly indicted for receiving bribes. Wilson later recovered his memory, and explained that he had not known what he was saying, having undergone a minor operation shortly before he was called to the stand, and being still under the influence of an anaesthetic. But Coffey stuck to his new story, and a few months later he was tried for receiving a bribe from Ford and Ruef in the trolley matter. Coffey was convicted, but eventually the state supreme court, by a four to three vote, set aside the conviction.

To the forgetfulness of witnesses Wilson and Coffey was added the disappearance of witness Alex S. Lathan, whose testimony would have been important in connecting Ford with the bribery. As Ruef's chauffeur, Lathan had driven Ruef to the United Railroads offices on May 25, 1906, when Ruef had entered Ford's office carrying an empty cardboard shirtbox, and emerged with the box bulging with packaged currency. Lathan failed to answer a call to the stand in the Ford trial, and the prosecution asserted that the father-in-law of Luther Brown had taken ex-chauffeur

Lathan and his bride on an automobile pleasure trip to some unknown point in Colorado.

Treasurer Starr of the United Railroads had been called to the bedside of a sick relative in the East shortly before the trial began. About the same time, some of United Railroads' books had been sent East, and could not be produced during the trial.

In spite of its various difficulties, the prosecution did succeed in bringing out a considerable body of evidence against Ford. Frank A. Leach, Superintendent of the Mint, produced records which showed that on May 22, 1906, Calhoun had sent $200,000 from the East by a telegraphic order depositing that amount to his credit at the mint in San Francisco; and that Ford had drawn $50,000 of this sum on May 25, $50,000 on July 31, and $100,000 on August 23. The supervisors had testified to receiving their money in two installments, one early in August, the other toward the end of the month. A clerk at the mint, Nathan Selig, who had helped to count and package the small bills which Ford had received on May 25, testified that he could fix the approximate date because he had noticed at the time that it was shortly after the mayor had signed the trolley ordinance; and Selig had remarked to another mint employee, as Ford was leaving with the money, "that I thought it was the supervisors' bit."

On October 2, the prosecution closed its case without calling Ruef as a witness. Heney had made up his mind not to call him unless Ford should take the stand in his own defense to deny that he had paid Ruef the $200,000; and Heney had surmised correctly that Ford would not do this. The defense called no witnesses. In closing arguments to the jury, A. A. Moore and Earl Rogers contended that the prosecution had established no direct evidence against Ford, and only faulty circumstantial evidence. Rogers' closing argument was so emotional that at the end of it he burst into tears and rushed from the courtroom.

Heney, in his closing argument, stated that the prosecution had not put Ruef on the stand "because we did not trust him," and because the defense on cross-examination could have "put words into his mouth."

At this point Lewis F. Byington, Ford's brother-in-law and one of his counsel, interrupted Heney to ask why the prosecution had kept Ruef for several months under threat of sentence and in an elisor's prison, if it did not intend to use him as a witness; and Byington charged that Heney's real reason for not putting Ruef on the stand was that Ruef "would not tell what you wanted him to," and that Ruef's testimony "might free an innocent man."

Heney replied that Ruef had been kept under careful guard because the prosecution feared that agents of the defense would try to tamper with him as they had tampered with other witnesses, particularly Lonergan and Wilson.

The jury retired on the evening of October 4. The next afternoon, the jury reported that it stood eight for acquittal and four for conviction after more than thirty ballots. It was discharged, and the eight members who had voted for acquittal told reporters that the absence of Ruef's testimony had been the decisive element.

Throughout the trial Ruef had been kept in constant attendance in the courtroom, ready to testify if he should be called. When he was not called, he became more anxious than ever. The *Examiner* speculated that "the little boss has decided to face an eternity in prison rather than tell the tale of his dealings with Ford in the way the prosecution wants him to tell it." But actually Ruef still nursed a desperate hope of patching up his immunity agreement, and when the second trial of Ford was beginning, Ruef made further overtures to Heney through Rabbi Kaplan. According to Heney, Dr. Kaplan attempted to arrange an agreement by which Ruef would give certain specific testimony. Heney refused to listen, and finally asked Kaplan to cease all further communication with him. Later Heney learned from Burns what Ruef had offered. This was to reply, when Heney should ask him whether he had received the money from Ford as an "attorney's fee": "Well, yes, that was what we *called* it"— implying by his manner and tone that Ford was perfectly aware of the subterfuge.

The San Francisco election of 1907 was held during Ford's second trial. On November 1, during the noon hour, Heney made a campaign speech in a workingmen's district, in which he advocated the reëlection of Langdon as district attorney. When he had finished, some one in the crowd called out, "Why didn't you put Abe Ruef on the stand?"

Heney replied: ". . . because he wanted complete immunity.

We had given him partial immunity, and when the Ford trial came up he thought he was the whole show. Ruef concluded we could not get along without him. He thought he had us where he wanted us, so he said he would not go on the stand and tell all he knew about the overhead trolley bribery unless we granted him complete immunity, and I told him to go to hell."

On the evening of the same day, in another political speech, Heney added: "We don't want his evidence. He is a liar and we don't want to convict any man on the evidence of such a man as Ruef."

The second trial of Tirey L. Ford was on the charge of bribing Supervisor Jennings Phillips, and in it the prosecution brought out substantially the same evidence as in the trial for the bribery of Lonergan. Again Ruef was not called, and this time Ford was acquitted, on the jury's sixth ballot, December 3, 1907. "Skirmishes never decide battles," Heney told reporters. But in the third and last trial of Ford, in April and May, 1908, for the bribery of Supervisor Coleman, the jury was out only seven minutes, and Ford was acquitted on the first ballot.

CHAPTER XX

"*Public opinion,*" *and the election of 1907*

At the beginning of the graft prosecution in the fall of 1906, every major newspaper in the city had treated it as an occasion for rejoicing, as a declaration of independence, and as a movement to regenerate San Francisco and liberate it from the venality of Boss Ruef, Mayor Schmitz, and other corrupt "Union Labor" politicians. At the outset, almost the only articulate opponents of the prosecution were the political adherents of the Union Labor party.

On October 31, 1906, supporters of the administration held a mass meeting in Dreamland Rink. Ruef made a speech which concluded solemnly: "As sure as there is a God in Heaven, they have no proof as they claim."

Another speaker was Thomas Eagan, who had captured the party's original convention for Ruef in September, 1901, and who was introduced as "the man who rocked the cradle of the Union Labor party." Eagan called the prosecution a "movement led by Rudolph Spreckels and engineered by James D. Phelan, conceived in iniquity and born in shame"—a movement designed to destroy the labor party and labor unions and to regain "control of our fair city."

James L. Gallagher, then acting mayor, issued a statement describing the prosecution as one more plot of the Citizens' Alliance.

San Francisco workingmen and their leaders, outside the inner circle of the Ruef-Schmitz administration, were bewildered, embarrassed, and resentful. Many of them had been proud of their handsome and colorful mayor, and had hoped for great things from him. Reluctant to believe that he had betrayed them, many workingmen preferred to attribute the attacks on him to reactionary employers. And many feared that if the San Francisco experiment should be discredited, it would greatly damage the cause of labor in politics in the eyes of the whole country. There was good reason for this fear. In the East, little was known of the Union Labor party of San Francisco except its name, and there was a tendency to blame the party's disgrace upon unionism as such. The *Nation,* for example, editorialized on November 22, 1906: "A defender of organized labor as a political force must be speechless in view of its San Francisco record."

P. H. McCarthy, president of the Building Trades Council, had originally opposed the Union Labor party, but since 1905 he had been one of its strongest supporters. Under his leadership the Building Trades Council passed resolutions, late in October, 1906, denouncing the prosecution, and endorsing Gallagher's attempt to replace Langdon with Ruef as district attorney. Several unions in the building trades, however, refused to follow McCarthy's lead.

In March, 1907, after the confessions of the supervisors had dealt a very damaging blow to labor's prestige, the San Francisco Labor Council passed resolutions pointing out that it was "a body organized and conducted for purely economic purposes"; that it had never had any connection with the Union Labor party; and that it was "in no way responsible for the conduct or misconduct of any such party organization." At the same time the local union of the United Brotherhood of Carpenters and Joiners resolved that "we repudiate and condemn the action of the gang of boodlers and grafters who have used the name of the labor unions to promote their own ends." Both the Labor Council and the carpenters denounced the private ownership of public utilities as the chief source of political corruption, and demanded the punishment of the bribers as well as the bribed.

During the early months of the graft prosecution, many San Francisco businessmen took pleasure in labor's embarrassment, and heartily endorsed the prosecution's efforts to break the Union Labor political machine. This was particularly true during the period when the prosecution's only important evidence con-

cerned the French restaurant extortion charges against Schmitz
and Ruef. For decades American businessmen had known that
there was an extraordinary amount of corruption in American
politics, especially at the municipal and state levels, and especially
at the points where politics and private business met. But many
businessmen had formed the habit of placing the blame for this
corruption entirely upon the politicians, and of regarding it not
as "bribery," in which the briber was as guilty as the bribed, but
rather as extortion, or "blackmail," in which businessmen who
wished to achieve perfectly honest and necessary ends were forced
to pay tribute to political highwaymen who happened to control
some agency of government. Often the difference between great
profit and great loss to a corporation, and sometimes its very life,
were at the mercy of venal politicians.

One of the most interested observers of the San Francisco graft
prosecution was Lincoln Steffens, who had recently popularized
the idea that wealthy and powerful "big business," in its quest
for special privilege, was itself responsible for the corruption of
American politics. Beginning in 1902 with a study of the railway franchise graft under Boss Ed Butler in St. Louis, and the
exposure of it by Joseph W. Folk as prosecuting attorney, Steffens had written a series of articles for *McClure's Magazine* on
a number of outstanding American city machines. In 1904 he
had gathered the articles together in a book, *The Shame of the
Cities*. Steffens had concluded: "The typical businessman is a
bad citizen. If he is a 'big businessman,' he is twice as bad. I
found him buying boodlers in St. Louis, defending grafters in
Minneapolis, sharing with bosses in Philadelphia, originating
corruption in Pittsburgh, deploring reform and fighting good
government with corruption funds in New York. He is a self-
righteous fraud. He is the chief source of corruption and it
would be a great boon if he would neglect politics."

Certain views which Joseph W. Folk had expressed to Steffens
in St. Louis had made a deep impression on him. Folk believed
that the crime of bribery had reached the proportions of treason
and revolution—that it destroyed democracy, and established
an invisible government, a "system," an inner oligarchy, a government by the worst who called themselves "the best people."
President Theodore Roosevelt expressed similar ideas occasion-

ally during these years. And in San Francisco, the leaders of the graft prosecution espoused this philosophy.

Steffens had met Heney while preparing a series of articles for the *American Magazine* on Heney's work in the Oregon land fraud cases. In November of 1906, and several times during 1907, Steffens came to San Francisco to observe what was to him a remarkable case study, and to prepare a series on the graft prosecution, for the *American*, under the title "The Mote and the Beam, a Fact Novel." One installment was on "Rudolph Spreckels, a Businessman Fighting for His City." Steffens and Heney became intimate and lifelong friends, and Steffens' ideas had an important influence upon Heney's. In many talks with Heney, and in several strategy conferences of the whole group of prosecution leaders, Steffens offered his advice.

On his first visit to San Francisco after the beginning of the prosecution, Steffens noticed the almost unanimous enthusiasm with which the wealthier classes of the city approved a movement which was financed by the president of the First National Bank of San Francisco, Rudolph Spreckels, and which then appeared to be directed entirely against the labor politicians who had "held up" so many businessmen. At this stage, the public had no inkling of the real nature and extent of Heney's plans. Heney told Steffens privately in February, 1907, that if he could trap the supervisors, he would let them go in return for evidence against Ruef; that he would let Ruef go, for evidence against William F. Herrin; and that he would let Herrin go if he would give testimony which would incriminate his superior, Edward H. Harriman, head of the Southern Pacific and Union Pacific railroad systems.

As late as a month after the confessions of the supervisors, when Heney spoke as guest of honor at a banquet of more than a thousand merchants at the Fairmont Hotel, he was applauded and cheered, although his speech strongly criticized businessmen for their share in the responsibility for political corruption. It was only gradually, in the succeeding weeks, that the wealthy businessmen who had for years been fellow members with Heney and Rudolph Spreckels in the Pacific Union Club began to realize the grim seriousness of Heney's intention to pursue graft to its "source" among the "higher-ups." But after the middle of

May, when Ruef turned state's evidence—when it became fully
apparent that the prosecution meant to give immunity to politicians in order to prosecute business executives—then there
were frowns and snubs instead of smiles and congratulations
when Heney and Spreckels went to their clubs for luncheon.
And officers of the Pacific Union Club asked Heney not to bring
Lincoln Steffens there again.

One of the most articulate organs of avowedly "conservative"
opinion in San Francisco was the *Argonaut*. According to general belief, it had long been subsidized by the Southern Pacific.
Certainly it had become the city's most substantial weekly journal, and the interesting trajectory of "conservative" opinion on
the graft prosecution during its first year can be traced with particular clearness in the *Argonaut's* editorial columns. During the
first winter, Ruef and Schmitz and their attorneys had seemed to
be holding the prosecution at bay. In February, 1907, the *Argonaut* asked the public to keep its confidence in the prosecution's
ultimate success, and emphasized that the delays in bringing the
boss and the mayor to trial for extortion were only the delays
"which the law allows to protesting criminals." In March, when
the Union Labor supervisors confessed that they had received
an almost incredible series of bribes from leading corporations,
the *Argonaut's* first reaction was one of shocked humility at these
"astounding" revelations, involving "certain criminals of higher
rank and pretensions. . . . The facts speak for themselves; they
point their own moral; they emphasize their own shame."

But in May, when Ruef entered a plea of guilty and announced that he would testify against his accomplices, the *Argonaut's* attitude toward the prosecution began to change. In particular it began to criticize the policy of granting immunity to
one class, the politicians, in order to prosecute another class, the
corporation executives. And after the street car strike had begun,
the *Argonaut* accused Spreckels and Heney of participating in it
on the labor side, in order to complete the ruin of Calhoun,
Spreckels' business rival; this, moreover, at a time when all decent and conservative men were admiring Calhoun's stand
against "an abandoned labor unionism" which had been "riding
San Francisco to her destruction."

Many wealthy men in San Francisco began to believe that the
graft prosecution was a socialistic attack upon the institutions of

private property, although this theory was inconsistent with the other charge which they often made, that Rudolph Spreckels and James D. Phelan were simply using the prosecution to enrich themselves by destroying rival operators.

The leaders of the prosecution often denounced and ridiculed the arguments of wealthy men who sympathized with the defendants. The *Bulletin,* for example, published a sarcastic cartoon portraying overdressed members of a fashionable set, whose conversation over the card table consisted of such clichés as "Poor Mr. Calhoun, he was held up"; or "He had to have it"; or "He needed it in his business." Heney asked repeatedly in public addresses why it was that if men like Calhoun and Glass had simply been "held up," they had not gone to the prosecution with the evidence of it during the winter of 1906–1907, when the prosecution was struggling to work out a case against Ruef and Schmitz. Mrs. Fremont Older complained that "the minds of the well-to-do and wealthy seem narcotized by the statement that 'the graft prosecution hurts business.'"

In March, shortly after the indictment of Louis Glass, the *Chronicle* reported that "at the clubs of which the indicted telephone magnate was a member, much sympathy is expressed for him. He was extremely popular because of his affability and good-fellowship, and he has a host of friends, who are loth to believe that he has committed a crime which may put him behind the bars of San Quentin for fourteen years." In speaking of Glass' club membership in the past tense, this report implied that he had either resigned from his clubs, or would promptly do so. But he did not resign, even after he was convicted in his second trial; and no pressure was brought upon him to resign. As the *Argonaut* put it: "The best among us, knowing perfectly well by what means public service companies have conducted their affairs, have not felt serious loss of social respect for the men who have been at the head of these companies, and who must in the very nature of things have been involved in questionable dealings with our rotten city government."

During the summer of 1907 there were other incidents which revealed strong anti-prosecution sentiment in the circles represented by some of the city's most exclusive clubs. In July, a member of the Olympic Club brought Patrick Calhoun, as a guest, to a "booster dinner." After the dinner there were cries from some of the members for Calhoun to make a speech. When he began to speak, one of the oldest members, Dr. Charles A. Clinton, protested that the presence of the indicted traction magnate was an "outrage," and that for him to make a speech was completely intolerable. Clinton was overruled and silenced; and Calhoun, after receiving the apologies of the chairman, finished his speech and received a round of applause. As a result of this episode, the protesting Dr. Clinton was expelled from membership in the club for "disturbing the harmony" of the organization, while Calhoun was soon admitted to membership.

A few weeks later James D. Phelan presented the name of Rudolph Spreckels for membership in the famous Bohemian Club, whose constitution described it as "an association of gentlemen connected professionally with art, music, and drama, and those having appreciation of the same." Among the members were Francis J. Heney, his partner Charles Cobb, Fremont Older, judges Lawlor and Dunne, and four relatives of Spreckels. But the membership also included Tirey L. Ford, William M. Abbott, and Thornwell Mullally of the United Railroads, and Eugene de Sabla and John Martin of the Pacific Gas and Electric Company, all of whom were under indictment; and also William F. Herrin and several prominent attorneys for various defendants. Spreckels was finally admitted to membership, but he was very nearly blackballed, and the controversy all but disrupted the club.

As the city began to divide into two camps, the many San Francisco businessmen who sympathized with "the defense" began to subject the members of "the prosecution" to an economic and social boycott. Wealthy depositors withdrew their accounts from Rudolph Spreckels' First National Bank, and large mercantile establishments withdrew their advertising from the *Bulletin*. Bartley P. Oliver, foreman of the grand jury, also suffered heavy business losses. Oliver had been a successful real estate dealer, who was deeply shocked by the revelations before the grand jury. "I realize for the first time," Oliver told a friend early in 1907, "that I have not been a good citizen. I have not taken much interest in politics; I have evaded jury duty when I could; and I have given myself up to the making of money; but since I have seen, in the grand jury room, what money will lead men to do, I have almost come to hate the rotten stuff. I don't care whether my children have any of it or not." And Oliver told Lincoln Steffens that "I wish the law required twenty or fifty thousand men on a grand jury. . . . They would all become good citizens first . . . and business men and heads of families second." Eventually Oliver was forced out of his real estate business as the result of a boycott on the part of former clients and business associates, who disapproved of his attitudes and actions.

Mrs. Fremont Older began to feel the force of her husband's social ostracism. "Members of the prosecution," she wrote, "were not bidden to entertainments where people of fashion gathered." In such circles "women reserved their sweetest smiles for the candidates for State's prison;" and "to ask whether one believed in looting the city became a delicate personal question."

Not all of the city's leading men of business and finance were hostile to the prosecution. Harris Weinstock, one of the largest department store owners in the West, supported it strongly, and often criticized the attitudes of his fellow businessmen in words which might have come from Lincoln Steffens, or from an editorial in the *Bulletin*. But among wealthy men generally, anti-prosecution sentiment steadily increased.

Thus in the summer and fall of 1907, with a San Francisco election approaching, two quite different groups had come to oppose the prosecution—one composed of members of the Union Labor party who wished to perpetuate their party as a political machine, the other composed of men who disliked the prosecution's attacks on "business." It was a remarkably strange alliance; and in 1907 the two groups together could still command only a minority in an election in which the prosecution was the main issue. For those whose real desire was that the prosecution should be stopped, it would have been politically hopeless in 1907 to say so openly. In the eyes of what was obviously still a majority of the voters, this would have been to take a stand against "good government." The question of whether criminals should be punished was not an issue which opponents of the prosecution could face.

The beclouding of issues, on the other hand, was a purpose for which the existing three-party situation and the party nominating convention system provided ample opportunity. Moreover, the election was complicated by personal ambitions, rivalries among intra-party factions, and jealousies among several leading newspapers.

The prosecution leaders wished to secure the reëlection of Langdon as district attorney and the election of Taylor to succeed himself as mayor. But because the nominating convention system was still in effect, the voters could not express their preferences for candidates directly in the party primary elections on August 13. In the Republican primary, a new organization headed by a previously obscure young man named Daniel A. Ryan succeeded in electing an overwhelming majority of its slate of delegates, over the slate put forward by the discredited "Herrin" or "regular" Republicans. Ryan had been recognized as the organizer and leader of the pro-prosecution wing of the party, and probably most of the Republicans who voted for his ticket of delegates assumed that the party convention would nominate Taylor and Langdon. But when the Republican convention assembled, a majority of Ryan's delegates, while nominating Langdon for district attorney, gave the mayoralty nomination to Ryan himself.

There was now a serious possibility that Taylor would also fail to secure the Democratic nomination. But at this point a group of supporters of the prosecution organized a non-partisan body called the "Good Government League," in which Rudolph Spreckels was one of the members of the executive committee. The League announced its support of Taylor as well as Langdon; and it soon acquired such a large membership that the Democratic convention, impressed with the value of an alliance with the Good Government League, abandoned all doubts it might have had, and nominated Taylor for mayor and Langdon for district attorney.

The imprisonment of Ruef and then of Schmitz had left P. H. McCarthy as the dominant figure in the Union Labor party organization. There were two minority factions. One was led by Thomas Eagan, who insisted that Schmitz, although in the county jail, was an "ideal candidate." Another group, headed by Walter Macarthur of the seamen, Michael Casey of the teamsters, and Richard Cornelius of the striking carmen's union, wished to place the party on record in favor of the prosecution. In the primary the McCarthy delegates secured control of the convention, which then proceeded to nominate McCarthy for mayor and Frank McGowan for district attorney.

Those who opposed the prosecution, for whatever reasons, now tended to support McCarthy and McGowan against Taylor and Langdon. The Union Labor platform pledged vigorous punishment of all criminals regardless of class. In campaign statements, McCarthy demanded that the prosecution be placed in better hands. Up to that time, he said, it had been conducted as an attempt by Rudolph Spreckels and other "millionaires" to press a crown of thorns upon the brow of labor. At the same time, however, McCarthy's own campaign was receiving the support of the public service corporations whose officials had been indicted; and these included the United Railroads, which was effectively engaged in crushing the carmen's union.

As the Union Labor candidate for district attorney, Frank McGowan took the line of demanding not a less vigorous but a more vigorous prosecution. "If elected," he said in a political advertisement on November 3, "I will prosecute every man accused of crime, regardless of his position in life. . . . The District Attorney's office will not be used for politics, nor to disturb business. I will be the District Attorney in law and in fact, and I will never allow any man to control the office for any purpose. I will honorably enforce the law without the aid of any millionaire's money." In criticizing the granting of immunity to the entire board of eighteen supervisors, McGowan was attempting to capitalize on an apparently plausible and rather widespread objection to the prosecution's methods. The reasons for the immunity policy had been somewhat too complex for many citizens to understand. Certainly a number of aspects of it were extraordinary. Sixteen supervisors had remained in office for five months after confessing that they were criminals. Ex-supervisors Wilson and Duffey, as state railroad commissioner and president of the board of public works respectively, had remained in office even longer before being forced to resign. Moreover, the ex-supervisors had kept the bribe money, and some of them were obviously enjoying comfortable small fortunes as a result of it. The fact was that the district attorney's office had been unable to discover any legal procedure by which the money could be returned to its original owners, when the original owners did not care to admit that it was theirs. Ex-supervisor Louis A. Rea, the board's one honest member, tried for years to find some legal method of returning the $1,225 which he had unwittingly received from the proprietors of the fight trust and the Pacific Gas and Electric Company. But it clung to him, as the *Bulletin* once remarked, like the Rheingold; and though several attorneys, intrigued by the theoretical aspects of the question, volunteered ingenious suggestions, no satisfactory method of returning the money was ever found.

To McGowan's disingenuous campaign promise that he would prosecute all criminals and give immunity to none, Heney replied with a sarcastic open letter. He inquired what direct witnesses there were to the briberies, other than those who were criminally involved themselves; and how McGowan would persuade any such witness to testify without giving him immunity. "In this prosecution," said District Attorney Langdon in a campaign speech,

> we have tried to be practical, to be effective. What would you have said if we had made a scapegoat of a petty criminal and let the giants go? What would you have said if in all this graft and corruption we had arrested and jailed two or three obscure Supervisors . . . and had let escape the giants in crime?
>
> There have been graft exposures before in the history of American municipalities and the graft has gone on. And it was bound to go on so long as the prosecutions failed to stop the sources of evil. . . . Profiting by the mistakes of previous prosecutions, this office has struck straight at the roots of public graft. . . .
>
> This prosecution has a moral as well as a legal significance. It is time to stop the cynicism of common men when they view democracy and say it is for the powerful and the rich; that the poor must go to jail for the theft of bread and the rich escape for the theft of privilege, the purchase of men's souls and the degradation of government. It is time to stop the brazen and confident effrontery of the criminal rich. . . .

None of the major daily newspapers opposed the continuance of the prosecution, and none supported the candidacy of McCarthy and McGowan. The *Bulletin,* the *Call,* and the *Chronicle* supported Taylor for mayor and Langdon for district attorney. The *Examiner* supported Langdon, whom Hearst had made his own protégé; but it refused to support Taylor for mayor, and instead advocated the election of Ryan, the Republican candidate. The *Examiner's* policy in this respect gave some credence to the *Bulletin's* charges that Hearst had turned against Spreckels and Heney in July, when they had selected Taylor rather than Hearst's choice, Dwyer, to fill out Schmitz's unexpired term.

In the vote cast on November 5, 1907, Langdon, with the Democratic and Republican nominations for district attorney, received nearly 35,000 votes to McGowan's 20,000. And Taylor, with only the Democratic nomination, still received more than the combined vote for his rivals McCarthy and Ryan in the race for mayor. Thus at the end of its first year "the prosecution" received a clear and overwhelming endorsement by majority opinion in the city. But "the defense" had only begun to fight.

CHAPTER XXI

Ruef's trials and conviction

D URING the fall of 1907, while the election campaign and the first and second trials of Tirey L. Ford were in progress, Ruef was in a position of uncomfortable suspense. He remained a prisoner awaiting sentence on the charge of extortion from the French restaurants, to which he had been forced to plead guilty as one of the conditions of his immunity contract. Moreover, he had good reason to fear that the prosecution would abrogate the contract and bring him to trial for bribery, since Heney had refused to accept his account of his relations with Ford as being true state's evidence.

On January 9, 1908, a decision of the district court of appeals invalidated the conviction of Schmitz, and thus made Ruef's relations with the prosecution more peculiar than ever. As sustained by the state supreme court a few weeks afterward, this decision meant that the French restaurant extortion charge had never actually been a charge of crime within the meaning of the law. Extortion, ruled the district court of appeals, would have been the obtaining of money by means of a threat to do an *unlawful* injury to the property of the French restaurant keepers. But the injury which Schmitz (and Ruef) were alleged to have threatened was not an "unlawful injury." A mayor, or anyone else, held the appellate court, had the right to ask the police commissioners to withhold a liquor license from a house of prostitution. A mayor, or anyone else, had the right to *threaten* to do so. It was true, said the court, that "a high standard of ethics" would not countenance the obtaining of money by a threat, even a threat to do a lawful act. But not every moral wrong was defined by the penal code as a crime.

This decision aroused a storm of bitter public controversy. Judge Dunne, whose rulings in the trial of Schmitz were thus reversed as errors, now issued an extraordinary and emotional statement to the newspapers, in criticism of the decision and of the court which had made it. Many of those who had come to regard the prosecution as a crusade now gave themselves up to passionate denunciations of the three appellate justices. Every day for six weeks after the decision, the *Bulletin's* editorial page was topped by a streamer headline referring to Justices Cooper, Hall, and Kerrigan as THE MEN WHO LEGALIZED BLACKMAIL AND FREED RUEF AND SCHMITZ. The *Call* asserted that "Even the lay mind is competent to reach the conclusion that this decision is bad law, bad logic and bad morals." And several ministers castigated the decision in their sermons. Undoubtedly the extravagance of much of the criticism of the appellate court by prosecution sympathizers went so far that it shocked many men, and caused some who had previously supported the prosecution to turn against it.

On March 9 the state supreme court unanimously sustained the ruling of the district court of appeals. Moreover, ruled the supreme court, the entire trial of Schmitz had been invalid for a further reason which the appellate court had not mentioned: the indictment had failed to state that Schmitz was mayor of San Francisco, and that Ruef was a political boss. Hence it had failed to show how the defendant had proposed to, or how it was understood that he would, accomplish his threat—whether by fair persuasion and lawful influence over the police commissioners, or by duress, menace, or fraud.

When this decision was announced, it provoked even more controversy than had the appellate decision two months earlier. There was discussion of it all over the country, often with much heat and little light. Chief Justice Beatty was finally goaded into issuing a long public defense of the supreme court's decision. On the most bitterly disputed point, the chief justice wrote: ". . . though the facts that Schmitz was Mayor and Ruef the political boss of the city may have been as notorious as the fire or the earthquake, no lawyer would contend for a moment that they were facts of which a court could take judicial notice in passing upon the sufficiency of the indictment." There were, however, lawyers who did so contend. Heney and Dean John H. Wigmore wrote burning public criticisms of the chief justice's views on the doctrine of judicial notice and on the law of extortion.

This reversal by the higher courts was a serious defeat for the prosecution; and several of those whom the prosecution had attacked now sought to embarrass it still further. Patrick Calhoun issued another of his communiqués "To the American People," in which he denounced the prosecution's methods. He changed his own tactics, and now demanded an immediate trial. William S. Tevis, president of the Bay Cities Water Company, brought a complaint charging R. A. Crothers and Fremont Older with criminal libel. Ironically, however, this proved to be a boomerang.

The "Crothers-Older libel proceedings" grew out of an article which the *Bulletin* had published on May 16, 1907, giving the details of the Bay Cities Water Company's scheme to secure the city's purchase of a water supply for $10,500,000, through the payment of a $1,000,000 attorney's fee to Ruef. Knowledge of this plan had come from one of Ruef's confessions to William J. Burns, and Burns had given the details to Older as a "scoop" for the *Bulletin,* in order to reward Older for his services to the prosecution. Tevis was not indicted, since the Bay Cities project had not passed the preliminary stage and no money had been paid. On January 13, 1908, Tevis filed a charge of criminal libel in a justice court in Bakersfield, California, against R. A. Crothers as publisher of the *Bulletin* and Fremont Older as its managing editor. The *Bulletin* promptly reprinted the article which was the basis of Tevis' complaint, and reasserted the truth of its charges. In addition, the *Bulletin* published a series of articles asserting that Tevis, through the Kern County Land Company, virtually owned Bakersfield in the manner of a feudal baron. And these articles clearly implied that Tevis also owned the court in which he hoped to have Crothers and Older brought to trial.

Soon afterward, and obviously in order to shift the proceedings from the Bakersfield court, an admirer of Older filed a similar complaint against Crothers and Older in the superior court in San Francisco. The shoe was now on the other foot, and Tevis' attorneys bitterly charged the San Francisco district attorney's office with collusion in a plan to give the graft prosecution the chance to "prosecute" two of its own leading sympathizers. District Attorney Langdon denied any such collusion, but the trial in San Francisco soon proceeded. In form, it was a trial of Crothers and Older for criminal libel; but in effect it was an opportunity to prove to the public that the charges in the Bay Cities matter were not libelous but true. Tevis left the state, apparently to avoid testifying; and Ruef was not called. But ex-supervisors Jennings Phillips and Andrew M. Wilson testified that Ruef had led them to expect far more money from the Bay Cities project than from any other. The jury acquitted Crothers and Older; and the charge that Tevis had planned a colossal fraud upon the city, a charge which the public would otherwise have known only as an unsupported newspaper story, was now, as a result of Tevis' own blunder, substantially proven by sworn testimony in court.

Undoubtedly one factor in Tevis' action against Crothers and Older, as well as in Calhoun's demand for an immediate trial, was the supposition of both Tevis and Calhoun that Ruef would not testify against them. This hope was based on the belief that the decision of the appellate court on January 9, invalidating the indictment on which Ruef had pleaded guilty, had freed Ruef from the prosecution's hold upon him. And on this same assumption Ruef himself was making a determined effort to obtain not only his freedom from the custody in which he had been held on the extortion charge, but also immunity from prosecution on the bribery charges.

Judge Dunne had originally placed Ruef in the custody of Elisor Biggy, rather than in the county jail, because he had disqualified Sheriff O'Neil as untrustworthy. But a reform candidate defeated O'Neil in the election of 1907, and on January 8, 1908, when the new sheriff took office, the legal basis of the elisorship expired. On that day Ruef was taken from the elisor's prison and placed in the county jail, where Schmitz and Glass were also confined. Ruef found the change most unwelcome. In his comfortable quarters with the elisor, he had been allowed to provide himself with whatever food he liked, at his own expense. Conditions in the county jail represented a drastic reduction in his standard of living. He complained that the place was ancient, overcrowded, and filthy. It was in a building which had originally served as a house of correction for boys. Schmitz complained that he could get little rest, since his body was not only longer than his bed, but actually longer than his cell. Glass was finally released on bail, in February, on the testimony of his doctors that he needed medical attention. In March, when the supreme court nullified the extortion charge, Schmitz was admitted to bail on the bribery indictments still pending against him. But Ruef was to be denied this privilege until July.

For several months rabbis Jacob Nieto and Bernard M. Kaplan had been puzzled and worried by the prosecution's policy toward Ruef. They believed that their own advice to Ruef had been largely responsible for his consenting to the agreement under which he had turned state's evidence. They had given Ruef their guarantee "as men and as ministers" that the prosecution would carry out its part of that agreement. Ruef convinced the two rabbis that he had fulfilled his part of the bargain by telling the whole truth, to Burns, to Heney, to the grand jury, and as a witness in rebuttal against Schmitz. In the opinion of Nieto and Kaplan, it was now a question of whether the prosecution meant to fulfill the conditions of the immunity contract. And from the beginning the rabbis had formed impressions which differed from the understanding of Heney and Langdon as to just what the conditions of the immunity contract were.

Rabbi Nieto was angered by Ruef's removal to the county jail, on January 8, because he believed that the prosecution had agreed never to send Ruef there. The next day, when the appellate court announced its opinion that indictment number 305 was null and void, Nieto and Kaplan asked Langdon and Heney to recommend that Ruef be permitted to withdraw his plea of guilty to the charge which that indictment contained. On January 11, the *Chronicle* published a statement by "Ruef's spiritual adviser," Rabbi Nieto, threatening that "unless the prosecution does the right thing in regard to Ruef, and does it within a short time, I will tell all I know of the affair, and it will make a startling story."

On January 14, District Attorney Langdon told Judge Dunne that "Ruef wished" to enter a motion for the withdrawal of his plea of guilty in the French restaurant case. Judge Dunne replied that he would not entertain such a motion; and a few moments later the judge said emphatically to a group of newspaper reporters that he never had been and never would be a party to any immunity contract. Rabbi Nieto now grew more angry than

ever, and issued another public statement saying that between
12 and 1 o'clock on the morning of April 28, 1907, Judge Dunne
had made an unequivocal promise to allow Ruef to withdraw
his plea of guilty in the French restaurant case.

Months before, Heney had told Ruef that he considered the
immunity contract void, and that if he had his way he would
prosecute Ruef on every one of the bribery charges. Langdon, as
district attorney, had hesitated for months before reaching the
conclusion that Heney was right. But about the middle of January, 1908, according to his own account, Langdon finally made
up his mind that Ruef "was still traitorous to the State he had
debauched"; that Ruef's sole objective had been to secure the
escape from punishment of himself and his accomplices; that
Ruef was secretly in league with Ford, Calhoun, and other defendants; and that Ruef had broken the immunity contract by
his own actions. Up to this time the details of the Ruef immunity agreement of May 8, 1907, while the subject of much specu-
lation, had never actually been revealed to the public. But on
January 18, Langdon gave the text of the document to the newspapers; defended his own action in approving it originally; and
declared it finally annulled, "for good and sufficient reasons."

That evening, when a reporter asked Rabbi Kaplan whether
he cared to make a statement, Kaplan replied that he was "too
stunned" to do so. But his colleague was not. Rabbi Nieto
promptly wrote and sent to several newspapers an intensely emotional letter which placed the actions of the prosecution in the
worst possible light. He described, for example, the "midnight
meetings" to which judges Dunne and Lawlor had been summoned by a private detective, and in which, Nieto asserted, the
judges had promised to do the bidding of the district attorney's
office. In a supplementary statement Nieto charged that the prosecution had given Ruef its "word of honor," and had broken it.

Rabbi Nieto's letters received particular comment in
Emanu-el, a weekly of wide circulation among San Franciscans
of the Jewish faith. In an editorial on the "Startling Revelations
in the Graft Prosecutions as Disclosed by Rabbi Nieto,"
Emanu-el remarked: "It is now more than whispered that the
reason for the breach between Ruef and the prosecution, is that
he has refused to perjure himself, [to] 'come through,' to use the
language of Burns." And this editorial asked how the officers of

the prosecution could know that Ruef's account of the facts had been false, and that certain particular testimony which they had demanded from him was "the truth."

For weeks after Langdon's final abrogation of the Ruef immunity contract, the air was thick with charges and counter-charges in what came to be known as the "war of the affidavits." Ruef, Nieto, Kaplan, Heney, Burns, and Langdon all prepared and made public their versions of the long and tortuous history of the immunity question. And judges Dunne and Lawlor filed statements accusing rabbis Nieto and Kaplan of distorting the facts of the "midnight meetings."

Ruef hoped to secure the dismissal of the bribery indictments on the ground that the prosecution had fraudulently induced him to become a witness against himself in criminal proceedings. In the trolley cases, in which he had been jointly indicted with Calhoun and others, he filed a series of affidavits charging that the prosecution had promised him complete immunity, and then denied it to him because he would not give perjured testimony. Heney countered with an affidavit of nearly two hundred typewritten pages, covering the whole history of his dealings with Ruef in exhaustive detail.

The war of the affidavits produced such a maze of accusations, denials and counter-assertions that it was extremely difficult for an open-minded observer to form intelligent conclusions from them. Many San Franciscans were already so emotionally committed, either in favor of the prosecution or against it, that they believed what they wished to believe. But the affidavit war intensified public argument on both sides; and the whole affair won more converts to "the defense" than to the prosecution. Heney's main affidavit, for example, was so long and involved that few newspapers attempted even a serious summary of it. On the other hand, someone interested in the defense subsidized the printing of the affidavits of Ruef, Nieto, and Kaplan in pamphlet form, with such pointed topical headings as: ATTEMPTS BY LANGDON, HENEY, AND BURNS TO SUBORN PERJURY. THEIR THREATS TO REPUDIATE IMMUNITY CONTRACT IF RUEF WOULD NOT TESTIFY TO WHAT THE PROSECUTION DEMANDED. Ruef denied any knowledge of the origin of these pamphlets; but the *Call* reported that they had been printed in the plant of the Oakland *Tribune;* that a box containing several thousand copies of them had been delivered to Ruef's attorney, Henry Ach; and that they were being distributed throughout the city.

Having made its final break with Ruef, the prosecution resolved to bring him to trial on the indictment which charged him with offering a bribe to Supervisor Jennings Phillips in the Parkside matter. Ruef pleaded not guilty, and with the aid of Henry Ach, who had long since resumed service as his chief counsel, he stubbornly resisted prosecution. After a series of technical pleas, he asked for a change of venue on the ground that Judge Dunne was biased. The judge, unnerved and exhausted by the controversies of recent months, announced that he would soon leave the city on an extended vacation, and that Judge Dooling of the superior court of San Benito County would preside in his place. Ruef and Ach then sought to disqualify Judge Dooling, on the ground that he was a close friend of Judge Dunne; that he had been indoctrinated with Judge Dunne's prejudices against Ruef; and that Judge Dooling himself, as Grand President of the Native Sons of the Golden West, in 1907, had sponsored and signed the order which had declared Ruef expelled from that organization although Ruef had already resigned from it. The appellate and supreme courts, however, denied Ruef's pleas for change of venue. Judge Dooling ruled that an immunity contract was not recognized by the law, and was not binding upon the court; and that "When the defendant traded with the District Attorney he did so at his own peril. He had to depend solely upon the good will of the District Attorney."

The selection of the jury for the trial of Ruef in the Parkside case began on April 7. Before the jury was completed another of the sensational incidents of the graft prosecution occurred. This was nothing less than an attempt to murder a key witness, ex-Supervisor Gallagher, by dynamite.

On the evening of April 22, a shattering explosion blew out the whole front of the house in which Gallagher was living. Remarkably enough, however, no one in the house was killed or even seriously injured.

Leaders and followers of the graft prosecution promptly charged that the dynamiter must have been employed by Ruef, or the United Railroads, or both. The explosion occurred on the evening after Gallagher had testified in the third trial of

Tirey L. Ford. In that proceeding, as well as in Ruef's pending trial in the Parkside case, Gallagher's evidence was highly important, since as Ruef's agent he had made the bribery offers to the supervisors. Heney and Spreckels issued statements attributing the outrage to "hired assassins," and the *Bulletin* published an editorial asking who would benefit by Gallagher's death. A cartoon in the *Call* showed a group of bloated millionaires in a room in their club, one of them touching his cigar to the end of a fuse leading out through the door. On the other hand, opponents of the prosecution resented and ridiculed these charges. The *Chronicle,* which was growing steadily more critical of Heney and Spreckels, concluded that "in the absence of any conceivable sufficient motive the dastardly act must be assumed the work of a wicked man gone crazy." Others suggested that the prosecution itself might have planned the explosion in order to inflame public opinion against the defense. The advocates of this theory conjectured that the reason Gallagher and his relatives has escaped serious injury in a house so nearly demolished was that they had been forewarned of the explosion, and had not been telling the truth when they claimed to be in the house at the time.

On May 26 another dynamite explosion wrecked three residential buildings which Gallagher and a partner had recently constructed. A few weeks later a young Greek, John Claudianes, was arrested, and confessed that his brother Peter had hired him to plant the dynamite. Peter was captured soon afterward in Chicago, and also confessed. He, it appeared, had been employed by still another member of the San Francisco Greek colony, Felix Paduvaris.

Paduvaris fled to Europe, and since he was never caught, the question of his motives has remained unanswered. Not a shred of reliable evidence was ever discovered to indicate that his schemes had originated anywhere but in his own brain. But there were bits of circumstantial evidence which many partisans of the prosecution regarded as justifying their suspicions that the "graft defense" was linked with the murder plot. The Claudianes brothers, in their confessions, expressed the belief that Paduvaris was "working for Ruef"; and it was discovered that Paduvaris' generally disreputable career had included periods of association both with Ruef and with the United Railroads. He had been a padrone, or labor employment agent; a usurer; and a minor politician, in which capacity, according to the *Bulletin*, he had "delivered the Greek vote" and most of the "law business" of the Greek colony to Ruef. Paduvaris had also been employed by the United Railroads as a "spotter." But these inconclusive circumstances served only to heighten the mystery, and to intensify in the public mind the emotions of fear and hatred which were growing with each new development in the surging panorama of the graft prosecution.

Heney had selected the Parkside franchise affair as the case offering the surest opportunity of convicting Ruef of bribery, because it was one case in which Heney was willing to grant immunity to the businessmen, as well as to the supervisors, in order to secure their testimony against Ruef. Heney felt privately that in the Parkside matter there had been a greater element of extortion on Ruef's part than in the other major bribery charges. The Parkside railway franchise project had not actually been carried through before the fall of the Ruef-Schmitz regime; but it was considered so important and necessary for the city's development that the reform board of supervisors under the Taylor administration had finally granted the franchise on 20th Avenue, in October 1907, even though some of the promoters of the scheme were under indictment with Ruef for offering bribes to the previous board.

J. E. Green, president and general manager of the Parkside Realty Company, took the stand on May 1. When he declined to answer questions concerning the employment of Ruef, on the ground that he might incriminate himself, Heney moved the dismissal of the fourteen indictments against Green, and over the objections of Ach, Judge Dooling granted the motion. Green then testified freely. G. H. Umbsen likewise received immunity, and with it freedom from the insomnia which had plagued him for months. At the next session of the trial he gave full testimony of his part in the arrangements with Ruef. Gallagher and the other former supervisors then repeated their stories. Thus the evidence showed that Ruef had asked for $50,000, and finally agreed to accept $30,000; that he had actually received $15,000 on account; and that through Gallagher he had offered the supervisors bribes of $750 dollars at one time and $1,000 at another, although he had never actually paid them any of the Parkside money.

The jury began its deliberations on May 19. On the 21st, after forty-three hours and thirteen ballots, it stood six to six, and was discharged. According to Foreman Isaac Penny, who had voted for conviction, the jurors who voted for acquittal had clung to one of the arguments which Ach had stressed in his closing address to the jury—the contention that Green, Umbsen, and Gallagher were all accomplices of Ruef in the alleged bribery offer, and that their testimony could not be credited.

Although he was unable to prove it, Heney was convinced that several members of the jury had been "fixed," either by agents of Ruef or by members of the United Railroads detective force, and that if these jurors were not guilty of taking bribes, they had at least perjured themselves by swearing that they were unprejudiced. Moreover, Heney believed that a conspiracy of wealthy criminals was steadily growing, and that Spreckels, Burns, and Heney himself were in increasing danger of assassination.

From its beginning the graft prosecution had placed an extraordinary burden upon the ordinary machinery of justice, and that machinery had often creaked under the strain. The jury system had produced its share of complaints. And the process of getting a jury in the summer and fall of 1908, for what proved to be the main trial of Ruef, for the trolley bribery, produced a climax of these difficulties, and brought the jury system to the verge of breakdown.

The longer the graft trials had continued, the more difficult it had become to secure jurors, other than illiterates, who could honestly claim that they had not been prejudiced for or against the defendants by reading the sensational articles in the newspapers. Some prospective jurors had undoubtedly claimed to hold even stronger prejudices than they actually possessed, in order to escape jury duty. But the type of venireman whom the prosecution and the defense both feared was the one who was anxious to get on the jury, and who concealed his prejudices under questioning in court. It became very important for attorneys on both sides, in examining prospective jurors for bias, to have in advance special information about each man's background and opinions.

Lists of prospective jurors were available to representatives of the defense and the prosecution before the veniremen themselves were aware that their names were on the lists. Before the Schmitz trial, there had been complaints that Chief of Police Dinan was using city detectives as jury investigators, on Mayor Schmitz's orders. Dinan had admitted this, and asserted that his men were only doing what agents of William J. Burns were doing on behalf of "the other side."

Many were called, but few were chosen; and as the lists of veniremen grew longer, hundreds and then thousands of ordinary citizens began to be subjected to a veritable plague of detectives. The detective force of the United Railroads was at the disposal of the defense. And on the side of the prosecution, a group of latter-day vigilantes began to offer their services to supplement the efforts of Burns and his men. Members of the Good Government League participated in this activity; and the "Citizens' League of Justice," organized after the attempt to murder Gallagher, furnished so many volunteer investigators that Burns began to mimeograph his lists of veniremen and their home addresses. No less than two hundred members of the Citizens' League of Justice received copies of the Ruef panel, and most of them sent in reports on the supposed opinions of veniremen whom they knew, or with whom they had talked.

Burns' detectives, in approaching prospective jurors to determine their views on the graft prosecution, developed ingenious methods of concealing their identity and their purpose, and one of these devices became the subject of court proceedings. In July some of Burns' agents, falsely representing themselves as partisans of the defense, approached a number of veniremen with the request that they sign a petition asking the state attorney general to put an end to the "so-called graft prosecution." Henry Ach then filed a complaint charging Burns and two of his agents with contempt of court, on the ground that they had attempted to influence members of the jury panel, and special proceedings were held on this question in the court of Judge Lawlor. But after hearing the testimony, Judge Lawlor dismissed the contempt charges. Burns' men, the judge ruled, had not attempted to influence or disqualify the veniremen. Instead they had merely tried to discover their real opinions and prejudices. This was within the law, and the court had no power to determine how it might or might not be done. "It is my personal opinion," said the judge, "that it is wrong for anyone to approach a prospective juror and ask questions as to his views. . . . However, I must admit that extraordinary conditions [exist] in San Francisco."

On September 1, Burns and twenty-three of his detectives were appointed special agents of the district attorney's office. Those who had denounced the employment of these men by a privately financed prosecution now began to denounce the payment of their salaries out of public funds. And one of Burns' agents, encouraged by his newly acquired official status, did unquestionably venture beyond the legal limits of jury investigating. Special Agent Charles F. Oliver, Jr., who was only twenty years old, went so far as to approach two men who had actually been drawn and temporarily accepted as jurors in the Ruef trial. Judge Lawlor sentenced Oliver to two days in jail for contempt of court, and he was dismissed from his position. Venireman Dennis Murphy asked to be excused from service as a juror because of his bitter resentment against the graft prosecution, since one of its agents had visited his native town and asked questions about his character and his past life.

To justify these activities, the prosecution argued that its only purpose was to secure honest jurors, and charged that in the previous Ford and Ruef trials the juries had been "packed." Much color was given to these charges when two of Ruef's lawyers were implicated in an attempt to bribe a prospective juror.

On July 31, E. A. S. Blake, a building contractor, approached John Martin Kelly, a real estate salesman whose name had been drawn for possible service on the jury in Ruef's coming trial. Blake offered Kelly $500 if he would qualify on the jury and vote for acquittal. Kelly refused this offer, and about an hour later, with the advice of his employer, he informed District Attorney Langdon of it. At the suggestion of Burns, Kelly then coöperated in a plan to trap Blake. In further negotiations with him, he demanded $1,000, instead of $500, and Blake agreed. On September 3 the district attorney's office was ready to spring its trap. But as Kelly stepped to the bar of Judge Lawlor's court on that day, prepared to make his sensational revelations, one of Ruef's lawyers, Frank J. Murphy, addressed the court before Kelly had a chance to speak. Murphy asserted that Kelly had solicited a bribe of $1,000 from Blake, and that Blake had carried the solicitation

to Murphy and to another of Ruef's attorneys. Murphy said that
it was his duty to ask for an investigation of the affair.

"This," said Heney, interrupting Murphy's statement, "is one
of the most audacious pieces of business I have yet met with." He
revealed Kelly's relations with the district attorney's office, and
asked "that Mr. Kelly take the stand and make the statement
. . . that he came here for the purpose of making, and that Mr.
Murphy didn't say anything about until he saw him standing
there ready to make it to your honor. He jumped up as soon as he
saw Mr. Kelly walk in here."

Murphy and A. S. Newburgh, another of Ruef's lawyers, testified before Judge Lawlor that they had suggested to Blake that
he interview Kelly to try to determine Kelly's views on the graft
prosecution. But they swore that while Kelly had offered through
Blake to accept a bribe, they themselves had never offered to
give one.

It was clear at least that Blake was guilty. He was arrested in
an attempt to board an outbound train the next morning, and
indicted that afternoon. A few weeks later he was convicted, and
when he was about to be sentenced he made a confession involving Murphy and Newburgh. He had met Newburgh, he explained, because their offices were in the same building. His con-
tracting business had been failing, and he had been desperately
in need of money. One day in Newburgh's office, Blake asserted,
Murphy and Newburgh had shown him the list of prospective
jurors, and when he said that he knew one of them, John Martin
Kelly, the lawyers had suggested that he offer Kelly a bribe. After
his conviction, he continued, Murphy had promised to pay him
$10,000, and also to pay his wife $100 a month during his term
of imprisonment. As security for this promise, Blake said, Murphy had offered several thousand dollars' worth of promissory
notes made out to Murphy and signed by Ruef.

Blake was sentenced to four years in the penitentiary. Murphy
was tried, but the case against him depended on the testimony of
the convict Blake. A number of reputable citizens testified to
Murphy's good character, and he was acquitted. The jury disagreed in the first trial of Newburgh, and his second trial resulted
in acquittal. But Blake's confession had been widely believed,
and had done much to revive public support for the prosecution.

In Ruef's trial for the bribery of Supervisor Furey in the

matter of the trolley ordinance, the selection of the jury, which had begun on August 27, 1908, was not completed until 72 days and 1,450 veniremen later. From the beginning it was evident that agents for both the prosecution and the defense had secretly canvassed the personal views of every man who was summoned. Both Heney and Ach had bulky sheaves of detectives' reports, and both consulted a report on each man before questioning him. Heney asked many veniremen whether they had ever expressed the opinion that "the graft prosecution was hurting business." Both Heney and Ach often asked a man what newspaper he read, and Ach sought to persuade Judge Lawlor to excuse from duty all subscribers to the *Bulletin* or the *Call*. At one point Ach protested that the sheriff had made up one of the special venires entirely from the list of registered voters in the 37th assembly district, allegedly a prosecution stronghold.

After nearly a month, on September 25, when twelve men had been temporarily accepted, they were again reduced to six by peremptory challenges, through which the prosecution and the defense each excused three whose bias they suspected but could not prove. The six who remained were then deprived of their liberty for forty-two days before the jury was completed. "Six more innocent men," said the *Chronicle* on September 28, "condemned to incarceration for an indefinite period and their feelings insulted, their business damaged and their families outraged by the plain intimation that they are not men who can be trusted to resist the offer of bribes."

At last, on November 6, a full jury was sworn, and the testimony began. The trial was proceeding when, about 4:30 in the afternoon of November 13, Henry Ach paused in his cross-examination of Gallagher, and the court took what was to have been a brief recess. Many persons left the courtroom. About two hundred remained, but few noticed that a distracted little man was walking down the aisle toward the attorneys' table, until he had taken a pistol from the pocket of his overcoat, raised it to within a few inches of Heney's head, and fired a bullet which entered just in front of Heney's right ear. It was supposed at first that Heney had been killed.

The name of the would-be assassin was Morris Haas, and he had nursed a grievance against Heney for nearly seven months. On April 20, Haas had been temporarily accepted as a juror for

Ruef's Parkside trial. Shortly afterward Heney had learned that Haas was an ex-convict who had served a term in San Quentin for embezzlement some twenty years before. The governor had pardoned him and restored his citizenship; he had returned to San Francisco to marry and raise a family of four children; and his early disgrace had been almost forgotten. On learning of his prison record, however, Heney assumed that Haas had deliberately concealed it in order to get on the jury, and that his purpose had been to earn a bribe by voting for an acquittal of Ruef. On April 24, while Haas was sitting among the provisional jurors, Heney had confronted him with a twenty-year old photograph, taken from the rogues' gallery and showing Haas with shaven head and in his convict's stripes. Reprimanded and excused from service, Haas had tried rather incoherently to explain himself, and then had stumbled out of the courtroom.

Heney could have secured Haas' dismissal from the jury without a sensational public exposure of this sort, and there was some criticism at the time to the effect that he had been needlessly cruel. But the Gallagher dynamite outrage had occurred only two days before the Haas exposure, and Heney's nerves were on edge. He saw the Haas case as another part of a conspiracy of evil men who would stop at nothing to defeat the prosecution, and he felt it his duty to denounce this conspiracy as often and as dramatically as he could. The newspapers had reported the exposure of Haas as a minor sensation, and then the public had forgotten it. But Haas had brooded over it for months.

The shooting of Heney on November 13 led to intense public excitement. Again, as in the case of the attempt to kill Gallagher, there was no real evidence that the assassin had any connection with the "graft defense," but supporters of the prosecution were ready to believe the worst. The *Bulletin* and the *Call* laid part of the blame upon the *Chronicle* and the *Examiner*, for having turned against the prosecution; and part of it directly upon "graft defense interests."

The Citizens' League of Justice held a mass meeting on the evening after the shooting, and to an impassioned audience Mayor Taylor, District Attorney Langdon, Rudolph Spreckels, and others made speeches asking that there be no mob action, but that the city rededicate itself to the prosecution's cause.

If Heney had died a new vigilance committee might have

arisen, and mob violence might have ensued. But an almost miraculous chance had spared Heney's life. He had happened to be laughing. The bullet had passed between his jaws and lodged in the jaw muscles under his left ear; and although the slightest variation from the bullet's actual course would have been fatal, it was announced that he would recover and that he would not lose his voice.

On the evening of November 14, while the mass meeting of the Citizens' League of Justice was being held, Morris Haas committed suicide in the county jail, thus frustrating the determined efforts of William J. Burns to get a coherent confession from him. While lying under a blanket on his cot, under the eyes of a policeman detailed to guard him, Haas shot himself through the head with a small derringer pistol. Burns, and also Police Captain Thomas Duke, had searched Haas at the time of the shooting, and both were convinced that the derringer had not been on his person when he was brought to the jail. Burns was beside himself with anger. He believed that if he could have continued to question Haas, he could have proven his suspicions that someone had hired Haas to kill Heney. In rage and frustration Burns placed the blame for Haas' death upon the negligence of the police department, whose chief was his former friend William J. Biggy.

Biggy was a conscientious man with a good record. During the period when he had been elisor for Ruef, he had coöperated effectively with Burns. But he had grown rather critical of some of Burns' methods; and since his appointment as chief of police, replacing Dinan, Biggy had resented Burns' readiness to interfere in his administration of the police department. Biggy now believed that Haas had shot Heney simply because he had been mentally deranged by Heney's exposure of his criminal record. Biggy disagreed with Burns' theory that someone had hired Haas; and apparently, during the day of November 14th, Biggy tried to dissuade Burns from continuing his efforts to get Haas to make some such confession.

Burns and Rudolph Spreckels became publicly critical of Biggy. The *Call* charged that the chief of police had "arrayed himself" on the side of the graft defense; that he had at least been guilty of gross negligence; and that he might have been a party to a conspiracy in which someone on the defense side, to silence Haas, had smuggled the pistol to him in his cell, or perhaps even murdered him. The coroner's inquest resulted in a verdict of suicide, but failed to discover how Haas had obtained the pistol with which he killed himself.

Burns began to detail special agents of the district attorney's office to shadow the chief of police, and the Citizens' League of Justice demanded the chief's removal. One foggy evening the unhappy Biggy boarded a police launch to travel over the bay to the home of one of the police commissioners, in Belvedere, and to submit his resignation. Commissioner Keil later testified that he had persuaded Biggy to continue at his post. But on the return trip across the bay, about midnight, Biggy disappeared from the launch. His body was found floating in the bay two weeks later. The only man who had been with him on the launch was the pilot, William Murphy, who could not explain how the chief had fallen overboard. Two years later Murphy was committed to an asylum, muttering over and over that he did not know what had happened to Biggy, but that he himself had had nothing to do with it. Opponents of the prosecution denounced Burns, Spreckels, the *Call,* and the *Bulletin* for having "hounded" Biggy, perhaps to suicide. But the mystery of Biggy's death remained unsolved.

In the midst of all the uproar over the shooting of Heney, the suicide of Haas, and the death of Biggy, the trial of Ruef went on. Hiram Johnson took Heney's place, and as special prosecutor of Ruef, Johnson had the assistance of attorneys Matthew I. Sullivan and Joseph J. Dwyer. Ruef and Ach protested that under the circumstances a fair trial would be impossible, and petitioned for a change of venue, for a months' delay, or for the dismissal of the jury. Ach read into the record a long affidavit quoting from dozens of newspaper articles and editorials which clearly showed the inflamed state of public opinion. Undoubtedly many people blamed Ruef for the shooting of Heney, and there had been cries that Ruef should be lynched. Ruef had been free on bail since July. Judge Lawlor now ordered him back to the county jail, and on his trips to and from court he was protected by a heavy guard of policemen. But the judge refused to stop the trial. The jurymen had not been in the courtroom at the time of the shooting, and they were excluded from it during the proceedings on motion for change of venue. Finally Judge

Lawlor informed them that Heney had been shot; that he would recover; that the circumstances were entirely irrelevant to the case before them; and that they should exclude the incident entirely from their minds. The trial proceeded.

The evidence was substantially a repetition of the evidence in the three trials of Tirey L. Ford for the trolley briberies. But where it had been difficult to prove a corrupt understanding between Ford and Ruef, it was much easier to prove a corrupt understanding among Ruef, Gallagher, and the supervisors. Henry Ach greatly prolonged the proceedings by objecting to almost every question of Johnson's, by taking exception to almost every ruling of Judge Lawlor, and by lengthy cross-examination. But in the testimony of Gallagher, Wilson, Furey, and the officials of the mint, with ample corroboration from circumstantial evidence, the prosecution had an extremely strong case.

In his closing argument, Hiram Johnson informed the jurors that trials for jury-bribing were then going on, and hinted strongly that if any of them should vote to acquit Ruef the people of California would never believe that he had done so honestly. Johnson undoubtedly knew that this was an improper argument, but he felt certain that some of the jurors had indeed been bribed. Ruef's attorneys protested, and Judge Lawlor instructed the jury to disregard Johnson's remarks on the subject. Several jurors later said that they had strongly resented Johnson's implied threat.

The verdict of "guilty" came on December 10, 1908, on the jury's fifth ballot. Two weeks later Judge Lawlor sentenced Ruef to confinement in San Quentin for fourteen years, the maximum sentence for the crime of bribery. Ruef returned to the county jail, to wait for the outcome of his appeal.

CHAPTER XXII

The shift in opinion and the prosecution's defeat in 1909

WITH the conviction of Ruef in the fall of 1908, the prosecution achieved its greatest success. If it had made no further efforts, or if it had set itself only limited objectives for the future, it might have retained the approval of majority opinion in San Francisco. But Francis J. Heney, as he recovered from his wound, was determined not only "to convict every one of the grafters," but to proceed next against the wealthiest and most powerful of the defendants, Patrick Calhoun. An obsession akin to martyrdom now intensified Heney's belief that he had a mission in which he must not fail, and many admiring letters, including one from President Roosevelt, encouraged him in this preoccupation.

In the three trials of Tirey L. Ford many months before, there had been one hung jury and two acquittals on essentially the same evidence of bribery in the trolley matter which could now be brought against Calhoun. Heney's case was also weakened by the fact that Calhoun had been one step further removed from the actual briberies than Ford had been; and the split in public opinion had widened and deepened in the interim. On January 12, 1909, the first day of the selection of the jury to try Calhoun for the bribery of Supervisor Nicholas, Heney sat grimly in the same chair he had occupied when Morris Haas' bullet had struck him two months before. This time, it required three full months and 2,370 veniremen to produce a jury. The Calhoun jury proceedings revealed almost every shade of opinion and prejudice, from fanatical loyalty to blind hatred, toward the prosecution. But a startling proportion of the veniremen expressed frank and unshakeable bias in favor of the defense.

Throughout the trial, Calhoun's attorney's kept up a barrage of attacks on members of the prosecution. In a welter of argument over such matters as the prosecution's finances, the motives of the prosecutors, the employment of detectives, the responsibility for the streetcar strike of 1907, and the responsibility for attempts at assassination, the jury had to try to consider the actual evidence that a bribe had passed from Patrick Calhoun through Tirey L. Ford, Abe Ruef, and James L. Gallagher, to Supervisor Fred Nicholas, for his vote on the trolley ordinance. Gallagher and Nicholas testified, but Calhoun, Ford, and Ruef did not.

No one was very surprised when on June 20 the jury announced that it had failed to reach a verdict. Its final ballot had been ten to two for acquittal. According to one of the two jurors who had held out for conviction, the majority had argued that evidence showed only the payment of an attorney's fee to Ruef, and not a bribe.

The selection of a jury for a second trial of Calhoun began on July 16, but it faced insuperable obstacles. Several continuances were granted, and at last the proceedings were postponed until after the fall election, which was to decide the prosecution's fate.

As the months and years of the graft prosecution had gone by, the people of San Francisco had become more and more bitterly divided. Loyalty or hatred for the prosecution became entangled with a remarkable number of other loyalties and antagonisms— economic, social, political, racial, and even sectional and religious.

There were many San Franciscans of southern origin, for example, who had not yet traveled all the way on the road to reunion; and the prosecution revived some of the feelings of the Civil War. When the *Call* quoted and ridiculed an editorial which Col. Henry Watterson had written in the Louisville *Courier-Journal,* there were San Franciscans who agreed with "Marse Henry." He had observed: "Calhoun is a shining mark. He was born a gentleman; a southern gentleman; and he bears a very distingished name. There exists in most of the great cities a mean and mousing class which, unable to raise itself, delights in pulling its betters down. There is in the North a still lurking sectionalism whose very soul would be rejoiced to see the name of Calhoun trailed through the mire."

The question whether large numbers of Jews and Catholics were sympathetic with the defense became a still more touchy subject, and discussion of it led to much ill-feeling. Many San Franciscans of the Jewish faith had felt pride in the rise of Abraham Ruef to a position of power and success, and had felt resentment when the prosecution attacked him. Some were quick to believe that the prosecution was an anti-Semitic movement, even though five members of the Oliver grand jury were Jews. The leading Jewish organ in San Francisco was *Emanu-el,* a weekly journal of considerable influence among the more prosperous members of the Jewish community. In the spring of 1908, Rabbi Bernard M. Kaplan became its editor. This was shortly after the affidavit war over the Ruef immunity negotiations, in which Kaplan and his colleague Rabbi Nieto had taken such an important part, and for most of the next two years Kaplan's editorials in *Emanu-el* reflected his anti-prosecution feelings. There were Jewish leaders who condemned this attitude, but they were mainly in other parts of the country. Rabbi Stephen S. Wise of New York wrote that "Israel is not responsible for Ruef's crimes. . . . Israel is unutterably pained by this blot upon its record of good citizenship in America." But in San Francisco by far the greater part of Jewish sentiment seemed to favor the defense.

The ranks of the Catholics, both clergy and laymen, were grievously split. Father Peter C. Yorke denounced the prosecution frequently and publicly, while several other Catholic priests, though less articulate, held equally strong opinions in the prosecution's favor. Within the Paulist order, especially, an unfortunate incident led to a most vexatious quarrel. The head of the Paulists in San Francisco was Father H. H. Wyman, a kindly man who once wrote that he felt it his duty "to do favors for saints and sinners alike." In December, 1908, in the trial of Frank Murphy for jury-bribing, Father Wyman testified to Murphy's good character, and many felt that his testimony secured Murphy's acquittal. Subsequently Murphy gave the Paulist church,

Old St. Mary's, on California Street, a present of a pulpit, bearing a metal plate inscribed: "Donation of Mr. and Mrs. Frank Murphy, December 14, 1908." This fixed the date of the gift at two days after the acquittal. Certain Paulist priests who sympathized with the prosecution were already vexed with Father Wyman for aiding Murphy, and they considered it scandalous that he should accept a present so obviously intended as a reward for his help. One evening they entered Old St. Mary's Church, removed the offending nameplate with a screwdriver, and threw it into the bay.

This quarrel grew still more bitter when it became public. The freelance journalist Franklin Hichborn was preparing a series of articles for the Sacramento *Bee*. Hichborn was strongly pro-prosecution, and his purpose was to show that the "higher-ups" had reached even into the ranks of the clergy in their attempts to poison the minds of the people of San Francisco, but that in spite of such efforts the majority of the clergy were "still sound on the side of civic righteousness." One of the Paulist priests who had removed the Murphy nameplate revealed the episode to Hichborn; then, fearing that he had been hasty and unwise in giving such a story to a reporter, he regretfully informed Father Wyman of what he had done. Father Wyman wrote to Charles K. McClatchy, editor and publisher of the Sacramento *Bee*, and himself a Catholic, asking him not to publish an article which would injure the Church. But McClatchy shared Hichborn's pro-prosecution sentiments. He refused to suppress the story; and when it appeared in the *Bee* Father Wyman wrote sadly that he would offer a Mass for the publisher's forgiveness. McClatchy replied in an indignant letter in which he protested that in entreating divine forgiveness for him when he had done nothing wrong, Father Wyman had virtually born false witness against him before God Almighty. He asked Father Wyman to offer Mass for those who had committed offenses against public integrity, not for those who exposed them.

Among the Episcopalians, the ethical controversies which the graft prosecution raised were particularly embarrassing because so many of those indicted, and so many wealthy persons who sympathized with them, were members of the Episcopal Church. Calhoun and Ford were members of St. Luke's. Glass, at the time of his indictment, was an official of St. Paul's. And William H.

Crocker, senior warden of Grace Episcopal Church at the time of the exposure of the Parkside affair, had recently been instrumental in his family's donation of the magnificent site of the old Crocker mansion on Nob Hill for the building of Grace Cathedral. On the other hand, the rector of Grace Church, Dr. David J. Evans, was an outspoken advocate of the prosecution, and his relations with most of his wealthier parishioners grew strained. On the Sunday morning after the shooting of Heney, when Dr. Evans eulogized the prosecutor and offered a prayer for his speedy recovery, there were audible murmurs of protest from the pews.

Several other Episcopal clergymen favored the prosecution; but the attitude of the Bishop, William Ford Nichols, was one of neutrality. In June, 1908, in an address at the annual service commemorating the landing of Sir Francis Drake in California, Bishop Nichols said: "Civic righteousness is the twin of civic truth. If we have 'spied unrighteousness and strife in the city,' we are bewildered by counter claims that show wilful untruth somewhere. . . . The profound concern of a good many citizens today is the simple question: 'Who is lying?' "

As strife over the issues of the prosecution continued, there were clear signs that more and more San Franciscans were growing profoundly tired of its constant demands for sustained righteous zeal. At the same time the public in the rest of the state, where the progressive reform movement was steadily increasing, found it difficult to understand why the tide of reform in the metropolis had begun to ebb. At the neighboring universities, for example, student and faculty opinion continued strongly on the prosecution side. Nearly 150 members of the faculty of the University of California, with the approval of President Benjamin Ide Wheeler, signed a letter to Rudolph Spreckels expressing "appreciation of the great work already accomplished," and recommending that it be "carried on to the end."

A similar letter came from Stanford University, addressed to Spreckels, Langdon, Heney, Burns, and their associates, and signed by President David Starr Jordan and by a very large majority of the faculty. This was shortly after the confession of E. A. S. Blake to jury-bribing, and the Stanford letter extended to the prosecutors "our earnest and sincere congratulations on having successfully demonstrated the nature of some of the obstacles blocking the way of the conviction of powerful criminals of our commonwealth."

Professor George H. Boke, head of the University of California's department of jurisprudence, became the executive officer of the Citizens' League of Justice, formed in May, 1908, for the purpose of "creating and reviving and crystallizing public interest" in the prosecution's cause. For more than a year the League published a weekly journal called the *Liberator*, dedicated to the proposition that "there are no two sides to right." One of the articles it published was a letter from the liberal warhorse Edward A. Ross, who had left the faculty of Stanford at the order of that university's matriarch ten years before. Ross was now a leading sociologist at the University of Wisconsin; and he had recently published a provocative volume called *Sin and Society*, describing the social menace of the "criminaloid," the powerful figure in business and politics who was committing "new varieties of sin," offenses which had evolved with the evolution of a huge, rich, and complex industrial civilization, and which law and public opinion had failed to check.

To the *Liberator* Ross wrote: "It is perfectly clear to me where honest men ought to stand in this San Francisco graft fight, and I am eager to line up on the right side. One might wait a lifetime before finding a simple moral issue presented in so clear-cut a form as you now have before you."

Generally, some of the most enthusiastic support for the prosecution came from outside the city. But the prosecution's fate was to be decided at the polls, and nonresidents were not voters. Nor were women, to many of whom the "moral issue" made a strong appeal. One of the most interesting activities of the Citizens' League of Justice, for example, was the work of its women's auxiliary. During Ruef's trial in the Parkside case, the *Bulletin* complained that the courtroom audiences were full of "thugs" hired by the defense to influence the jury. "Hundreds of earnest, good citizens" were needed, said the *Bulletin*, to fill the seats instead and to encourage justice by their presence. Since male "good citizens" were usually too busy with their own affairs, the Women's League of Justice was organized to perform this duty, and during the later trials a large and earnest group of its members faithfully attended court, defying the taunts of the "pro-graft press," which compared them to the women of Paris who had sat knitting beside the guillotine during the reign of terror.

The power of the press was undoubtedly an important factor in the defeat of the prosecution in the election of 1909, in which it was supported only by the *Bulletin* and by E. W. Scripps' *News*. The *Examiner*, as well as the *Chronicle*, charged that the prosecution had been incompetently and improperly conducted and that it was lasting too long. "It would have benefited California," said an *Examiner* editorial, "to have had a brief and brilliant prosecution"; but it could do only harm "to have the state advertised as a sort of criminal community where there is a perpetual prosecution."

For several months in 1908 the *Examiner* made use of the weapon of ridicule, in the form of the "Mutt" cartoons. In February, Bud Fisher's comic strip character "Augustus Mutt" became involved in a long and sensational trial which satirized the San Francisco graft cases. Heney was "Beany"; Rudolph Spreckels was "Pickels"; Burns was "Detective Tobasco"; and judges Lawlor and Dunne were respectively judges "Crawler" and "Finished." This ridicule was in a medium which reached a large public, and some of it was undeniably effective. After the supreme court had invalidated the conviction of Schmitz, for example, "Detective Tobasco" was pictured as commenting: "The decision merely prolongs the matter and as Pickels is paying me by the day, I should worry. I have lots of time and Pickels has lots of money." Heney in particular was unmercifully satirized, up to the time of his near-assassination in November. But when that event occurred, prosecution sympathizers pointed out that the shooting of Heney, like that of President McKinley seven years before, had followed a long period of abuse by the Hearst newspapers—abuse which might have suggested the idea of assassination to such deranged minds as those of Czolgosz and Haas. "Once more," said the *Call*, "Hearst cartoons have directed a Hearst-sped bullet at a faithful, fearless servant of the people." Thereafter, the prosecution theme did not reappear in the "Mutt" cartoons.

The support of the *Call*, a leading morning daily, was one of the mainstays of the prosecution until June, 1909, and its defection at that time was a critical blow. Its owner, John D. Spreck-

els, was one of the brothers of Rudolph. But the *Call* once remarked that it had supported the prosecution in spite of this
relationship, not because of it; and the fact was that John and
Rudolph had not spoken to each other in all the years since the
family quarrel in the nineties. On June 7, 1909, in a newspaper
interview in New York, while explaining some of his reasons
for having thrown the support of the *Call* behind his brother's
fight, John D. Spreckels revealed that he was growing weary of
it. He and his brother Rudolph, he explained, had "built homes
on Pacific Avenue that we believed would be an ornament to the
city." Both had been equally angered when Calhoun proposed
a trolley line on Pacific Avenue, and both had tried to keep "San
Francisco, where our family had lived since 1855, from being
disfigured by trolley poles." But Heney, John D. Spreckels told
the reporters, had tried to "do too many things at once."

Supporters of the prosecution believed and charged that all
of the opposition newspapers were being subsidized by the defense. There were frequent denunciations of "the reptile press,"
and several groups passed resolutions deploring the "prostitution" of the *Examiner,* the *Chronicle,* the *Globe,* and the Oakland *Tribune* to the cause of the defense of crime. Heney asserted in a public statement that "both the *Chronicle* and the
Examiner have sold their news columns to the wealthy criminals."

Generally these charges were made without proof. But in the
case of the *Globe,* there was definite evidence of a large daily
newspaper being subsidized, and in fact created, to attack the
prosecution. Early in 1908 the Calkins Newspaper Syndicate,
which had previously published a few obscure journals in the
interior parts of the state, began to expand remarkably. It received much of the printing of the Southern Pacific, including
the printing of the railroad's monthly *Sunset Magazine.* It also
acquired the Fresno *Herald* and the Sacramento *Union,* and in
July, 1908, it began to publish the *Globe* as an evening daily in
competition with the *Bulletin.* The newsprint and typography
of the *Globe* were of high quality, but its reporting and editorials were not. Its praise of Calhoun, Ford, and the United Railroads was too obvious, and its attacks on the prosecution were
overdone. In the spring of 1909 it went into bankruptcy. Leigh
H. Irvine, its managing editor, testified that the auditor of the

United Railroads was in charge of the business affairs of the Calkins Newspaper Syndicate. In July, 1909, the *Globe* was merged with the moribund *Evening Post,* and continued its anti-prosecution campaign under the name of the *Post-Globe.*

For many years a profusion of weeklies had catered to San Franciscans of some leisure and means, to the upper and middle classes or those who liked to feel themselves identified with those classes. Of the weekly journals, only James H. Barrie's *Star* favored the prosecution. The *Argonaut, Emanu-el,* the *News Letter, Town Talk,* and the *Wasp* formed a chorus of protest against it.

Supporters of the prosecution had a tendency not only to attribute all press criticism to subsidies, but also to attribute all public sentiment against the prosecution to the "lies" of the opposition press. This was an exaggeration of the actual power of the fourth estate. While there is no accurate method of measuring the effect of newspaper opinion upon "public opinion" in general, there can be no doubt that a part of the newspaper opposition to the prosecution was the result of a shift in majority opinion, rather than its cause.

In magazines of national circulation, in 1908 and 1909, the prosecution received little aid. *Harper's Weekly* published a series of articles accepting the main contentions of the defense, and treating the prosecution as a failure. After the close of the Calhoun trial, an editorial in the *Nation* cited the views of the *Globe* without apparent realization of the fact that the *Globe* was a subsidized organ.

"Even a reformer," the *Nation's* editorial concluded, "cannot turn despot and run the machinery of government himself without provoking an immediate reaction. The best kind of reform is that which comes from the people themselves by regular democratic means, and not that which emanates from a handful of men financed by the well-filled purse of a business rival of some of the men accused of wrong."

Will Irwin denounced the tactics of the defense in an *American Magazine* article called "They Who Strike in the Dark." But he began with the sentence: "Complicated beyond all understanding, the graft prosecutions in San Francisco drag along." And even Lincoln Steffens, in an *American* article called "An Apology for Graft," suggested that the further punishment of individuals in the San Francisco cases was of little importance. The prosecution's real service to the country, he wrote, had been to expose the conditions resulting from the system of special privilege in American city government, the chain of circumstances which confronted both businessmen and politicians with a universal and overwhelming temptation to commit bribery. "Sympathy and understanding," Steffens wrote,

> are the needs of the hour. We Americans have been out on a manhunt. Some of us still are at it. We are crying to make some individual suffer; and we may, mob-like, catch some victim . . . and wreak upon him our hate. I hate this hate and this hunt. I have bayed my bay in it, and I am sick of it. . . . It is things, not men that hurt us; it is bad conditions, not ill-will, that make men do wrong. . . . There is something unspeakably painful in the spectacle of men—able, proud, successful; holding themselves and being held to be the best citizens of their city—suddenly summoned into a dirty, criminal court of justice to give bail as felons.

The continuance of the graft prosecution became the main issue in the San Francisco election of 1909, and this issue was presented to the voters chiefly through Heney's candidacy for the office of district attorney. It was also interrelated with national and state politics. Theodore Roosevelt had given the prosecution his personal support. Rudolph Spreckels had made public a long letter which he had received from the President, exhorting him not to be discouraged because men of wealth and power were "banded together" against him. "I want you to feel," Roosevelt had written to Spreckels, "that your experience is simply the experience of all of us who are engaged in this fight." At this time, however, Roosevelt's support was of doubtful value. His name had been considerably less popular in San Francisco since his intervention in the affair of the school board order segregating Japanese schoolchildren.

For two years the prosecution had been associated with a statewide progressive movement in California politics, which Heney and Rudolph Spreckels had hoped would succeed in exposing criminal actions by William F. Herrin, head of the Southern Pacific political machine. This hope had not been fulfilled. But in 1907 a group of progressive Republicans had formed the "Lincoln-Roosevelt League" for the purpose of breaking the

Southern Pacific's hold on the state government. Heney had made a large number of speeches for the Lincoln-Roosevelt League in various parts of the state, and Rudolph Spreckels had become the League's manager for the San Francisco area.

Heney was now convinced that he must "go into politics" in order to save the graft prosecution from defeat, and in 1909, when Langdon declined to run for a third term as district attorney, Heney decided to run in his place. He made this decision with some reluctance. The shock of his wound and the intense nervous strain of the prosecution had left him exhausted and overwrought, and he had been considering a move to New York City, where he might engage in private practice and enjoy some of the fruits of his national reputation.

The election of 1909 was the first to be conducted under the direct primary system, which the California legislature had established earlier in the year. In the party primaries under this law, the voters were to cast their ballots directly for candidates for their party's nomination for an office, rather than for delegates to a party nominating convention as before. One feature of the law had the effect of permitting the name of a primary candidate to appear on the ballot as a candidate for the nomination of one party only; and that party must be the one with which he had been affiliated at the last general election. In 1908 Heney had registered as a Republican and had supported Taft. But it became apparent that if he should file for the Republican nomination for district attorney he would be defeated; and defeat in the party primary, under the new law, would bar him from running as an independent in the fall election.

The registration figures showed that an extraordinary number of anti-prosecution voters had registered as Republicans, obviously for the purpose of voting against Heney in the only party column in which he could file. The Republican registration was almost 48,000, nearly twice as large as the Democratic and Union Labor registrations together. Thus Heney was effectively barred from filing in any party primary, and in the primary elections on August 17 his name did not appear on any party's ballot. The man who filed as a Republican and received the Republican nomination at the polls was Charles M. Fickert, formerly a Stanford football hero, and later notorious for his framing of evidence in the Mooney case. Fickert's candidacy was sponsored by a group of anti-prosecution businessmen. In the Union Labor primary, no one filed for the office of district attorney, but Fickert received the party's nomination with over 3,000 write-in votes. Heney's only chance lay in securing write-in nomination by the Democrats, and in this he succeeded by an extremely narrow margin, with 2,386 write-in votes to Fickert's 2,298.

Mayor Taylor, like District Attorney Langdon, refused to run. In the mayoralty contest the Union Labor nomination went to P. H. McCarthy, as it had in 1907. The Republicans nominated William Crocker, an obscure businessman who was no relation to his well-known namesake. And the Democratic nominee for mayor was Dr. Thomas B. W. Leland, a former coroner.

While Fickert did not say so explicitly, it was generally understood that he would ask for the dismissal of the graft cases if he were elected to the district attorney's office. P. H. McCarthy implied that "the stagnation of business in our city during the last two years" was due to the strife caused by the prosecution, and promised that as mayor he would give the city a "business like," "liberal," and "tolerant" administration which would restore "the get-together spirit" and bring back prosperity. Pleasure-loving San Francisco, he promised, would become "the Paris of America." The *Bulletin* charged that what this really meant was simply a "wide-open town." But to many San Franciscans in the fall of 1909, the idea of putting an end to moral crusades had a strong appeal. Anti-prosecution forces both of business and of labor mobilized behind McCarthy for mayor and Fickert for district attorney.

The tone of Heney's campaign speeches, in the opinion of some of his own supporters, lost him many votes. In one speech after another he demanded a second chance to convict Calhoun. Many of his hearers felt that he was seeking to try Calhoun in the court of public opinion rather than in the courts of justice, and that his frequent resort to personalities was out of place in a campaign for a quasi-judicial office such as that of district attorney.

A few days before the November election, Heney wrote to Steffens that he expected to win by 10,000 votes. But when the ballots were counted, he had lost by slightly more than that number. Heney's vote was 26,075, to Fickert's 36,192. It was true that Fickert had both the Republican and the Union Labor nominations, and Heney only the Democratic, and that the "party circle" on the ballot probably gave Fickert many straight-ticket votes. But the prevailing sentiment for an end to the prosecution was clear, as even the *Bulletin* conceded. In the race for mayor, McCarthy was elected by a plurality of nearly 10,000 votes over Leland, who had received most of the pro-prosecution support.

Again, as in the campaign of 1907, Heney had called for "moral stubbornness" in the punishment of sins against the community. But in the interim, stubborn righteousness had palled on thousands of San Francisco voters, many of whom might have compared their feelings to those of the Athenian citizen who cast his ballot for the banishment of Aristides because he was tired of hearing him called "the Just."

CHAPTER XXIII

Conclusion

EARLY in the fall of 1909, when the selection of the jury for a second trial of Calhoun had been half completed, Judge Lawlor had granted a postponement until after the election. When Charles M. Fickert defeated Heney, the case was further postponed until after the new district attorney had taken office early in 1910. In the meantime, ex-Supervisor James L. Gallagher, indispensable witness for the prosecution, quietly left San Francisco, after explaining to some of his friends and relatives that he had "been under fire long enough."

On February 7, 1910, District Attorney Fickert moved the dismissal of the case against Calhoun on the ground of insufficient evidence. Fickert pointed out that in three trials of Tirey L. Ford and one trial of Calhoun, upon the same state of facts, forty-two of the forty-eight jurors had voted "not guilty."

"I am convinced," said Fickert, "that the only evidence that might . . . strengthen the position of the People in this case would be the testimony of one Abraham Ruef, a co-defendant"; and Ruef, after the abrogation of his own immunity contract, had filed an affidavit which exonerated Calhoun and Ford by saying that they had never mentioned to him the subject of the payment of money to any public official.

In addition to these remarks of the new district attorney, his very presence in the courtroom was a reminder that the electorate of the city had voted, in effect, to dismiss the case against Calhoun. But Judge Lawlor did not feel that his court should follow the election returns. He denied the motion for dismissal, and ordered the district attorney to make every effort to bring back the witness Gallagher. In subsequent proceedings he

300

strongly hinted that he did not believe the district attorney was doing his duty.

On April 25, Fickert joined with attorneys for the defense in moving the dismissal of all the indictments still pending against Calhoun, on the ground that the trial had been postponed for more than sixty days without the defendant's consent, and over his protest. Judge Lawlor observed that the penal code required a dismissal under these circumstances, "unless good cause to the contrary is shown"; but he expressed the view that the absence of a material and indispensable witness, Gallagher, was "good cause" for further continuance. His ruling on the motion for dismissal was postponed until August 3.

On that date, he read a long and detailed opinion denying the motion. In the meantime it had been learned that Gallagher was in Vancouver, British Columbia. Judge Lawlor implied that he suspected the existence of an "arrangement" under which Gallagher was remaining outside the jurisdiction of the court by agreement with the defense, or the district attorney, or both. "At practically every turn," said Judge Lawlor, the district attorney had "followed the lead" of the defense. "Through the influence of unusual agencies," the judge's ruling continued, the law had broken down. Bribery was a very serious crime, because it tended "to sap the very foundations of government." And the disposition of such charges other than on their merits "is not to be encouraged and should not be allowed, except in the face of a strict legal necessity."

An extraordinary scene followed. There were bitter and defiant protests from defense attorneys Stanley Moore, A. A. Moore, and John J. Barrett; from District Attorney Fickert; and from Calhoun himself. Stanley Moore described Judge Lawlor's ruling as "a political document," and charged him with "doing politics from the bench that you stultify with your occupancy." He received a sentence of five days in the county jail for contempt of court. Thereupon his father and partner, A. A. Moore, remarked: "I fully agree, your Honor, that you are a partisan, a bitter partisan, and doing dirty politics."

A. A. Moore was also ordered to the county jail for contempt. So was John J. Barrett, who referred to the fact that Judge Lawlor was a candidate for the state supreme court, and accused him of wishing to keep the case alive until the 1910 election. District

Attorney Fickert insisted upon saying "that the statements and aspersions you have tried to cast upon me are false in each and every particular." And Patrick Calhoun addressed Judge Lawlor as follows:

> May it please your Honor: I have been educated, sir, to have respect for the courts. I have sat in your court under circumstances that would have tried the patience of any American. Throughout these trials I have sought, sir, to give you under most trying circumstances that respect to which your office entitles you. But, sir, I cannot sit quiet and listen to the vile insinuations which you yourself have stated there was no evidence before you to justify. There have been periods, sir, when the greatest honor that could come to a man was to go to jail; and as an American citizen I say to you that if you should send me for contempt it will be heralded all over this country as an honor. You have seen fit, sir, to send three of the most distinguished counsel of this state to jail. Why? Because they have sought to express in terms of respect, and yet in terms of strength, their protest against injustice——
>
> THE COURT. Mr. Calhoun——
>
> MR. CALHOUN. There is a time—pardon me, your Honor—when every man has a right to be heard——
>
> THE COURT. Mr. Calhoun——
>
> MR. CALHOUN. Now before I take my seat, I desire further to say this, that any insinuation that implies either that I was party to any obstruction of justice, or that I was a party to the absence of this witness, or that I have sought to control the District Attorney's office of this city is untrue. There is no evidence before this court. You yourself know it.

On August 10, the Moores and John J. Barrett began serving their five-day sentences in the county jail at Ingleside. They received special consideration, and regarded their confinement as something between an honorable martyrdom and a festive holiday. Their own servants brought in their meals from the Fairmont Hotel. They were free to receive visitors, including Calhoun and some of their other distinguished clients; and the *Daily News* observed that the three attorneys had "hung out their shingles" at their temporary "law offices."

During a period of a little more than a year after this incident, judges Lawlor and Dunne repeatedly refused to dismiss the case against Calhoun. At last, on August 15, 1911, the district court of appeals issued a writ of mandate ordering Judge Lawlor to dismiss the indictments, not only against Calhoun but against the other officials of the United Railroads, Tirey L. Ford, William M. Abbott, and Thornwell Mullally. "The law," said the appellate court, "will not tolerate repeated postponements on the vague hypothesis that perhaps in the future a fugitive witness may return to the court's jurisdiction." Two days later Judge Lawlor carried out this order as directed, and applied it also to the similar indictments against Frank G. Drum, Eugene de Sabla, and John Martin of the Pacific Gas and Electric Company. He predicted, however, that when all other similar indictments were finally disposed of, James L. Gallagher would return to San Francisco; and this prediction was eventually borne out.

With the dismissal of the indictments against him, in the summer of 1911, Calhoun was free from the threat of imprisonment, and as the largest stockholder in the United Railroads of San Francisco he remained in full control of that corporation's affairs. But the long and expensive fight to keep out of prison had been a heavy drain both upon his own fortune and upon the finances of the company. In 1912 he conceived a grandiose plan to recoup his losses. The United Railroads' board of directors, of which Calhoun, Ford, Mullally, and Abbott were members, passed a resolution which not only "ratified, approved, and confirmed" all payments which President Calhoun had made out of the company's treasury in the past, but also authorized him to make any further disbursements which he deemed to be in the company's best interests. By July, 1913, he had taken $1,096,000 out of the United Railroads treasury for investment in a large real estate scheme, the Solano Irrigated Farms Company. He conceived this plan as an imitation of what Henry E. Huntington had accomplished with the Pacific Electric system in southern California. The United Railroads were to expand into an interurban system extending throughout the entire bay region, and with this development the lands which Calhoun's new syndicate had purchased in Solano County would greatly increase in value. Huntington had built up a tremendous fortune in the area around Los Angeles by essentially similar methods.

In the meantime, in November, 1912, the United Railroads had applied to the state railroad commission for approval of a new bond issue; but the commission would not grant its approval without an inspection of the company's books. Presumably these books contained records not only of the $200,000 which had been paid to Ruef in the trolley matter, but also of the much larger sums which Calhoun must have disbursed in his long fight against the graft prosecution, for legal and detective expenses, and for his ventures into the publishing business, especially his interests in the Calkins Newspaper Syndicate, the *Globe,* and the *Post.* The books of the United Railroads had been sent East at the time of the trials. Calhoun now refused to bring them before the railroad commission; and the commission refused to permit the new bond issue.

The Solano land enterprise then failed. In the summer of 1913 the New York bankers who held part of the United Railroads stock rebelled against Calhoun's plans for further investment in the land scheme, and forced him out of the presidency of the United Railroads. Calhoun gave that corporation his personal note for the $1,096,000 he had lost in the land venture; but Jesse W. Lilienthal, his successor as president, ordered Calhoun's note recorded in the company's books as of a value of $1.00. As for the books for the period 1902–1912, President Lilienthal complained that they had disappeared.

Calhoun went into bankruptcy in 1916, testifying that he was penniless and that his wife was supporting him. For a number of years he lived in relative obscurity, and in 1931 the first edition of Lincoln Steffens' *Autobiography* asserted that he was dead. An irate Calhoun, seventy-five years old but very much alive, promptly threatened suit over this and other statements, and Harcourt, Brace and Company hastily recalled the erring first edition from the market. At the age of eighty Calhoun returned to California to build up a new fortune, which he accomplished by negotiating a lease on a rich new oil field in the lower San Joaquin valley. When he died, at eighty-seven, it was from accidental and not natural causes. Late one night as he was returning from a convivial party he stepped from an automobile into the middle of the street in front of his home in Pasadena, and was killed by a passing car.

In the end, not one of the public utility corporation executives indicted in the San Francisco graft prosecution went to the penitentiary. Abram K. Detwiler of the Home Telephone Company, who had been in hiding for years since his indictment in 1907, returned to San Francisco in 1910, and eventually secured the dismissal of the indictments against him. Theodore V. Halsey, political agent for the Pacific States Telephone and Telegraph Company, had made the direct and obvious bribery payments to the supervisors in the bare rooms in the Mills Building; but his trial in 1907 had been postponed when he suffered an attack of appendicitis. Later he became ill with tuberculosis, from which he recovered very slowly. At last, in September 1910, Judge Dunne charged Halsey's doctors with misrepresenting the state of his health, and ordered him brought to trial. Prosecuted by one of District Attorney Fickert's assistants, he was acquitted.

Halsey's superior, Louis Glass, vice-president and general manager of the Pacific States company, had been convicted and sentenced in the summer of 1907. The process of appeal took more than three years. On November 30, 1910, the state supreme court nullified the conviction on highly technical grounds, notably the admission at the trial of certain incompetent, and to the lay mind, relatively unimportant evidence. Theoretically this ruling would have meant a new trial, but a new trial was no longer practical. The remaining indictments against Glass and Halsey were dismissed in 1912. Both men continued to hold positions of honor and responsibility in the telephone business, and both continued to enjoy the esteem of most of their fellow corporation executives. Glass was president and Halsey vice-president of the Philippine Telephone and Telegraph Company, with offices in San Francisco. When Glass died in 1924, Halsey succeeded him in the presidency.

Some of the leaders of the prosecution, on the other hand, felt the weight of disapproval of big business. Rudolph Spreckels was eventually forced out of the presidency of the First National Bank. Francis J. Heney's later career was a series of disappointments. In 1910 he stepped aside in favor of Hiram Johnson in the gubernatorial contest. His fellow leaders of the Lincoln-Roosevelt League felt a strong sense of loyalty and gratitude to him, but they realized that if Heney were the candidate his personality would be an issue which might lessen their chances of victory over the Southern Pacific machine. By tantalizing combinations of circumstances Heney also missed a senatorship in 1914, and the governorship in 1918. In his law practice in San Francisco he found himself boycotted by wealthy clients, and he finally moved to Los Angeles.

As forerunners of the California progressive reform movement, the leaders of the San Francisco graft prosecution were prophets without honor in their own city. Throughout the rest of the state, however, they were held in higher esteem. Hiram Johnson's part in the prosecution enabled him to capture the governorship in 1910, with a promise, forcefully repeated during the campaign and highly successful afterward, to "kick the Southern Pacific Railroad out of politics."

To William J. Burns, the prosecution also proved to be an experience of great value. Capitalizing on his reputation as a detective, Burns organized his famous private detective agency in 1909. He soon obtained the contract of the American Bankers Association, and went on to other triumphs, such as the arrest of the McNamara brothers for the bombing of the Los Angeles *Times*.

To Abraham Ruef, of all the figures in the history of the graft prosecution, fortune was most unkind. Following his conviction in December, 1908, for bribing Supervisor Furey in the trolley franchise matter, Ruef was in the county jail for a year while his appeal was being prepared. He was admitted to bail in December 1909, giving bond of $600,000. At last, in the summer of 1910, his appeal was ready to be filed. In its preparation, he had spared no expense, and his attorneys had spared no effort. Every word of the proceedings of the trial was printed in the transcript on appeal—from the indictment through the examination of jurors, the arguments and testimony, and the affidavits. The result was a five-foot shelf of twenty-four printed volumes, containing nearly two and a half million words. In addition there were several volumes of printed briefs, with such titles as "Misconduct of Judge" (541 pages); "Misconduct of District Attorney"; "Furey, the Alleged Bribee, was an Accomplice"; "Erroneous Examination of Witness"; and "Erroneous Admission of Evidence." But in spite of the quantity of material submitted to it, the district court of appeal upheld Ruef's conviction, in a unanimous decision announced on November 23, 1910.

On December 31, Ruef petitioned the state supreme court for a rehearing. This petition could be granted if four of the seven supreme court justices should sign the rehearing order within sixty days of the appellate court's ruling, that is, by January 22, 1911. Justice Frederick W. Henshaw had planned to be out of California for several weeks, beginning on January 11. He signed the rehearing order on January 10, and left the state the next day. Justices Melvin and Lorigan signed the order a few days later. Justices Angellotti, Shaw, and Sloss declined to concur in it. But on Sunday, January 22, the last legal day, Chief Justice Beatty attached the necessary fourth signature, and it was announced the next morning that the supreme court had granted Ruef's petition for a rehearing of his appeal.

Many observers anticipated that the outcome of the rehearing would be to invalidate Ruef's conviction on technical grounds, and to order a new trial, as the court had done in the case of Glass. Under the existing conditions in San Francisco, if a new trial were held at all there was a strong chance that it would result in Ruef's acquittal. Consequently the announcement that the supreme court would grant a rehearing was greeted with angry protests, notably in the current session of the legislature, which contained a majority of reform-minded members from the interior of the state, chosen in the elections of 1910. The judiciary committee undertook to investigate the supreme court's action, and there was talk of a constitutional amendment to provide for the recall of judges.

Before the rehearing of Ruef's appeal could begin, however, someone noticed that Justice Henshaw had been out of the state on the day when the rehearing order had supposedly become effective, that is, on January 22, the day when the fourth signature on the document, Chief Justice Beatty's, had been attached. It was now contended that Henshaw's absence from the state on that day had annulled his signature, and that with only three valid signatures the rehearing order lacked a majority and was without effect. This argument was presented before the supreme court itself, and to their considerable embarrassment the justices discovered that the argument was correct, and that their own procedure had been faulty. For years the court had seldom met in session to sign such orders. The individual justices had often looked over the cases and signed the orders at their leisure. Absence of justices from the state had also occurred before under similar circumstances. These practices were now questioned for the first time. But the court confessed its error, and on February 28, 1911, in a unanimous ruling, it declared its own order for a rehearing to be void. By this ironic fiasco Ruef lost his last chance to keep out of the penitentiary.

In the meantime, the actions of Justice Frederick W. Henshaw had appeared in a particularly unfavorable light when it was discovered that he had signed the rehearing order, on January 10, two days before Attorney General Webb had filed his brief in reply to Ruef's petition. In other words, Justice Henshaw had voted to grant Ruef a rehearing before he had even read the state's argument against such action. When this was revealed, William Denman, a prominent San Francisco attorney, appeared before the judiciary committee of the legislature to demand Henshaw's impeachment.

Henshaw had been the subject of gossip and suspicion for several years. The *Examiner* had once described him as "the brains" of the Southern Pacific's political machine in California. He had been renominated for the supreme court at the Santa Cruz convention of 1906, which Ruef had controlled; and he had been a member of the group in the famous photograph, taken that same evening, in which Ruef had occupied the place of honor. It was learned later that it was Henshaw who had first suggested the candidacy of Charles M. Fickert for district attorney of San Francisco, in 1909, and that he was Fickert's constant advisor. And many leading California lawyers suspected, though they could not yet say publicly, that Justice Henshaw had accepted a huge bribe to change his vote in the case of the estate of James G. Fair in 1901. The impeachment project was abandoned, however, and Henshaw continued to occupy his seat on the court until 1917, when he resigned, a few months before it was revealed that the suspicions against him in the Fair will case were true.

On March 7, 1911, Ruef entered the state prison at San Quentin. The *Call* reported that he was "the most conspicuous prisoner ever to enter the gray stone walls of a California penitentiary"; that his fellow-convicts treated him with respect and almost with awe; and that his two cellmates, one serving a life term for murder, and the other a seven-year term for grand larceny, insisted that he occupy the lowest bunk, which was the least uncomfortable. Newspapermen were permitted to interview him, and he received them in good spirits. "This is a modern Utopia," he told the reporters. "Here all men are equal. . . . Here is a great opportunity to study sociology." While he worked in the jute mill his mind was busy with plans for prison reform, and he soon wrote a letter to the state board of prison directors, proposing a self-help plan for convicts and ex-convicts, a voluntary coöperative society which would help its members to prepare for the difficult period of readjustment following their release, and then help them to secure employment.

Ruef's presence in San Quentin made life a great deal more interesting for its inmates. For many years, on each Fourth of July, the convicts had presented a play in the prison chapel. When it was reported that Ruef had written a farce to be presented with an all-convict cast on July 4, 1911, many San Franciscans clamored for tickets, but unfortunately the public was denied admission.

Ruef had scarcely entered the penitentiary when an agitation began for his release. For some time not only Jews, but others also, had asserted that Ruef was a victim of persecution. A visiting Congregational minister from New York, in an address to a Jewish group in San Francisco, compared Ruef's case to the Dreyfus affair, and concluded: "If you believe that a scapegoat is being made of one of your co-religionists . . . stand up and say so." Many thought it unfair that of all the men involved in the political corruption of San Francisco, Ruef alone should be in prison.

The movement in favor of granting Ruef an early parole received its most remarkable ally in Fremont Older. On the day Ruef went to San Quentin, Older wrote in a *Bulletin* editorial: "One need have a lively sense of self-righteousness to hold the key to another man's cell. One should be very sure of his own rectitude before he feels a pharisaical gladness over the humiliation of Abe Ruef." Older's conscience began to plague him. It was he who had first begun the fight to put Ruef in convict's stripes, and now that his long fight was successful his triumph turned to ashes. He began to believe that Ruef had been a victim of corrupt conditions of life for which the whole people of San Francisco shared the responsibility, conditions which the mere imprisonment of individual men would not cure. Older came to feel that the leaders of the prosecution had stooped to the use of methods almost as reprehensible as those of the defense; that they had wrung a confession from Ruef with a promise of immunity, and then broken their promise; and that Judge Lawlor had been bitterly prejudiced. In the summer of 1911 Older visited Ruef at San Quentin, asked his forgiveness, and offered to help him win an early release from prison.

Ruef's sentence had been fourteen years. Good behavior would reduce this to a "net" sentence of nine. The state board of prison directors had established a rule under which it did not grant paroles until a convict had served half of his net sentence; and as applied to the case of Ruef this meant that he would have to serve four and a half years, or until 1915. But Older began to lead an agitation to have this rule set aside, and to have Ruef paroled in 1912.

In December, 1911, the state supreme court pronounced a decision in the case of ex-Supervisor Michael Coffey which seemed to strengthen the argument for Ruef's release. The prosecution had revoked Supervisor Coffey's immunity contract because it accused him of withholding testimony in the first Ford trial. In 1909, Coffey had been convicted of receiving a bribe from the United Railroads, through Ruef and Gallagher, in the trolley affair. The points raised in his appeal had been similar to the points raised in Ruef's. In both cases, the district court of appeals had sustained the convictions. But late in 1911 the supreme court granted Coffey a rehearing, after which it nullified his conviction on the ground that Gallagher, the only direct witness to his crime, was his accomplice. Older and others now argued that except for the ridiculous accident of Justice Henshaw's absence from the state on January 22, 1911, Ruef would also have had a rehearing, and the supreme court might have applied the same doctrine on the testimony of accomplices to his case.

Early in 1912 ex-Mayor Schmitz, whom the supreme court had freed of the charge of extortion in the French restaurant matter four years earlier, was finally brought to trial in San Francisco for bribery. The public had almost forgotten that Schmitz had been indicted along with Ruef for conspiring to bribe the supervisors in the gas rate and trolley matters; and in 1912 few seriously supposed that Schmitz could still be convicted. Nevertheless a trial was held before Judge Lawlor on one of the gas rate indictments, and Ruef was brought from San Quentin to testify. One consideration which might affect Ruef's parole was the fact that many indictments for bribery were still outstanding against himself. He refused to testify against Schmitz unless all these indictments were dismissed, and Judge Dunne, in whose court some of the indictments were still pending, refused to dismiss them. Thus Ruef did not testify against Schmitz, and Gallagher was still absent without leave. The evidence was obviously insufficient, and Judge Lawlor instructed the jurors to acquit Schmitz, which they did.

In the fight for Ruef's parole, Ruef and Older next adopted a remarkable piece of strategy. Ruef was to write his memoirs, and Older was to publish them in a long series of installments in the *Bulletin*. In a bid for public sympathy, they were to be advertised as the confessions of a fully repentant boss whose main desire was to help the American people to understand and reform the conditions which had made his career possible.

Ruef's "Foreword" to this extraordinary document, written in San Quentin, appeared in the *Bulletin* of April 6, 1912. He wrote:

> Solitude, restraint, confinement make for introspective thought. Since the heavy doors of the state prison closed behind me, I have given much consideration to the events and influences which ended so ignominiously a life full of hope. I have reflected; I have studied; I have considered the causes, the effects, the surrounding conditions, the inevitable consequences of the destructive social and civic forces which brought about that result. I believe much good can come from a straightforward statement of my experiences. I have determined to make such a statement. It will embrace all the leading events of my political life. It will show the roseate colored ideal of the dawn turning into the sombre darkness of the night.
>
> I shall endeavor to make it autobiographical but at the same

time specific and far-reaching. I feel that the narration will have much educational value and will, in some degree, conduce to the benefit of society, of the city, of the state, and perhaps of the nation. In the preparation of this document, which I shall begin at once, and which will necessarily be of some length, I shall not undertake to spare myself or to extenuate in the smallest degree any act of mine. . . .

Without malice or bitterness, without personal feeling or illwill, I shall endeavor to show the political system which made politics what they have been, and the influences which controlled and corrupted. . . . I shall show the relation between big business and big and little politics. . . . In doing which I hope not only to give the public an insight behind the scenes which will be of benefit to them, but also in some measure to compensate for any participation in the events which I shall relate.

In its announcement accompanying this foreword, the *Bulletin* proudly published the comments which it had received from many prominent men in reply to the question, "Do you think such a document would be of educational value to the American people?" Such well-known figures as Lincoln Steffens, Gifford Pinchot, Charles Edward Russell, Samuel Untermeyer, Norman Hapgood of *Collier's,* and several United States senators had replied enthusiastically. On the other hand, the *Bulletin* charged that certain powerful persons were doing everything they could to prevent publication; and the *Bulletin* also stated that the first regular installment would not appear until and unless Judge Dunne should dismiss the indictments still hanging over Ruef's head.

A few weeks later the district court of appeals issued a writ of mandate directing Judge Dunne to dismiss all of the 123 indictments still remaining out of the 383 which the San Francisco graft prosecution had produced. Judge Dunne dismissed these last remaining indictments on May 18, 1912, including eighty against Ruef, eleven against Schmitz, eight against Halsey, and a scattering of others.

Three days later the *Bulletin* published the first regular installment of "The Road I Traveled: An Autobiographic Account of My Career from University to Prison, with an Intimate Recital of the Corrupt Alliance between Big Business and Poli-

tics in San Francisco," by Abraham Ruef. With his considerable
literary talent, Ruef set forth a detailed, vivid, and fascinating
account of his political career.

Ruef's story had been running for a little more than two
weeks, and was still describing the political conditions of the
'eighties and 'nineties, when, on June 8, 1912, the state board
of prison directors held a very unusual open session to consider
the application of Fremont Older for the parole of Abraham
Ruef. Tirey L. Ford was still a member of the board of prison
directors. Older believed, and said in the *Bulletin,* that Ford
owed his own freedom to Ruef—that if Ruef had not refused to
give testimony which would incriminate Ford, then Ford would
have gone to San Quentin as a convict rather than a director,
and Ruef would now be free. But Ford abstained from voting
on the question of Ruef's parole; and the other directors voted
three to one to refuse it.

Ruef's memoirs continued to appear in the *Bulletin,* in almost unbroken daily installments, for more than three months.
In July, they described the great briberies of 1906. But they revealed little of an incriminating nature that had not already
become public during the prosecution; and while Ruef confirmed the fact that he had received the huge fees from Ford,
Drum, and Detwiler, and had passed parts of the money on to
the supervisors and the mayor, he continued to insist that the
corporation executives had paid the money as attorney's fees,
and had had no knowledge of his bribery payments.

Early in September, having carried the story through the
Santa Cruz convention of 1906, the series suddenly ended, without going on to the story of the graft prosecution. A letter from
Ruef explained that the labors of composition had proved too
exhausting. Another consideration was probably that to publish
an account of the prosecution from Ruef's point of view would
have ruffled too many tempers, and might have defeated the
purpose of increasing public sympathy for him. Instead, in the
latter part of September and occasionally during October, there
appeared a series of eighteen articles under the title: "Civic
Conditions and Suggested Remedies." Here, in the style of a
professor of political science, Ruef advanced many proposals
for reform. The use of private money in elections should be
barred, and the state should pay all campaign expenses. The

functions exercised by bosses in party organizations should be made official, and turned over to responsible, salaried public officers. Proof of bribery should invalidate a franchise (although this might have proved unconstitutional). There should be public classes for the political education of voters, in school and out. And there should be a new alignment of parties, one made up of conservatives standing for property rights, the other a new "party of the people."

In the upper corners of many of the installments of Ruef's articles, Older had inserted a petition to the prison directors, which the reader might clip, sign, and send in to the "Society for the Parole of Abraham Ruef." The *Bulletin* announced that eleven of the twelve jurors who had convicted Ruef now joined in favoring his parole. Many prominent men and a number of organizations added their support.

This agitation, however, accomplished nothing. The prison directors would set aside their rule of "half the net sentence" only on petition of both the district attorney and the trial judge. District Attorney Fickert was willing to sign a petition, but Judge Lawlor refused. As for hopes that the governor might intervene—the governor was Hiram W. Johnson, who had not changed his opinion of Ruef since the day when he had delivered the closing argument to the jury as special prosecutor in Ruef's trial. In 1914, Governor Johnson issued a long public statement, criticizing the parole agitation and insisting that in the interest of justice Ruef must receive exactly the same treatment as any other convict.

When Ruef had served four years and seven months, a little more than half of his net sentence, the board of prison directors granted him a parole, on August 21, 1915, and he left San Quentin two days later. Forbidden to return to San Francisco for ninety days, he retired to a cottage near Ukiah, in Mendocino County, until this period elapsed. Then, late in the fall of 1915, he returned to his native city, to manage his still extensive properties and to extend his operations in real estate.

Ruef had been disbarred by order of the state supreme court in 1912. But while his criminal record had disqualified him from the practice of law, it was apparently no disadvantage in his activities in the real estate business. He opened a new office in one of his downtown buildings, and prospered. Delighted

San Franciscans began to go there to see whether it was true, as was rumored, that his office door was inscribed: "A. Ruef, Ideas." Actually, the inscription was "A. Ruef, Ideas, Investments, and Real Estate." Ruef described himself as an "idea broker," and in this capacity he began to promote a number of interesting schemes. There was a process for removing the alcohol from wine while preserving the flavor; and later there was a project, which was more successful, for a café on the property he owned at Fishermen's Wharf, with "colorful stores and bizarre sea food dispensaries."

His name was often in the news. In 1916 he purchased property adjoining Rudolph Spreckels' mansion on Pacific Street, and announced plans for a six-story apartment building which would have cut off Spreckel's view of the bay. This project, however, was not carried out. In 1917 the tenants of one of his properties, the Hotel Marquise, were charged with conducting a house of prostitution, but Ruef was able to prove that he had ordered these tenants to move as soon as the charges were made. In January, 1920, he was pardoned by Governor William D. Stephens. The governor said that he had no doubt of the justice of Ruef's conviction, but that many judges, attorneys, newspapers, bankers, labor leaders, and clergymen had recommended the pardon, and had praised Ruef for exemplary conduct in prison and on parole.

Ruef never reëntered politics, even after his pardon restored his rights of citizenship. But Eugene E. Schmitz, in spite of the fact that he had been removed from office as mayor on conviction of a felony, later enjoyed a remarkable political career. After several unsuccessful ventures in the oil and mining businesses and in the writing of an operetta, Schmitz announced that he would run for mayor against the incumbent James Rolph in 1915. Rolph was a successful businessman who had first been elected mayor in 1911, following the exceedingly undistinguished administration of P. H. McCarthy. For Schmitz to run against the popular Rolph seemed utterly fantastic. But many San Franciscans felt an impish admiration for a colorful figure like Schmitz, and a warm-hearted sympathy for a man who was down and trying to get up again. The *Examiner*, although opposing his election, recounted his unhappy career since the beginning of the graft prosecution, and concluded:

"Now this man, whom his friends consider one of the noble army of martyrs, will come before the people in the great dramatic appeal of his life." True, he had been convicted of extortion, but the supreme court had reversed the conviction; and in his only trial for bribery he had been acquitted. Schmitz maintained that he had thus been vindicated in court against the attacks of his enemies. And he promised that if elected mayor he would bring back the prosperity which the city had enjoyed during his first two administrations, before the earthquake and fire.

Though Rolph defeated him for mayor in 1915, Schmitz received no less than 35,000 votes. And in later years, beginning in 1917, the people of San Francisco elected him to a series of two-year terms—on the board of supervisors!

Throughout his life Schmitz always firmly denied, both publicly and in the bosom of his family, that he had ever received a dishonest dollar or committed a dishonest act. The only direct evidence to the contrary rested upon the statements of Ruef.

Schmitz died on November 20, 1928, having lived, said the *Chronicle*, "a life as vivid, adventurous and splashed with color as the beloved city in which he made his home." For his funeral, the police and fire departments furnished a guard of honor, and Mayor Rolph and ex-Mayor McCarthy were among the honorary pallbearers. The church was full to overflowing, and the cortege was long. Ruef was among the many who attended Schmitz's funeral, although the broken friendship between the ex-mayor and his former attorney had never mended.

Ruef's own last years were more obscure, and his passing less honored. Although his fortune before the graft prosecution had been well over a million dollars, and although he had restored it to about half a million in 1925, his real-estate enterprises steadily failed in the following decade. After his death, on February 29, 1936, in San Francisco, his estate was found to be bankrupt.

It was Ruef's misfortune to have been born too late. Had his unquestionably remarkable abilities appeared on the political scene a generation earlier, instead of in the age of the "muckrakers" and of progressive reform, it is interesting to speculate upon the power and success which might have been his.

Notes

Notes

T H E following paragraphs list the most important sources for each chapter. For scholars and others who may be interested, I have deposited a more fully and specifically annotated manuscript of the book in the Bancroft Library, University of California, Berkeley.

CHAPTER I. A REFORMER TURNS OPPORTUNIST

On Ruef's early career, the chief source is his own account in his memoirs, "The Road I Traveled: an Autobiographic Account of My Career from University to Prison, with an Intimate Recital of the Corrupt Alliance between Big Business and Politics in San Francisco," published serially in the San Francisco *Bulletin*, May 21–September 5, 1912. Quotations from it are made with the permission of the San Francisco *Call-Bulletin*. Other important sources are Martin Kelly, "Martin Kelly's Story," edited by James H. Williams, in the *Bulletin*, September 1–November 26, 1917; Jeremiah Lynch, *Buckleyism, the Government of a State* (1889); and files of the San Francisco newspapers, notably the *Bulletin*, the *Call*, the *Chronicle*, and the *Examiner*.

CHAPTER II. THE UNION LABOR PARTY OF SAN FRANCISCO

Frederick L. Ryan, *Industrial Relations in the San Francisco Building Trades* (1936). Ray Stannard Baker, "A Corner in Labor," *McClure's Magazine*, February, 1904. Thomas W. Page, "The San Francisco Labor Movement in 1901," *Political Science Quarterly*, December, 1902. Ira B. Cross, *History of the Labor Movement in California* (1935). Edward J. Rowell, "The Union Labor Party of San Francisco, 1901–1911," unpublished Ph.D. thesis in the Univer-

319

sity of California Library. Walter Macarthur, "Political Action and Trade Unionism,"*Annals of the American Academy of Political and Social Science* (1904), pp. 316–330. Fremont Older, *My Own Story* (1919, 1925, and 1926), quotations by permission of the Call-Bulletin Publishing Company, the Post-Enquirer Publishing Company, and the Macmillan Company. Ruef's memoirs, in the *Bulletin,* especially June 28 and 29 and July 1 and 2, 1912. San Francisco *Bulletin, Call, Chronicle, Daily News,* and *Examiner,* and the *Coast Seamen's Journal,* especially May–November, 1901.

CHAPTER III. THE FIRST SCHMITZ ADMINISTRATION

Ruef's memoirs; *San Francisco Municipal Reports* for 1901, 1902, 1903; and the daily newspapers.

CHAPTER IV. FREMONT OLDER'S CRUSADE

Fremont Older, *My Own Story.* Mrs. Fremont Older, "The Story of a Reformer's Wife," *McClure's Magazine,* July, 1909. George Kennan, "Criminal Government and the Private Citizen. A Study of San Francisco," *McClure's Magazine,* November, 1907. Files of the *Bulletin,* 1904–1905. On the French restaurant case, see also the testimony before the grand jury, November and December, 1906, Hichborn Collection, Haynes Foundation, Los Angeles; testimony in *People* v. *Schmitz* in June, 1907, transcript on appeal; Ruef's memoirs, the *Bulletin,* September 4, 1912; San Francisco, Committee on the Causes of Municipal Corruption, *Report,* pp. 18–19; and the account of the trial of Schmitz for extortion, in Chapter XVII of the present work.

CHAPTER V. "A CLIMAX IN CIVICS"

Ruef's memoirs, *Bulletin,* July 20–29, 1912; Older, *My Own Story;* daily newspapers, 1904–1905. A typed draft of Walter Macarthur's manuscript, "San Francisco—A Climax in Civics," on the election of 1905, is in the Bancroft Library.

CHAPTER VI. THE ORIGINS OF THE PROSECUTION

Older, *My Own Story.* Mrs. Older, "The Story of a Reformer's Wife." Lincoln Steffens, "The Making of a Fighter; How Frank Heney Prepared in Arizona for the Work He is Now Doing in San

Francisco," *American Magazine,* July, 1907; "The Mote and the Beam, a Fact Novel. Chapter One—The Clash of Classes in San Francisco," *ibid.,* November, 1907; "Chapter Two—Breaking into San Francisco," *ibid.,* December, 1907; and "Rudolph Spreckels, a Business Man Fighting for his City," *ibid.,* February, 1908. Testimony of Older and Burns in the Crothers-Older libel proceedings, as quoted in the *Bulletin,* March 14, 16, and 17, 1908. Testimony of Rudolph Spreckels in *People* v. *Schmitz* and in *People* v. *Calhoun.*

CHAPTER VII. LABOR AND CAPITAL

Ruef's memoirs in the *Bulletin,* July 23–August 15, 1912. Testimony before the grand jury, transcripts in the Hichborn Collection at the Haynes Foundation, and in the San Francisco *Call,* April 26, 1907; notably the "confessions" of the supervisors. Testimony in *People* v. *Ruef,* no. 840, the trial of Ruef in the Parkside case, transcript in Records of the San Francisco Graft Prosecution, Bancroft Library. The evidence that Justice Henshaw was guilty of accepting the bribe in the Fair will case is conclusive; see texts of affidavits of Dingee and Lash, in San Francisco newspapers, November 23, 1918; statements of Henshaw, *Examiner,* November 23 and 24, 1918, and *Chronicle,* June 3 and 6, 1919; and Older, *My Own Story,* Ch. XXII.

CHAPTER VIII. TELEPHONE COMPETITION

Testimony, particularly that of the supervisors and of officials of the Pacific States Telephone and Telegraph Company, before the grand jury and in the two trials of Louis Glass. Ruef, in the *Bulletin,* especially August 8–14, 1912. H. N. Casson, *History of the Telephone* (1910).

CHAPTER IX. CABLE CARS AND TROLLEYS

Ruef's memoirs, in the *Bulletin,* especially July 5, 6, 7, 21, and 31, and August 17, 19–24, and 29, 1912. *Poor's Manual of Railroads,* 1902–. Franklin Hichborn, *"The System," as Uncovered by the San Francisco Graft Prosecution* (1915), pp. 32–48. San Francisco newspapers, 1905–1906.

CHAPTER X. EARTHQUAKE, FIRE, AND EMERGENCY GOVERNMENT

San Francisco Municipal Reports, 1905–1907, appendix, pp. 701 ff. *Report on a Plan for San Francisco by Daniel H. Burnham Assisted by Edward H. Bennett,* published by the city, September, 1905. Newspapers of the period. Ruef, *Bulletin,* August 29, 1912.

CHAPTER XI. BUSINESS AS USUAL

Ruef's memoirs, *Bulletin,* July 31–August 28, 1912. *Journal of Proceedings of the Board of Supervisors,* vol. I. On the trolley matter, see also testimony of supervisors, especially Gallagher, before the grand jury and in the trials of Ford, Ruef, Coffey, and Calhoun. On Parkside, testimony of company officials, Ruef, Gallagher, and several other supervisors, before the grand jury and in the Ruef Parkside trial. On the scheme of the Bay Cities Water Company, Ruef's memoirs are silent, but see testimony in the Crothers-Older libel proceedings in March, 1908, as reported in the *Bulletin.*

CHAPTER XII. RUEF'S STAR REACHES ITS ZENITH

Ruef, in the *Bulletin,* July 11, August 1, 23–31, and September 2 and 3, 1912. San Francisco newspapers of the first week in September, 1906. Ruef's memoirs ended at this point.

CHAPTER XIII. THE PROSECUTION BEGINS

Heney, "Parts of the Story of the Prosecution," *The Liberator,* July 17, 1909. Testimony of Spreckels in *People* v. *Calhoun.* Testimony of Older and Burns in the Crothers-Older libel proceedings, March 16, 1908. Older, *My Own Story.* Langdon, "The Story of the Great Struggle," *Cosmopolitan,* August, 1907. Dwyer, "A Review of the Battle," *ibid.* "Confessions of a Stenographer," anonymous, but probably by George Keane, *Overland Monthly,* August, 1907.

CHAPTER XIV. RUEF FIGHTS TO STAVE OFF DISASTER

Older, *My Own Story.* Hichborn, *"The System."* San Francisco newspapers, December 1906–March 1907. On the "Oriental school" incident, see especially the report of the board of education in *Municipal Reports,* 1905–07, pp. 683–685.

Notes

CHAPTER XV. THE PROSECUTION BREAKS THROUGH

Heney, in *The Liberator,* July 24, 1909, and affidavit of March 10, 1908, in *People* v. *Calhoun*. Steffens, in the *American Magazine,* December, 1907 and April, 1908, based on many intimate conversations with Heney and Burns. Testimony of Roy, Burns, and Spreckels, in *People* v. *Calhoun,* May and June, 1909; of Boxton, in the first trial of Glass; of Gallagher, in the first trial of Ford; and of Wilson, in the trial of Ruef on the trolley matter.

CHAPTER XVI. RUEF NEGOTIATES

The inner history of the negotiations leading up to Ruef's plea of guilty is told, in conflicting versions, in the affidavits filed by Heney, Burns, Nieto, and Kaplan in March, 1908, and by Ruef in March and November, 1908, transcripts in Records of the San Francisco Graft Prosecution, Bancroft Library, vol. 81; the affidavit of Judge Dunne, in the *Bulletin,* March 31, 1908; and the affidavit of Judge Lawlor, in the *Examiner,* August 23, 1908. See also "Ruef, a Jew Under Torture," by "Q.," *Overland Monthly,* November, 1907; Steffens, in the *American Magazine,* April, 1908; and Gatlin, in *McClure's Magazine,* February, 1911.

CHAPTER XVII. THE CONVICTION OF MAYOR SCHMITZ

People v. *Schmitz,* transcript on appeal, Records of the San Francisco Graft Proseuction, Bancroft Library, vol. 14. Heney, affidavit of March 10, 1908, pp. 136 ff. "San Francisco's Ferment," by "Kew," *Outlook,* August 31, 1907. Newspapers for May, June, and July, 1907.

CHAPTER XVIII. THE TELEPHONE CASES

Testimony of the supervisors on March 18 and of telephone officials on March 19 and 21, 1907, before the grand jury, published in the *Call,* April 26, 1907; and testimony in the two trials of Glass, transcripts in Records of the San Francisco Graft Prosecution, Bancroft Library, vols. 18–22. Newspapers, July and August, 1907.

CHAPTER XIX. THE TRIALS OF TIREY L. FORD

Transcripts of the first two trials of Ford, and of the trial of Coffey, in Records of the San Francisco Graft Prosecution. Newspapers during the trials. Gertrude Atherton, in *Harper's Weekly,* November 2, 1907. Cohn and Chisholm, *Take the Witness* (1934), a rather eccentric biography of Earl Rogers. Will Irwin, "They Who Strike in the Dark," *American Magazine,* April, 1909. Older, *My Own Story* (1926), pp. 126–136.

CHAPTER XX. "PUBLIC OPINION," AND THE ELECTION OF 1907

San Francisco daily and weekly newspapers. Hichborn, *The System,* Chapter XXI. Steffens, *Autobiography* (1931), especially p. 372, letters to Heney, mss., Bancroft Library, and articles in the *American Magazine,* November and December, 1907. Mrs. Fremont Older, in *McClure's Magazine,* July, 1909.

CHAPTER XXI. RUEF'S TRIALS AND CONVICTION

Higher court decisions on the Schmitz case, 7 Cal. App. 330 and 369. Extensive quotations from testimony in the Crothers-Older libel proceedings, *Bulletin,* February 25 to March 28, 1908. On the Ruef immunity contract, affidavits in Records of the San Francisco Graft Prosecution, vol. 81. Theodore Bonnet, *The Regenerators* (1911), chapters VIII, IX, and X. The best record of the main Ruef trial is the complete transcript on appeal, a five-foot shelf of printed volumes in the Hichborn Collection, Haynes Foundation, Los Angeles; reporter's transcripts are in Records of the San Francisco Graft Prosecution. On practices in relation to prospective jurors, see also proceedings "In the matter of the Alleged Contempt of W. J. Burns, *et. al.,*" Records of the San Francisco Graft Prosecution, vol. 43. Newspapers throughout most of 1908. Notes made by Hiram W. Johnson during the main Ruef trial, mss., Johnson Papers, Bancroft Library, University of California.

CHAPTER XXII. THE SHIFT IN MAJORITY OPINION AND THE PROSECUTION'S DEFEAT IN THE ELECTION OF 1909

Calhoun trial, Records of the San Francisco Graft Prosecution. Calhoun, *Some Facts Regarding Francis J. Heney* (San Francisco, 1909). Elizabeth Geberding, "Woman's Fight against Graft in San Francisco," *Delineator,* October, 1910. Hichborn, *"The System,"* pp. 405–424; his appendix, *ibid.,* pp. xxxiv–xl, on the prosecution's finances; and his articles in the Sacramento *Bee,* July 20 and August

12, 1909. Steffens-Heney correspondence, in Bancroft Library, and in Ella Winter papers. Heney-Lissner correspondence, Meyer Lissner papers, Stanford University Library. Roosevelt-Heney correspondence, Yale University Library. Records of the League of Justice, Hichborn Collection, Haynes Foundation. Newspapers and magazines.

CHAPTER XXIII. EPILOGUE

On the dismissal of the graft cases, Records of the San Francisco Graft Prosecution, vols. 82–83, and Hichborn, *"The System,"* Chapter XXVIII. Supreme court decision in the Glass case, 158 Cal. 650. *People* v. *Ruef,* No. 1437, transcript on appeal, Hichborn Collection, and briefs, Records of the San Francisco Graft Prosecution, vols. 54–61; higher court decisions, 14 Cal. App. 576 and 581, and 161 Cal. 433. On Justice Henshaw, see also notes for Ch. VII, above. Older, "Shall Abe Ruef Be Pardoned?" *The Survey,* September 2, 1911; and *My Own Story* (1926), pp. i–vii, 102–103, and 158–182. Newspapers.

Bibliography

Bibliography

Manuscripts and Public Documents

Franklin Hichborn Collection, Haynes Foundation, Los Angeles.

Hiram W. Johnson Papers, Bancroft Library, University of California.

Meyer Lissner Papers, Stanford University.

Records of the San Francisco Graft Prosecution, Bancroft Library, University of California. The collection of A. A. Moore and Stanley Moore, attorneys for the United Railroads and its officials.

Letters of Theodore Roosevelt to Francis J. Heney, Yale University Library.

Chester Rowell Papers, Bancroft Library, University of California.

San Francisco. Board of Supervisors. *Journal of Proceedings.*

San Francisco. Committee on the Causes of Municipal Corruption. *Report on the Causes of Municipal Corruption in San Francisco, as Disclosed by the Investigations of the Oliver Grand Jury, and the Prosecution of Certain Persons for Bribery and Other Offenses against the State.* William Denman, Chairman. Committee appointed by Mayor Edward R. Taylor, November 10, 1908. Published by order of the Board of Supervisors, January 5, 1910.

San Francisco Municipal Reports.

Steffens-Heney Letters, Bancroft Library, University of California.

Steffens-Heney Letters in the custody of Ella Winter, transcripts by Helene M. Hooker.

Unpublished Theses

Rowell, Edward J., "The Union Labor Party of San Francisco, 1901–1911," manuscript in the University of California Library.

Wiens, Henry W., "The Career of Franklin K. Lane in California Politics," manuscript in the University of California Library.

Books and Articles

"Abe Ruef's Scheme to Help Prisoners," *The Survey,* 26 (September 2, 1911), 771–772.

Adams, H. Austin, *The Man John D. Spreckels* (1942).

Asbury, Herbert, *The Barbary Coast: an Informal History of the San Francisco Underworld* (1933).

329

Atherton, Gertrude, "San Francisco and her Foes," *Harper's Weekly*, 51 (November 2, 1907), 1590–1593.

Bailey, Thomas A., *Theodore Roosevelt and the Japanese-American Crises; an Account of the International Complications Arising from the Race Problem on the Pacific Coast* (1934).

Baker, Ray Stannard, "A Corner in Labor. What is Happening in San Francisco, where Unionism Holds Undisputed Sway," *McClure's Magazine*, 22 (February, 1904), 366–378.

Bancroft, Hubert Howe, *Retrospection Political and Personal* (1912).

Bonnet, Theodore F., *The Regenerators; a Study of the Graft Prosecution in San Francisco* (1911).

Buell, Raymond L., "The Development of the Anti-Japanese Agitation in the United States," *Political Science Quarterly*, 37 (1922), 605–638.

Burnham, Daniel Hudson, *Report on a Plan for San Francisco* (1905).

Burns, William J., *The Masked War* (1913).

Byington, Lewis F., and Oscar Lewis, editors, *The History of San Francisco* (1931).

Calhoun, Patrick, *Some Facts Regarding Francis J. Heney* (1909).

Casson, Herbert N., *History of the Telephone* (1910).

Caughey, John W., *California* (1940).

Cleland, Robert G., *California in our Time (1900–1940)* (1947).

Cohn, Alfred A., and Joseph F. Chisholm, *Take the Witness* (1934).

"Confessions of a Stenographer," *Overland Monthly*, second series, 50 (August, 1907), 101–109. Probably by George Keane.

Cross, Ira B., *History of the Labor Movement in California* (1935).

Daggett, Stuart, *Chapters on the History of the Southern Pacific* (1922).

Dosch, Arno, "Rudolph Spreckels—the Genius of the San Francisco Graft Prosecution," *Overland Monthly*, second series, 50 (November, 1907), 476–481.

Dwyer, Joseph J., "A Review of the Battle," *Cosmopolitan*, 43 (August, 1907), 442–444.

The Fate of the San Francisco Grafters [by the] Benedict Arnold of his Native City (1908). Purports to be written by Eugene E. Schmitz.

Gatlin, Dana, "Great Cases of Detective Burns; How Abe Ruef Confessed," *McClure's Magazine*, 36 (February, 1911), 386–400.

Geberding, Elizabeth, "Woman's Fight against Graft in San Francisco," *Delineator*, 76 (October, 1910), 245–246 and 322–323.

Hamilton, Edward H., "The Liberating of San Francisco," *Cosmopolitan*, 43 (August, 1907), 435–437.

———, "What are You Going to Do About It? Part 8. What San Francisco Has Done About It," *Cosmopolitan*, 51 (July, 1911), 149–159.

Heney, Francis J., "Parts of the Story of the Prosecution," *The Liberator*, I (July 17, 24, and 31, and August 7, 1909).

Hichborn, Franklin, *"The System," as Uncovered by the San Francisco Graft Prosecution* (1915).

"The History of William J. Burns," *The Nation*, 125 (November 23, 1927), 561.

"Impressions of a Careless Traveler," *The Outlook*, 78 (September 17, 1904), 164–167.

Inglis, William, "Celebrities at Home: Patrick Calhoun," *Harper's Weekly*, 52 (November 21, 1908), 25–26.

——, "For the Kingdom of California. The True Story of San Francisco's Civil War between the Grafters and the Elaborate Forces of the Prosecution," *Harper's Weekly*, 52 (May 23 and 30 and June 6 and 13, 1908).

Irwin, Will, *The City that Was* (1906).

——, "They Who Strike in the Dark. True Story of Plots, Abductions, Dynamiting, and Attempted Murder against those Concerned as Witnesses, Lawyers, or Supporters of the San Francisco Graft Prosecution," *American Magazine*, 67 (April, 1909), 564–575.

Jordan, David Starr, *The Days of a Man* (1922).

Kauer, Ralph, "The Workingmen's Party of California," *Pacific Historical Review*, 13 (September, 1944), 278–291.

Kelly, Martin, "Martin Kelly's Story," edited by James H. Williams, San Francisco *Bulletin*, September 1 to November 26, 1917.

Kennan, George, "Criminal Government and the Private Citizen. A Study of San Francisco," *McClure's Magazine*, 30 (November, 1907), 60–71.

——, "The Fight for Reform in San Francisco," *McClure's Magazine*, 29 (September, 1907), 547–560.

"Kew" [pseud.], "San Francisco's Ferment," The *Outlook*, 86 (August 31, 1907), 950–956.

Kipling, Rudyard, *American Notes* (189_).

Lane, Franklin K., *The Letters of Franklin K. Lane*, edited by Anne W. Lane and Louise Herrick Wall (1922).

Langdon, William H., "The Story of the Great Struggle," *Cosmopolitan*, 43 (August, 1907), 437–441.

Leake, W. S., "When King Mazuma Ruled," San Francisco *Bulletin*, March 16 to April 26, 1917.

Lewis, Oscar, *The Big Four; the Story of Huntington, Stanford, Hopkins, and Crocker, and of the Building of the Central Pacific* (1938).

Lynch, Jeremiah, *Buckleyism, the Government of a State* (1889).

Macarthur, Walter, "Political Action and Trade-unionism" *Annals of the American Academy of Political and Social Science*, 24 (1904), 316–330.

——, "San Francisco: a Climax in Civics" (1906). Reproduced from typewritten copy.

Marberry, M. M., *The Golden Voice. The Biography of a Lusty American* (1947). On Isaac Kalloch.

Marx, Guido H., "Reform in San Francisco," *The Nation*, 89 (July 1, 1909), 10.

Millard, [Frank] Bailey, *History of the San Francisco Bay Region* (1924).

Mowry, George E., *Theodore Roosevelt and the Progressive Movement* (1946).

Older, Cora (Mrs. Fremont Older), "The Story of a Reformer's Wife; an Account of the Kidnapping of Fremont Older, the Shooting of Francis J. Heney, and the San Francisco Dynamite Plots," *McClure's Magazine*, 33 (July, 1908), 277–293.

Older, Fremont, *My Own Story* (New edition, revised, 1926).

——, "Shall Abe Ruef be Pardoned?" *The Survey*, 26 (September 2, 1911), 772–773.

Page, Thomas W., "The San Francisco Labor Movement in 1901," *Political Science Quarterly*, 17 (December, 1902), 664–688.

Palmer, Frederick, "Abe Ruef of the 'Law Offices,'" *Collier's*, 38 (January 12, 1907), 13–16.

"Patrick Calhoun and the Carmen's Union in San Francisco," *Harper's Weekly,* 51 (December 21, 1907), 1869.

Perlman, Selig, and Philip Taft, *History of Labor in the United States, 1896–1932,* edited by John R. Commons (1935).

Phelan, James D., "The Regeneration of San Francisco," *Independent,* 62 (June 20, 1907), 1448–1451.

Ray, P. O., "Claus Spreckels," *Dictionary of American Biography,* 17: 478.

Ross, Edward A., *Sin and Society; an Analysis of Latter-day Iniquity* (1907).

Ruef, Abraham, "The Road I Traveled. An Autobiographic Account of my Career from University to Prison, with an Intimate Recital of the Corrupt Alliance between Big Business and Politics in San Francisco," San Francisco *Bulletin,* April 6, and May 21 to September 5, 1912.

——, "Civic Conditions and Suggested Remedies," San Francisco *Bulletin,* September 14, 21, 24, 26, 27, and 28, and October 1, 2, 3, 5, 9, 10, 12, 15, 17, 19, 22, and 26, 1912.

"Ruef, a Jew under Torture," *Overland Monthly,* second series, 50 (November, 1907), 516–519.

Ryan, Frederick Lynne, *Industrial Relations in the San Francisco Building Trades* (1936).

Ryder, David Warren, "The Unions Lose San Francisco," *American Mercury,* (April 7, 1926), 412–417.

"The San Francisco Trial," *The Nation,* 88 (June 3, 1909), 550–551.

Steffens, Joseph Lincoln, "An Apology for Graft," *American Magazine,* 66 (June, 1908), 120–130.

——, *The Autobiography of Lincoln Steffens* (1931).

——, "Hearst, the Man of Mystery," *American Magazine,* 63 (November, 1906), 3–22.

——, "The Making of a Fighter; How Frank Heney Prepared in Arizona for the Work He Is Now Doing in San Francisco," *American Magazine,* 64 (July, 1907), 339–356.

——, "The Mote and the Beam, a Fact Novel. Chapter One—The Clash of Classes in San Francisco," *American Magazine,* 65 (November, 1907), 26–40; "Chapter Two—Breaking into San Francisco" (December, 1907), 140–151.

——, "Rudolph Spreckels, a Business Man Fighting for his City," *American Magazine,* 65 (February, 1908), 390–402.

——, *The Shame of the Cities* (1904).

——, *The Struggle for Self-Government* (1906).

——, "The Taming of the West: Discovery of the Land Fraud System, a Detective Story," *American Magazine,* 64 (August, 1907), 489–505; "Heney Grapples the Oregon Land Graft" (October, 1907), 585–602.

——, "William J. Burns, Intriguer," *American Magazine,* 65 (April, 1908), 614–625.

Wells, Evelyn, *Champagne Days of San Francisco* (1939).

——, *Fremont Older* (1936).

Young, John P., *San Francisco, a History of the Pacific Coast Metropolis* (1912).

——, *Journalism in California* (1915).

Zink, Harold, *City Bosses in the United States* (1930).

San Francisco Daily Newspapers

Bulletin	*Evening Post*
Call	*Examiner*
Chronicle	*Globe*
Daily News	

San Francisco Weeklies

Argonaut	*Organized Labor*
Coast Seamen's Journal	*News Letter*
Emanu-el	*Star*
Labor Clarion	*Town Talk*
Liberator	*Wasp*

Index

Index

337